Prison Landscapes

Published by Four Corners Books
56 Artillery Lane, London E1 7LS
www.fourcornersbooks.co.uk

Text and images © Alyse Emdur 2012
Front cover painting by Darrell van Mastrigt

Designed by Fraser Muggeridge studio
Repro by DawkinsColour
Print production by Martin Lee Associates
Printed in Italy by Conti Tipocolor

Distributed in the UK by Art Data
www.artdata.co.uk
Distributed in North America by
Distributed Art Publishers
www.artbook.com

ISBN 978 0 9561928 6 8

Many American prisons do not allow inmates
to receive hardcover books. This book's
soft cover makes it possible for incarcerated
contributors to receive copies.

Prison Landscapes

Alyse Emdur

Introduction

In 2005, I found a Polaroid photograph of myself, at age five, in a family
photo album. I was pictured with my older brother and sister in front
of a tropical beach scene in the visiting room at Bayside State Prison
in Leesburg, New Jersey. Growing up, I was accustomed to the tradition
of posing in front of backdrops for school pictures, holidays, and at
amusement parks, but the backdrop in prison felt different. It amplified
the sadness of visiting him. The painting behind us represented
freedom, the exact opposite of the prison's mission and the reality
my brother was living. My sister and I could go to the beach, but
our brother could not go with us. We posed in front of this painting
of a beach instead and it made us feel more comfortable showing
our friends the picture. We could say, "This is our brother," instead
of saying, "This is our brother in prison." From the picture, no one
would know he was incarcerated.

On my first visit, after waiting in an unbearable line with other visitors,
a guard patted us down and led us through a metal detector and a series
of locking doors to the closely surveilled visiting-room where Bruce,
serving his second prison sentence, waited for us anxiously. Noticing
a couple reprimanded for kissing, he pointed out that kissing was
prohibited to deter visitors from passing drugs stuffed in balloons
from mouth to mouth.

From 1988 to 1998, my brother was in and out of three prisons, serving
time for car theft and possession of illegal substances. In each institution,
my family posed in front of backdrops hand-painted by talented inmates.
Bruce explained that artists capable of photorealism are highly respected
for their skills in prison. Many run micro businesses selling ballpoint
pen portraits, greeting cards, or hand calligraphed love letters. These
artworks are often used as currency and traded for commissary items
including stamps, cigarettes, and snacks. Although it is technically illegal
for inmates to engage in economies outside of prison walls, some manage
to sell artworks through craft fairs, the Internet, and prison art advocacy
organizations.

Internal art programs rarely facilitate the production of visiting room
backdrops. Most prisons do not have the resources to offer art classes
nor are they even interested in giving educational tools to criminals.
In these facilities, the administration oversees the painting. There is

no official competition to select the painters, but rather a kind of
consensual emergent agreement. The chosen artists paint the backdrops
directly on walls or on a type of canvas that hangs and rolls up. Institutions
that prefer the canvas backdrops usually have several in storage that
are rotated to offer frequent visitors a variety of landscapes to choose
from. The visiting room in State Correctional Institution, Houtzdale,
Pennsylvania features eight backdrops that electronically roll down at
the push of a button. When the backdrops are painted directly on walls,
guards are assigned to accompany the artists throughout the process
of painting. Instead of involving inmates, a growing number of prisons
today use mass-produced store-bought backdrops.

Photographs are occasionally taken during special events like holidays,
graduations, performances, and weddings but, in most American
prisons today, photographs can only be taken in front of a backdrop
in the visiting room. If inmates do not receive visitors, they are not
permitted to take photographs of themselves. Prisons provide cameras
and inmates volunteer in shifts to work as in-house photographers during
visiting hours in the makeshift portrait studios. This is an appealing task
for volunteers who enjoy watching the intimate scenes that unfold in
the visiting rooms. A single photograph costs $2–$4. In the New York
State Department of Corrections, the Click-Click program organizes
the portrait studios. Profits generated from the program are used
to donate school supplies and Christmas presents to children visiting
their incarcerated parents.

Prison Landscapes explores this little known and largely physically
inaccessible genre of painting and portraiture seen only by inmates,
visitors, and prison employees. Created specifically for escape
and self-representation, the idealized paintings of tropical beaches,
fantastical waterfalls, mountain vistas, and cityscapes invite sitters
to perform fantasies of freedom. As inmates and their visitors pose
for photos in front of these backdrops, they pretend, for a brief moment,
that they are someplace else. The portraits are given to these visitors
as gifts to take home and remember the faces of their loved ones while
they are locked up.

This collection acknowledges an important perspective that is rarely
seen or heard – the experience of friends and family who are forced
to relate to this system. The images show prisoners representing
themselves for their families. Nearly one and a half million American
children have a parent in prison. Many of the criminals pictured, who

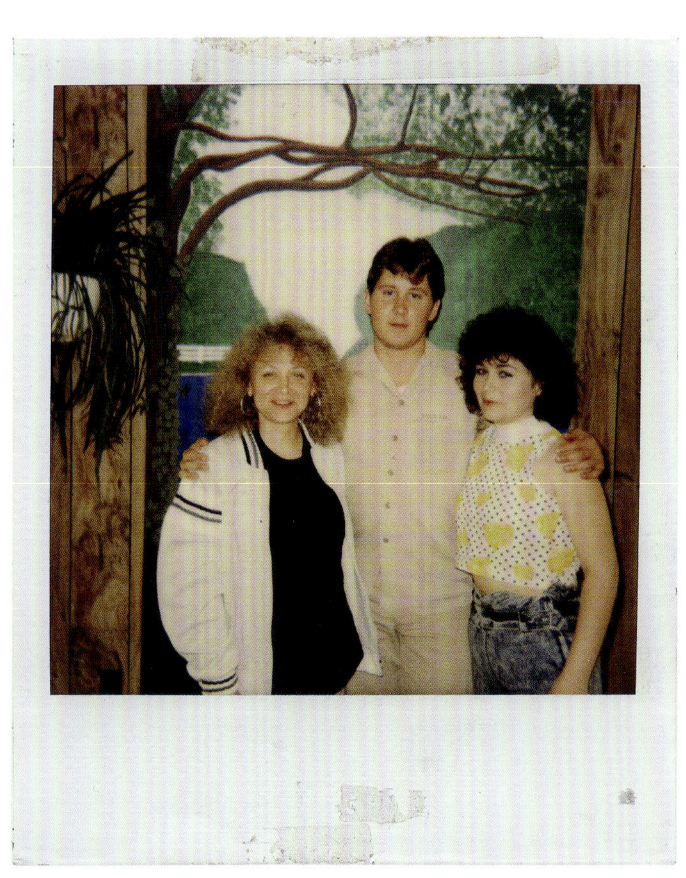

Bruce Emdur, Bayside State Prison,
Leesburg, New Jersey

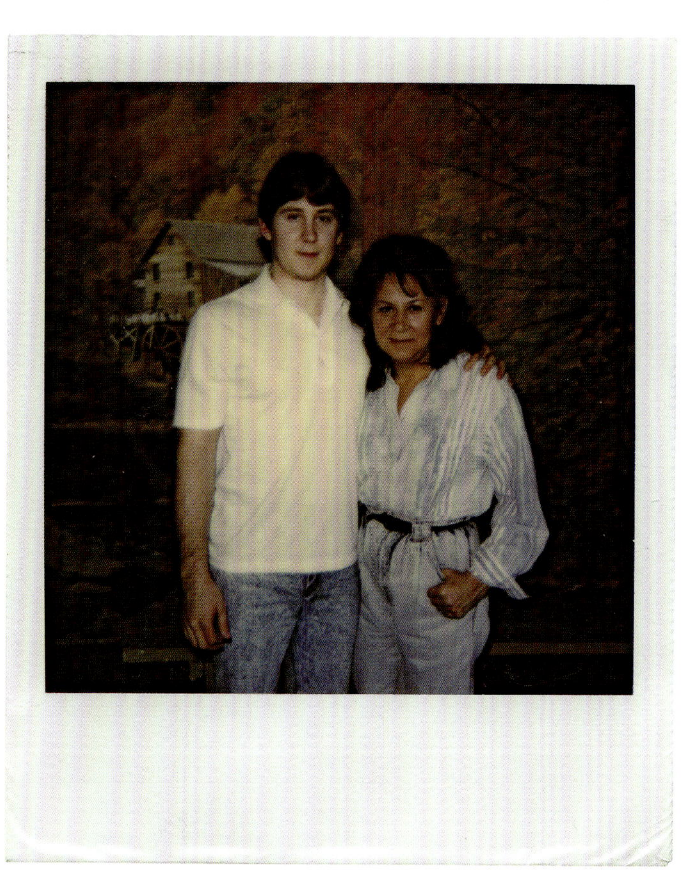

are also parents, took these photographs for their children. These images offer an opportunity to see America's prison population, not through the usual lens of criminality, but through the eyes of inmates' loved ones. In addition to distributing the images to family, some prisoners also use them to attract pen pals through dating websites like, writeaprisoner.com, inmate-connection.com, and friendsbeyondthewall.com.

While many sitters act out fantasies of freedom, others see the backdrops as just another part of the prison routine. After all, murals similar to the backdrops are commonly painted throughout prisons. While photographing in Gadsden Correctional Facility in Florida, a private women's facility operated by Management and Training Corporation, I toured most of the prison's murals – in hallways, classrooms, dorm rooms, and in medical exam rooms. These paintings, like the portrait studio backdrops, are used to create a brief escape from the architecture and culture of confinement. Richard Crutcher, Gadsden's Public Information Officer, noted that the production of murals is a positive activity employed to keep inmates busy and out of trouble.

Portrait studios in visiting rooms are often prisoners' sole mode of visual self-representation but, ironically, they also function as instruments of power for prisons because they are the only place where images can be produced. The backdrops are a means to exercise control over the imagery that circulates inside and outside of institutions. In New York state prisons, I spoke with wardens who pointed out that the backdrops are not only used to facilitate a more pleasant experience for visitors, they serve prisons' primary mission – to keep inmates incarcerated. From a security perspective, an image with a fence, door, security mirror, or surveillance camera in the background could potentially aide an inmate in a physical escape. For this reason, prisons do not want images revealing these architectural details to circulate.

While photographing portrait studios in Pennsylvania and New York State prisons, I was closely supervised to assure that I only left with the one image I was approved to photograph. My experience was very different from that of other outside photographers like Danny Lyon, Douglas Kent Hall, and Ethan Hoffman who, in the 1970s and 1980s, were granted seemingly unrestricted access to photograph inside cells, yards, visiting rooms, weight rooms, offices, libraries, corridors, showers, and factories in state prisons. With this access, they provided significant, in-depth looks into our prison system. Since the late 1980s, gaining access to photograph in American prisons has grown more and more difficult. Consequently, our prison system has become increasingly opaque. Walls not only lock criminals in, they also keep society out. In most prisons today, the only images that inmates are permitted to participate in, are in front of backdrops. These visiting room portraits, which intentionally hide what is outside the frame and gloss over the struggles of being locked up, are one of the few accessible visual entrances into this system.

I began *Prison Landscapes* in 2005 by writing letters to a few incarcerated individuals whom I found on inmate pen pal and dating websites. One of my first pen pals was a muralist who painted a backdrop in the Columbia River Correctional Institution in Oregon. I wrote a letter to the prison's warden, requesting permission to document his painted backdrop in the visiting room. Although my proposal was rejected, it became a starting point for the project. Since, initially, I could not attain access to these backdrops through the institutions, I asked my pen pals to send me their own photographs. The portraits sent to me were originally given to mothers and girlfriends, sisters, brothers, children, and fathers. The project gradually shifted – instead of photographing the backdrops myself, I wanted to see how people represented themselves without the interruption of my presence. Over the next three years, I casually collected photographs of pen pals. Then in 2008, I mailed out a solicitation to around three hundred inmates across the United States directly asking them to send me photographs to be included in this book. From those three hundred solicitations, about half sent me their most valued images.

My correspondence with hundreds of prisoners is an action that explores the complex relationship between the incarcerated and the free. When I began collecting the images for *Prison Landscapes*, I used the alias Lee Lana, a combination of my sister's middle name and mine. Eventually, as the book started taking shape, I sent release forms to contributors with both my legal name and my alias; it was then that a number of inmates stated that they too had used aliases, and clarified their legal names.

The prisoners' decisions to participate may seem ambiguous insofar as some viewers may doubt their ability to make the decision. But it would be patronizing not to trust them. The fact that someone is incarcerated does not mean that he or she is incapable of making decisions for him or herself.

The individuals pictured have different reasons for choosing to engage with my proposal. Many participated because they felt forgotten and wished to draw attention to the politics of incarceration. Others explained that they sent me their photos because they wanted to be seen, not only as criminals, but as sensitive people with emotions, and families, and worth. Some participated simply because they wanted to be my pen pal. Others noted that being part of something outside of prison feels good. Some contributed because they wanted to be in a book, or because they wanted a copy of the book. Incarcerated artist Darrell Van Mastrigt noted that he participated, in part, because he wants to see what artists in other prisons are painting. Jason Jordon recently wrote that he is looking forward to giving his copy of the book to his son. Although he is not proud of being incarcerated, he nevertheless takes pride in being part of this book.

I do not have the authority to speak for all of the individuals pictured in this collection, I believe that their decision to participate speaks for itself. In sending me their pictures, contributors have agreed to become objects of our gaze. They have expressed their agency and acted on their desire to be seen by a world from which they are locked away. In prison, decision-making is limited. While the decision to engage or not engage with this proposal is a small gesture, it is also an act of freedom and a rare choice. Together, we are exploiting ourselves to offer a window into the American prison system.

There is something inherent in these images that makes us uncomfortable, myself included. I believe that is because it pushes us to face a difficult reality. A reality that involves a victim, a criminal, a prison system that incarcerates over 2.3 million Americans, collateral damage (the families of victims and criminals), and the biases and experiences that us as viewers bring to bear. This collection is an affirmation of the humanity of prisoners – something that society often finds troubling in and of itself.

Alyse Emdur

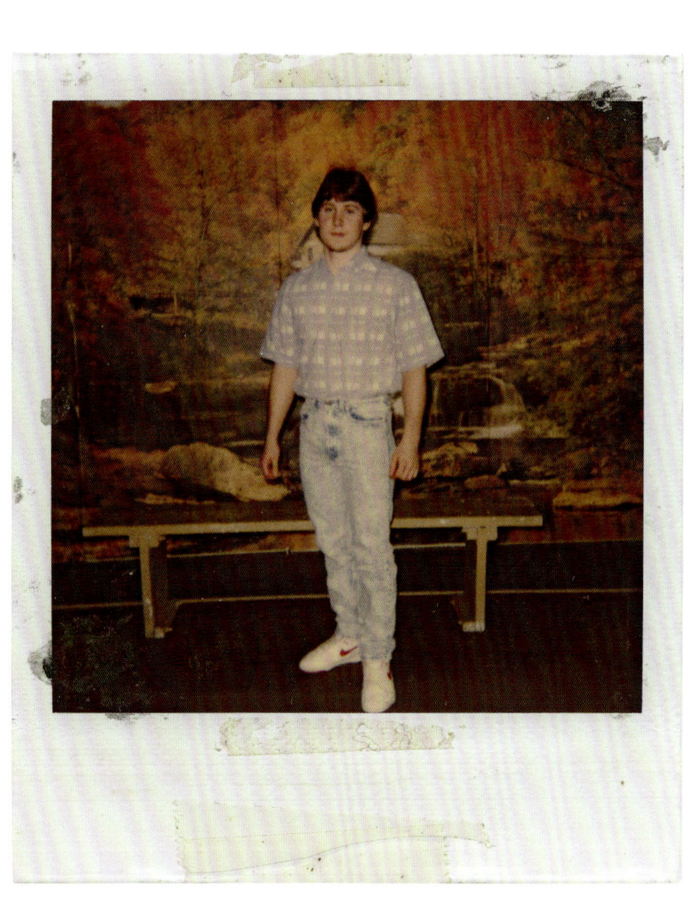

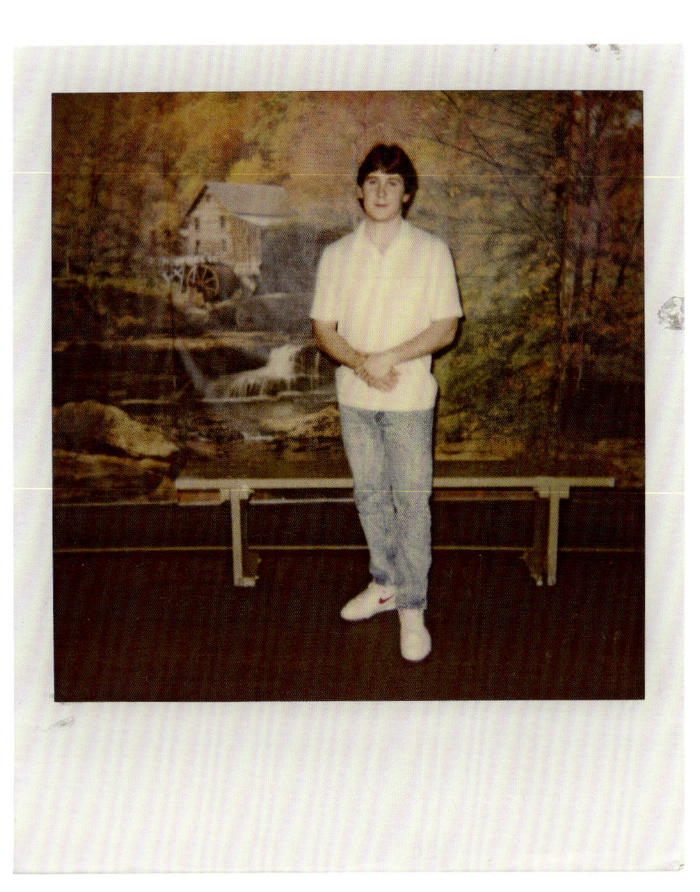

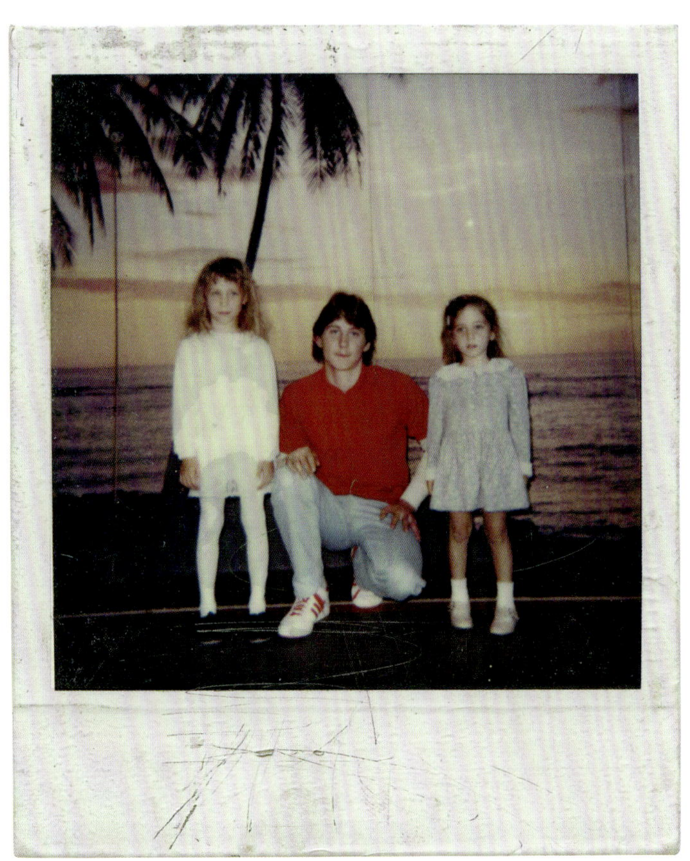

When I initially began collecting the images for *Prison Landscapes*, I used the alias Lee Lana, a combination of my sister's middle name and mine. During my correspondences with contributors, I sent a release form with both my legal name and my alias; it was then that a number of inmates stated that they too had used aliases, and clarified their legal names.

March 8, 2008

Dear Melvin,

Hello, I saw your picture and profile on www.writeaprisoner.com
and would like to invite you to contribute to a book that I am
working on. Growing up, my older brother spent many years
in and out of prison. Memories of visiting him remain significant
to me. In a family photo album, I recently found Polaroid pictures
of him posing in front of various scenic backdrops. He tells me
that murals painted by talented inmates of tropical beaches,
flowing waterfalls, cityscapes, and mountain vistas are commonly
used as backdrops in prison visiting rooms. Enclosed is a picture
of myself with my brother in front of a tropical beach mural.
I'm the youngest one on the right.

I am collecting photographs of people in prison in front of these
backdrops. The photographs will be compiled into a book of
portraits.

Can you send me a photograph of yourself in the visiting room
where you are? Represent yourself. The picture(s) can be of you
alone or with a friend or loved one. Let me know if you would like
your name included, if you prefer to remain anonymous, and if you
want your photograph returned. If you would like to include a brief
caption, please write it on a separate sheet of paper. All
contributors will receive a copy of the book directly from the
publisher. I understand that you posted your profile online to find
pen pals, not to be solicited. Thank you for your consideration and
thoughts. I am looking forward to hearing from you soon.

Sincerely,

Lee Lana

655 South Flower Street #166
Los Angeles, CA 90017

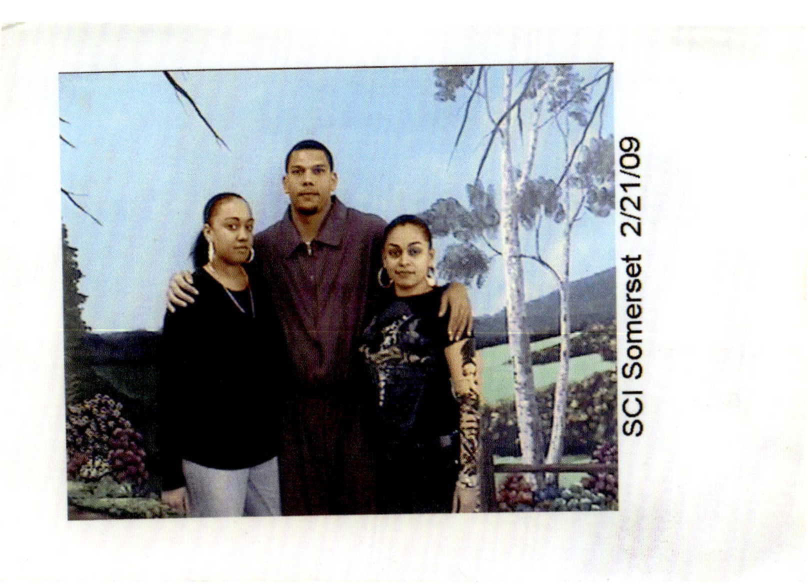

Samuel Perez, State Correctional
Institution, Somerset, Pennsylvania

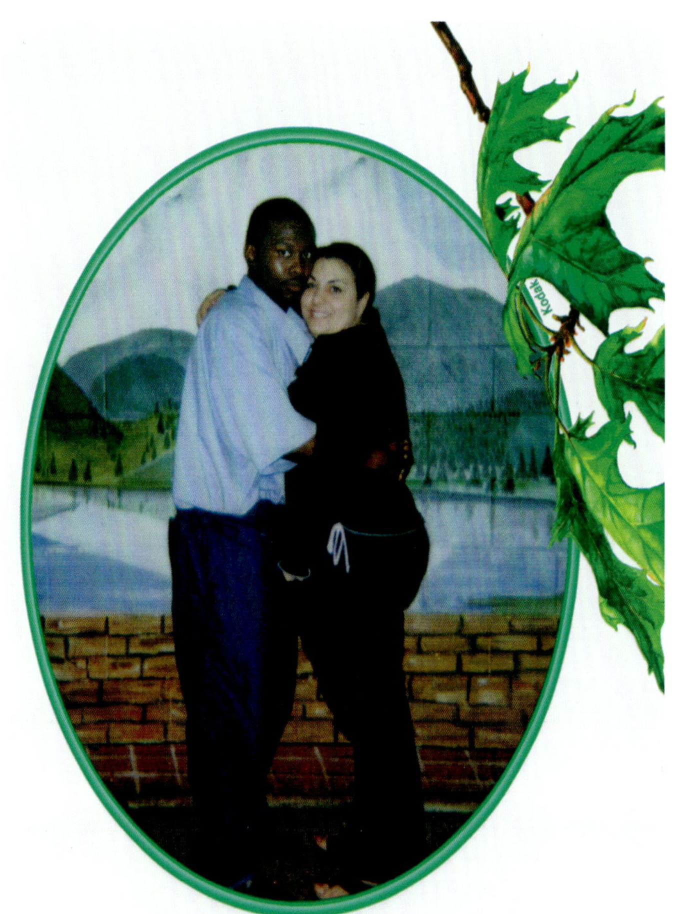

GENESIS & CATRINA

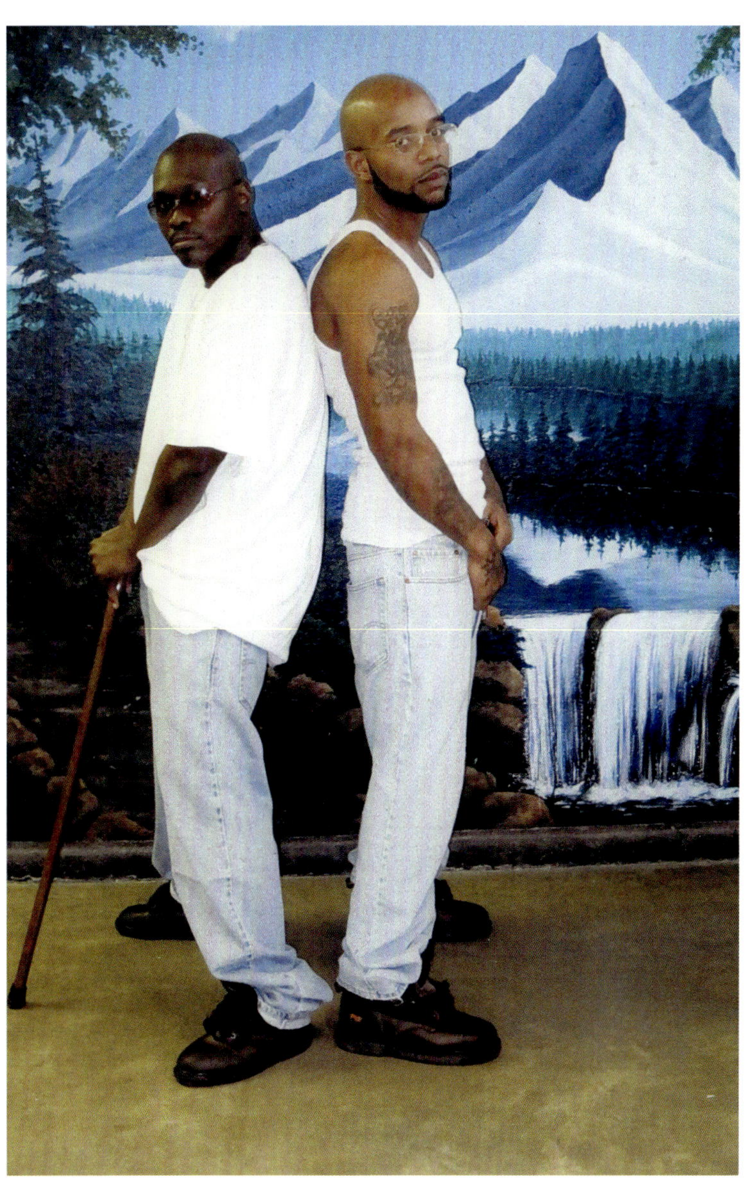

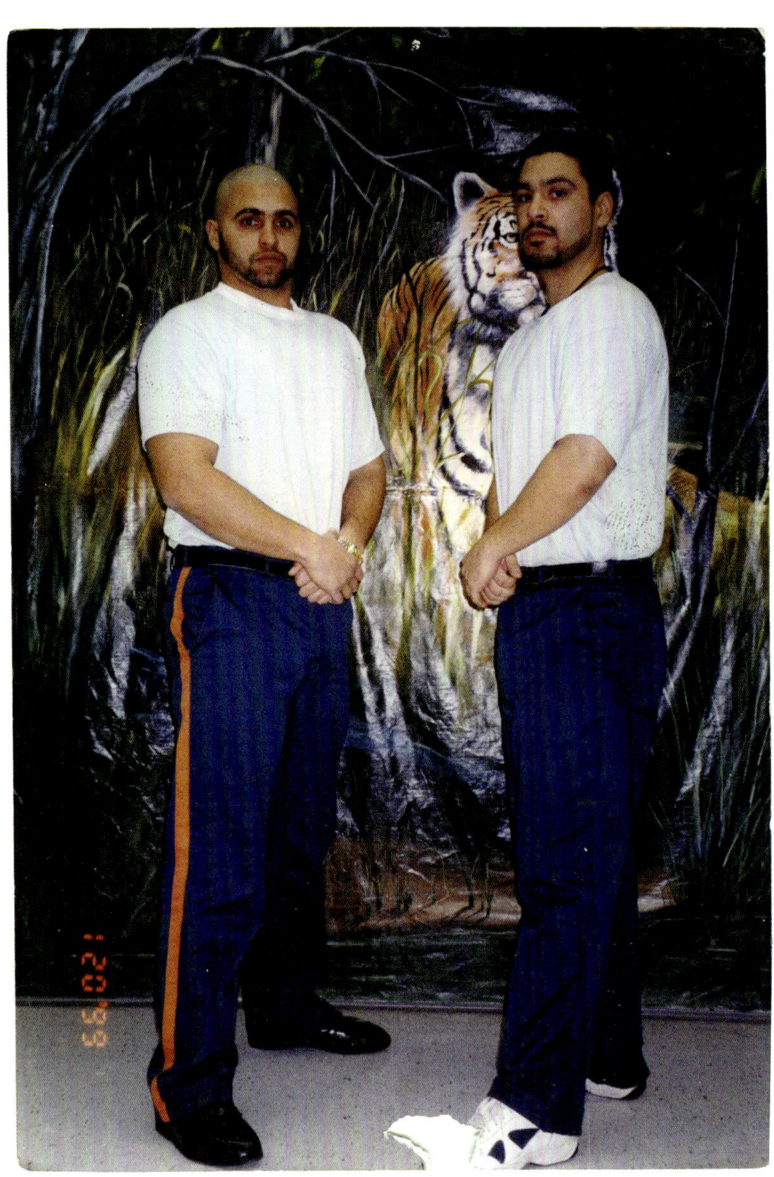

Dimas Antonio Garza (right),
Alger Maximum Correctional Facility,
Munising, Michigan

"WHAT EVER IT TAKE'S
I'M THERE!!"
1-LOVE!

April 7, 2009

Dear Lee Lana,

Hello right back atcha! I received your letter and initially thought a new pen pal had wrote, and me being a native Californian, I was delighted to see CA. on the return address. You see in prison, we are often very appreciative of the little things so a letter is like a blessing to some… but then I got to reading it and was like… huh? I don't mean that in a negative way, it was (your request) just very unique to say the least to receive something like that out of the blue. I am though nonetheless thankful that you considered me and of course I will do what I can to help. Enclosed you'll find the most recent photo I have, hopefully enough of the mural is in focus because as you can see, the mural in our visiting room is situated sorta at waste-level so the photographer would have to be positioned from a downward angle (looking up) in order to get a larger scope of it. If you need something better, let me know and I'll try and work something out.

No need to return the photo as it wouldn't be allowed in to me. The prison prohibits it, speaking of which – even the photo you sent me was rejected because it was taken in a prison, so I would appreciate it if you would send another of you alone or not one that was taken inside – if you don't mind. I've been in prison in California and Nevada also and still know people in those places that I could refer you to if that would help your efforts, and I don't mind if you publish my name, number, or address – if you need any sort of release for me to sign – send it and I'll respond immediately. I applaud your endeavor as well as your achievements – you do your thing baby girl and keep reaching for and wanting more in life.

Thank you.

Sincerely,

Robert Barfield #6836148

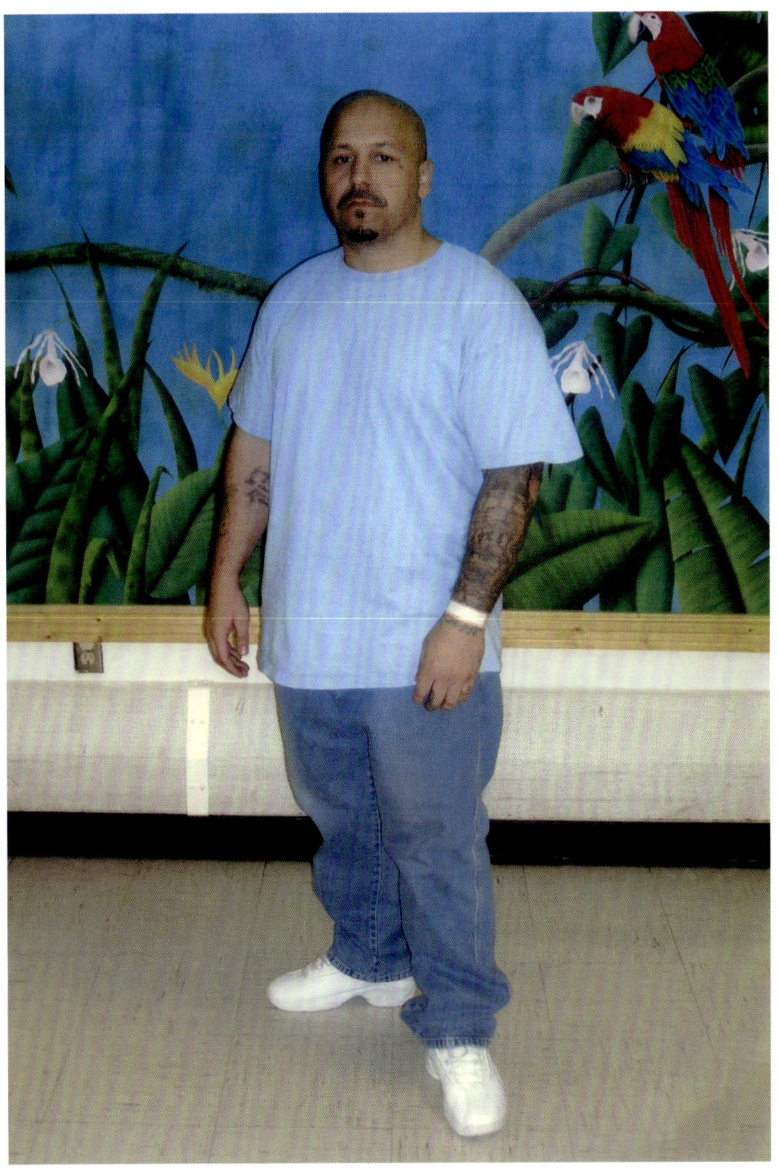

I took this picture during the second
visit I've received in 16 years. My only
thoughts were of the love I felt for the
friend who cared enough to come see me.

Robert Barfield, Anamosa State
Penitentiary, Anamosa, Iowa

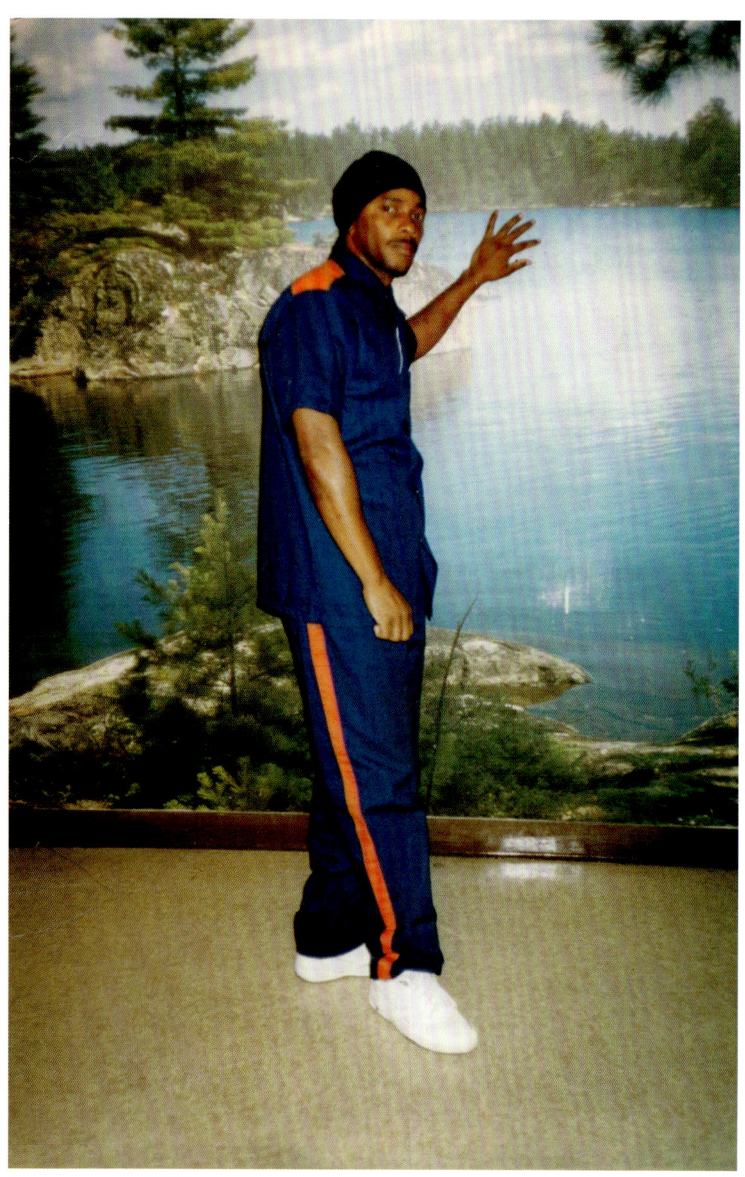

Anonymous, Ionia Maximum
Correctional Facility, Ionia, Michigan

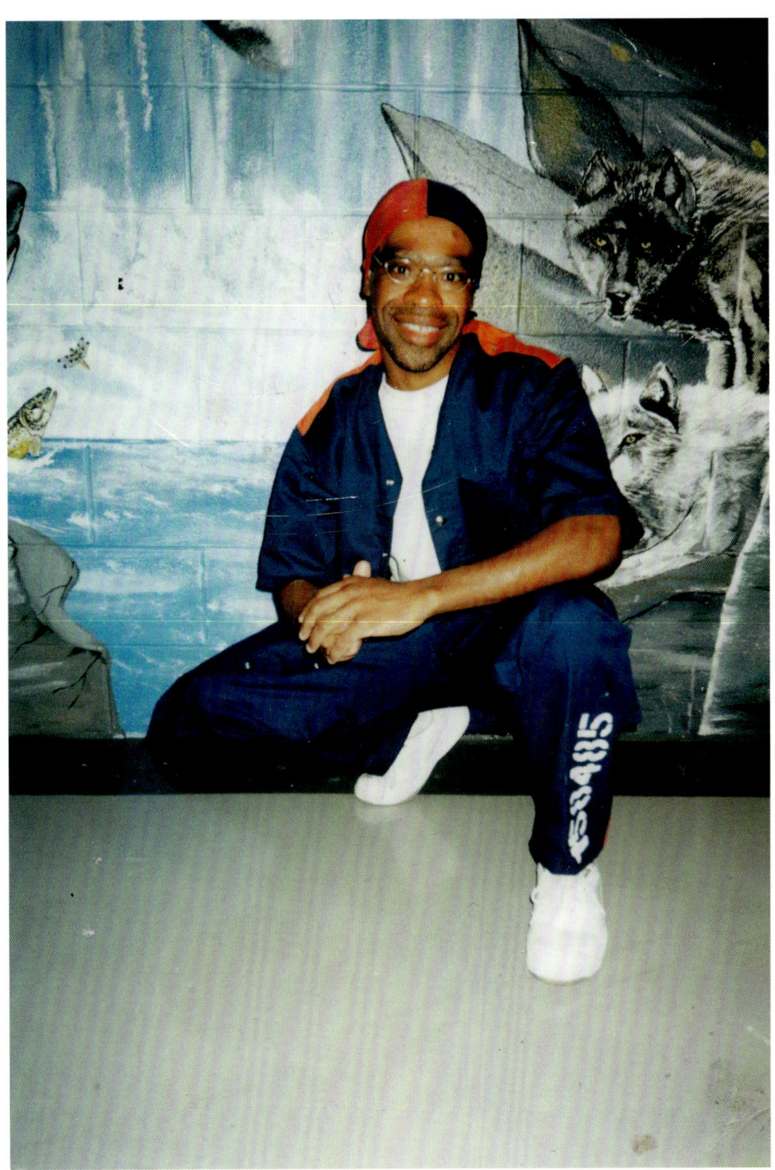

Anonymous, Ionia Maximum
Correctional Facility, Ionia, Michigan

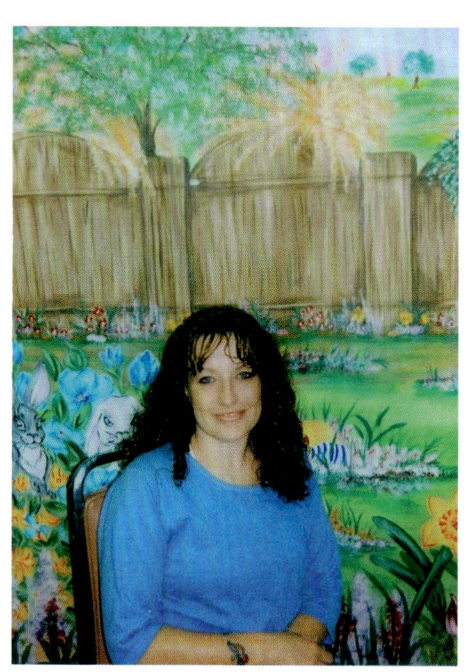

Moranda Trimble, Valley State Prison
for Women, Chowchilla, California

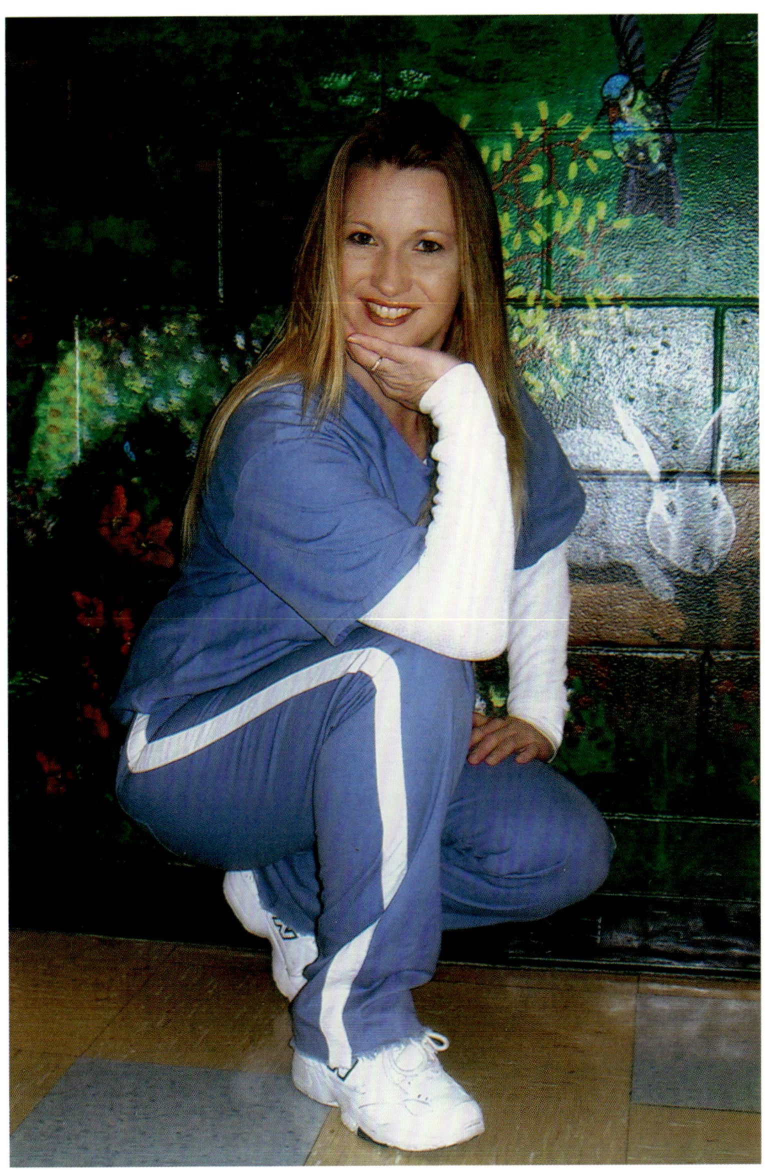

Jackie Foley, Gadsden Correctional
Facility, Quincy, Florida

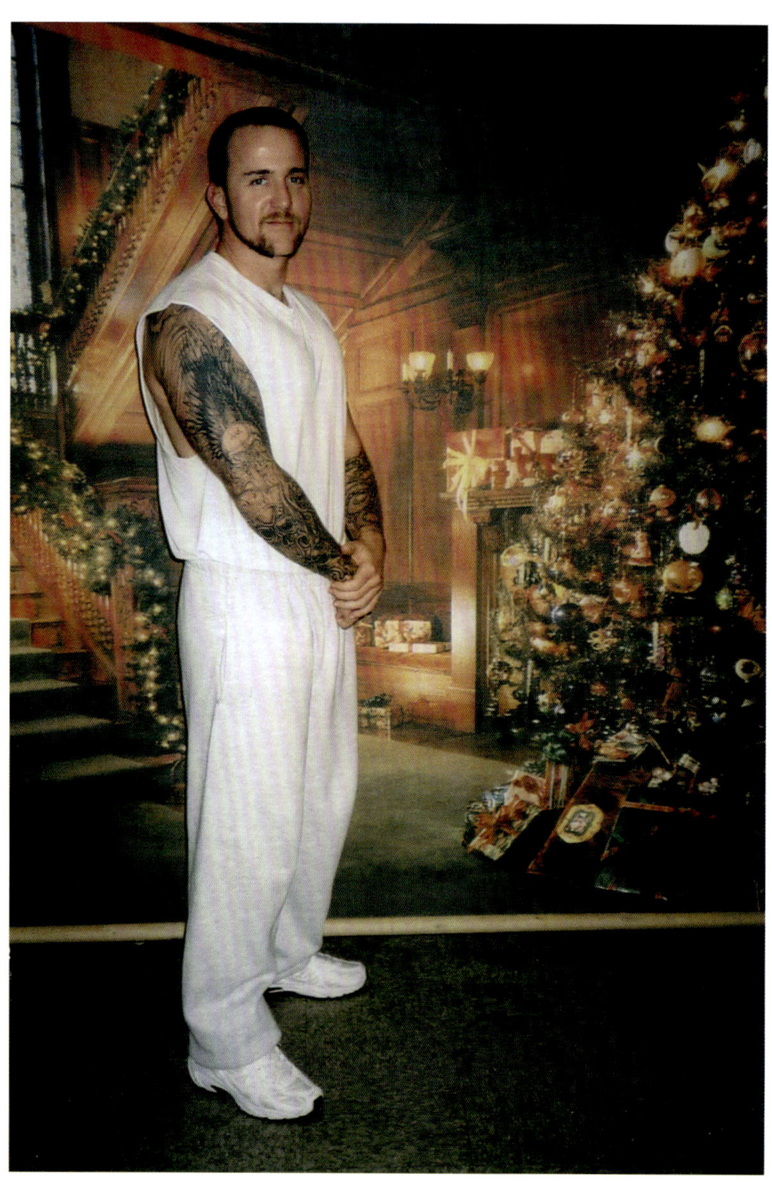

Brandon Jones, United States
Penitentiary, Marion, Illinois

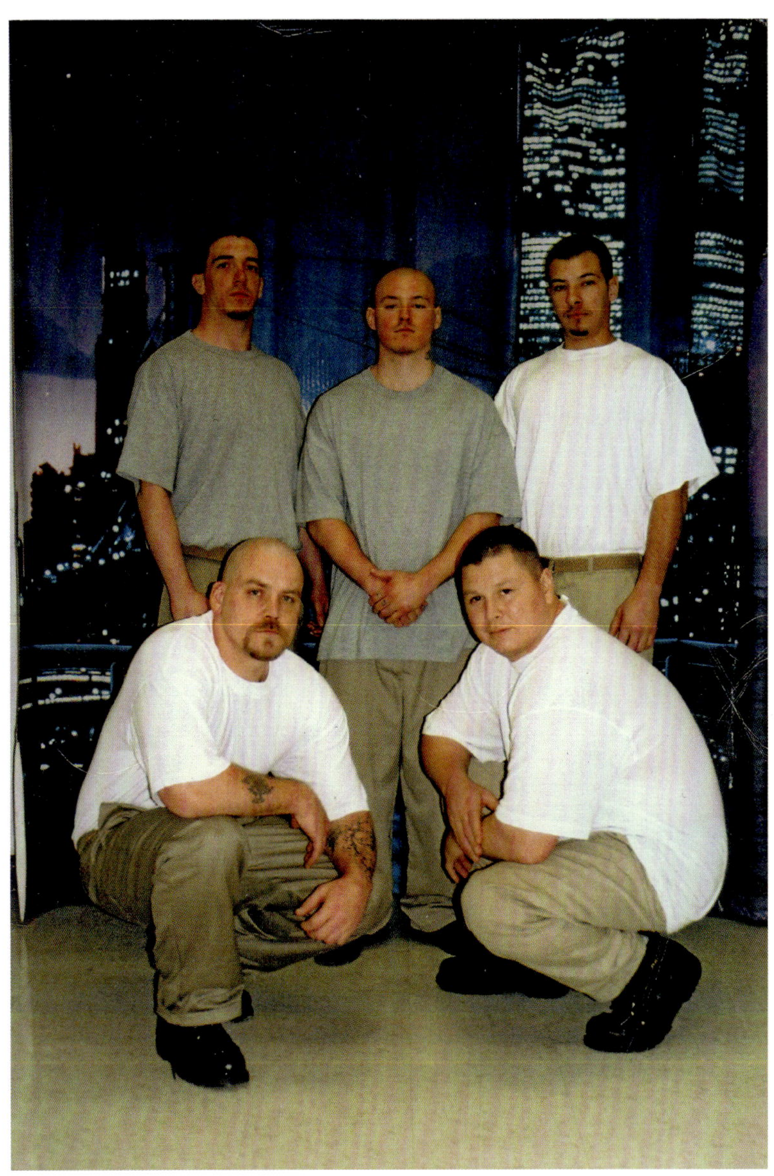

Dustin Jordon (back row, middle),
Federal Correctional Institution,
Pekin, Illinois

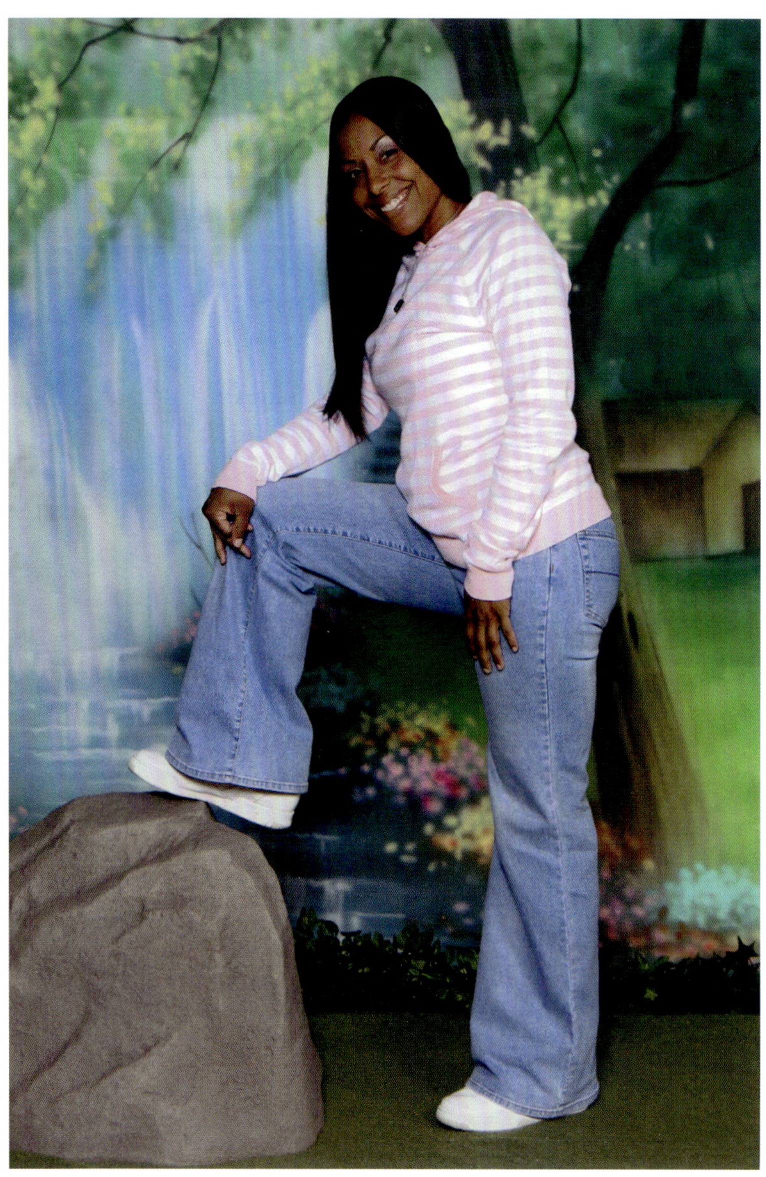

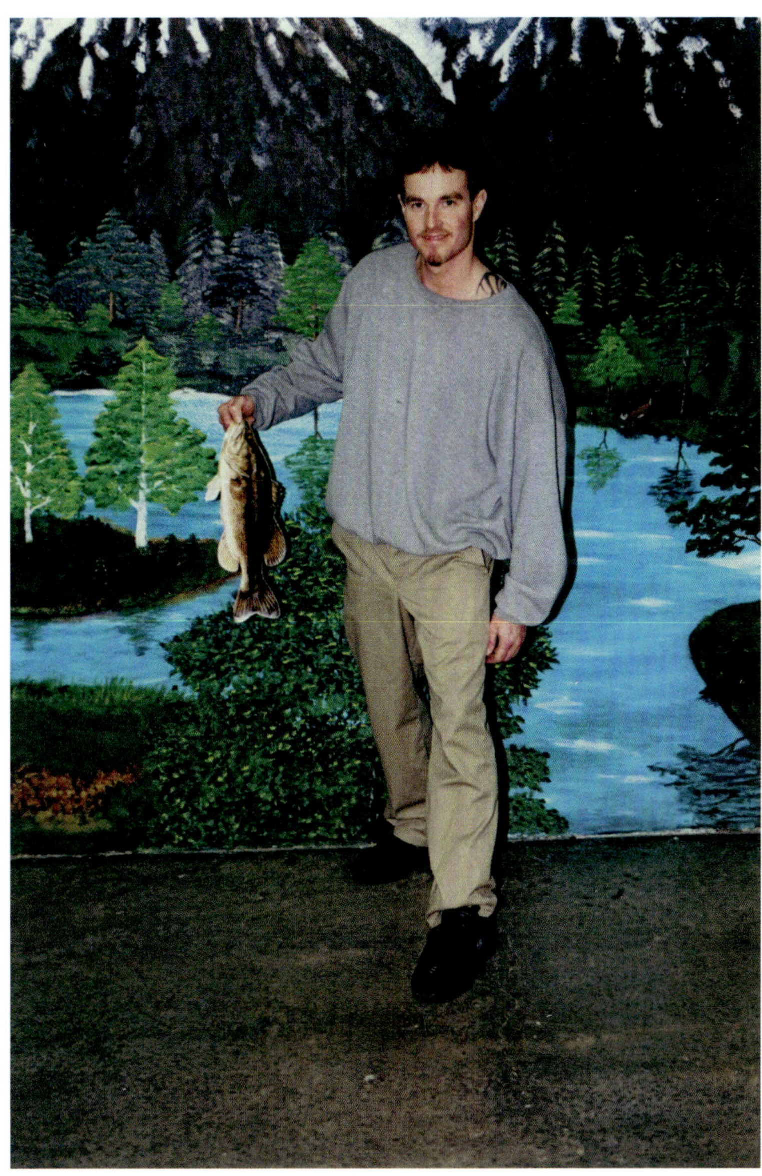

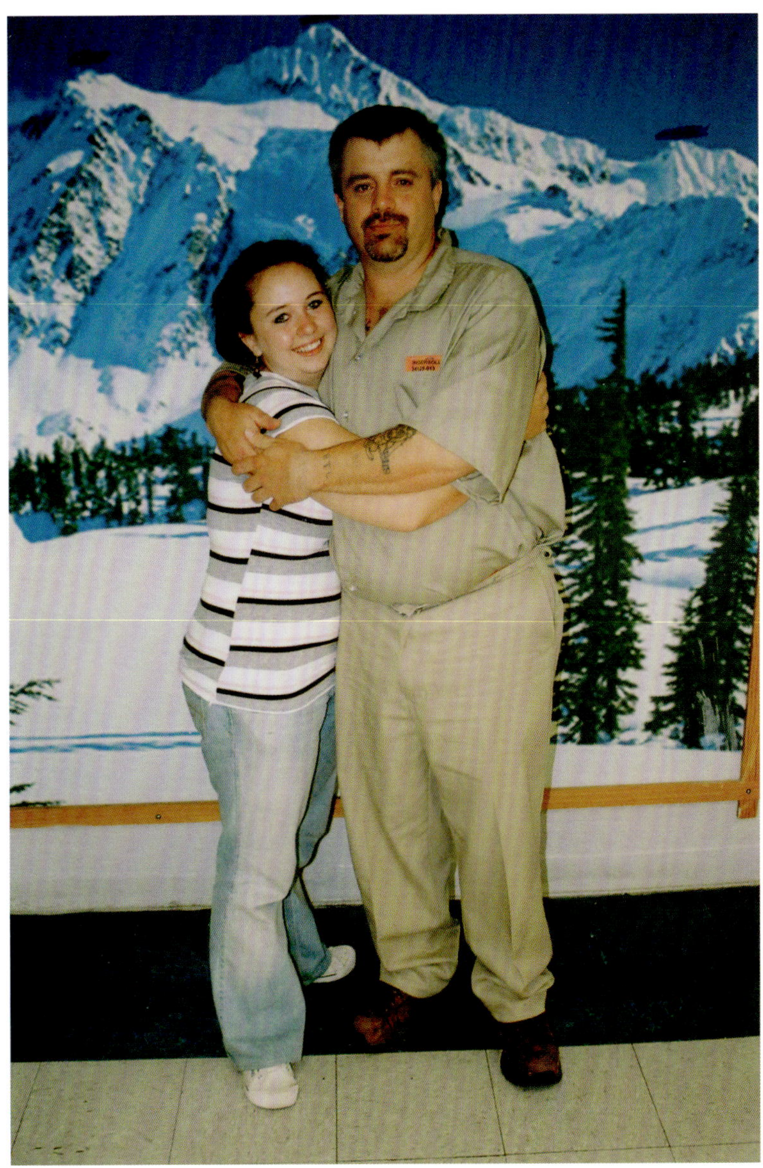

James Ingensoll, United States
Penitentiary, Leavenworth, Kansas

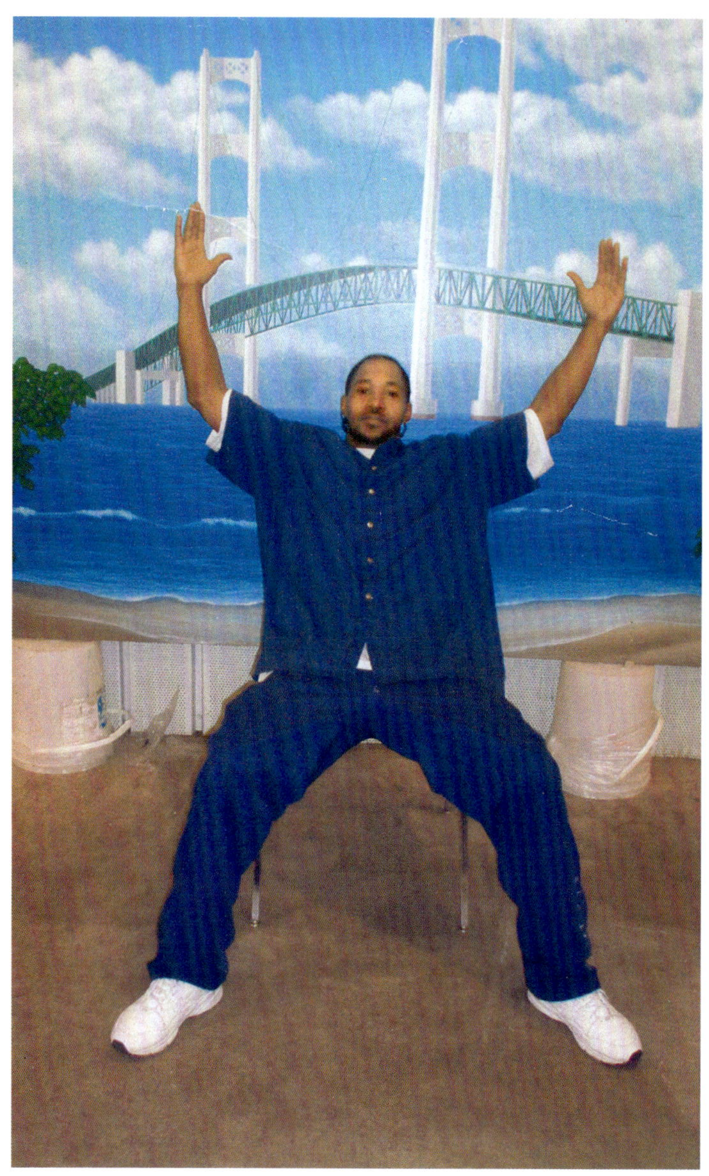

Anonymous, Ionia Maximum
Correctional Facility, Ionia, Michigan

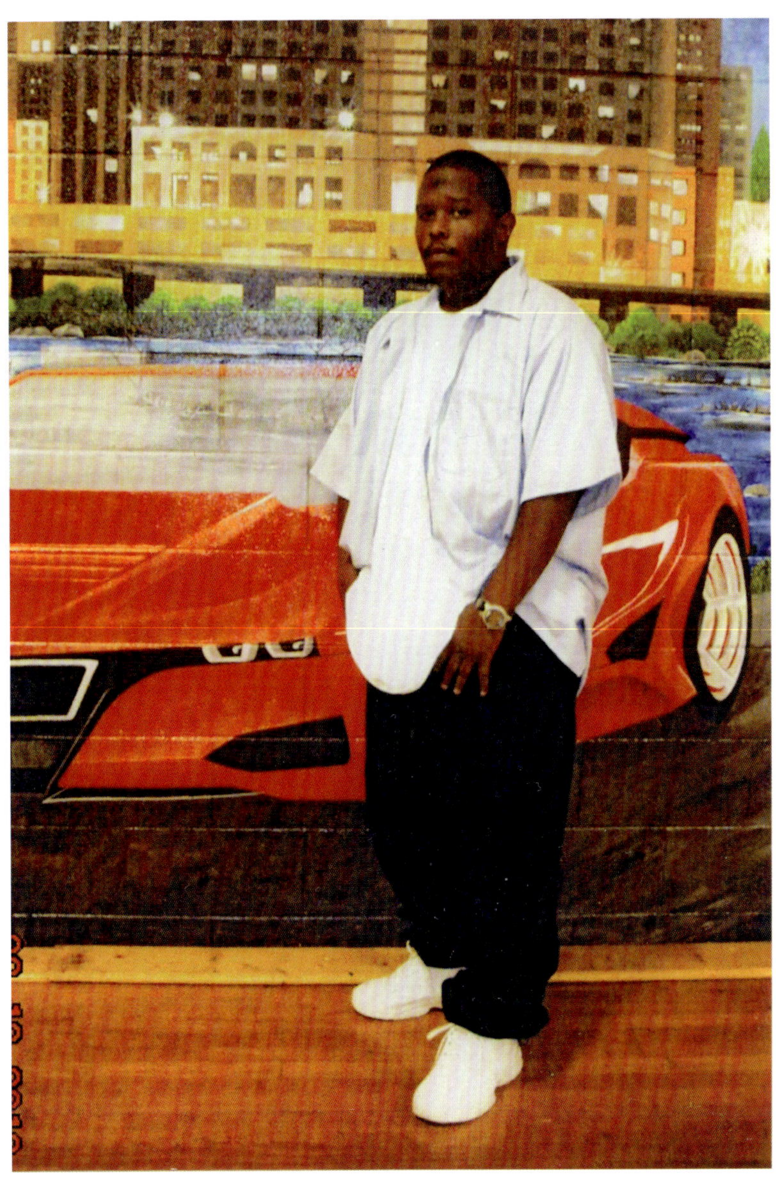

Haleem Baker, Nottoway Correctional
Center, Burkeville, Virginia

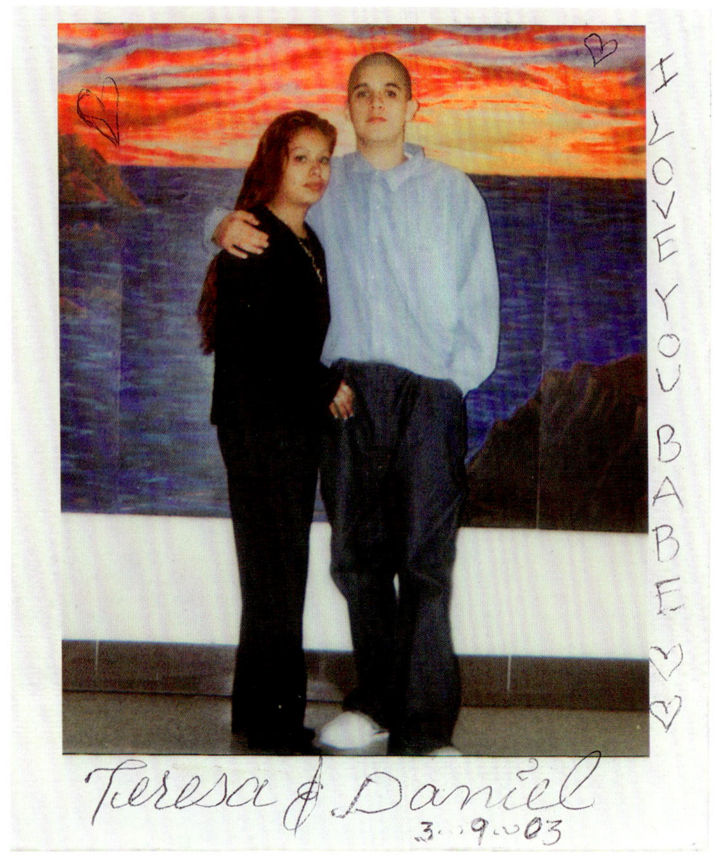

When these pictures were first taken,
I was very nervous and happy holding
my Kool-Aid smile. Here in the box it
is not often that we receive visits since
the majority of us are from Southern
California. To have someone drive from
Los Angeles to Crescent City means
they care for you deeply. Our families
and friends who care for us are a great
part of our so-called "rehabilitation".
They are our hope and inspiration, what
keeps us going in life. I say, treasure
the moments you spend with those you
love and love you. Don't let nothing come
between you. Sometimes little things
mean a lot to a person incarcerated.
A letter, a card, a picture, but the best
is always a visit!

Daniel Ascencio, Pelican Bay State
Prison, Crescent City, California

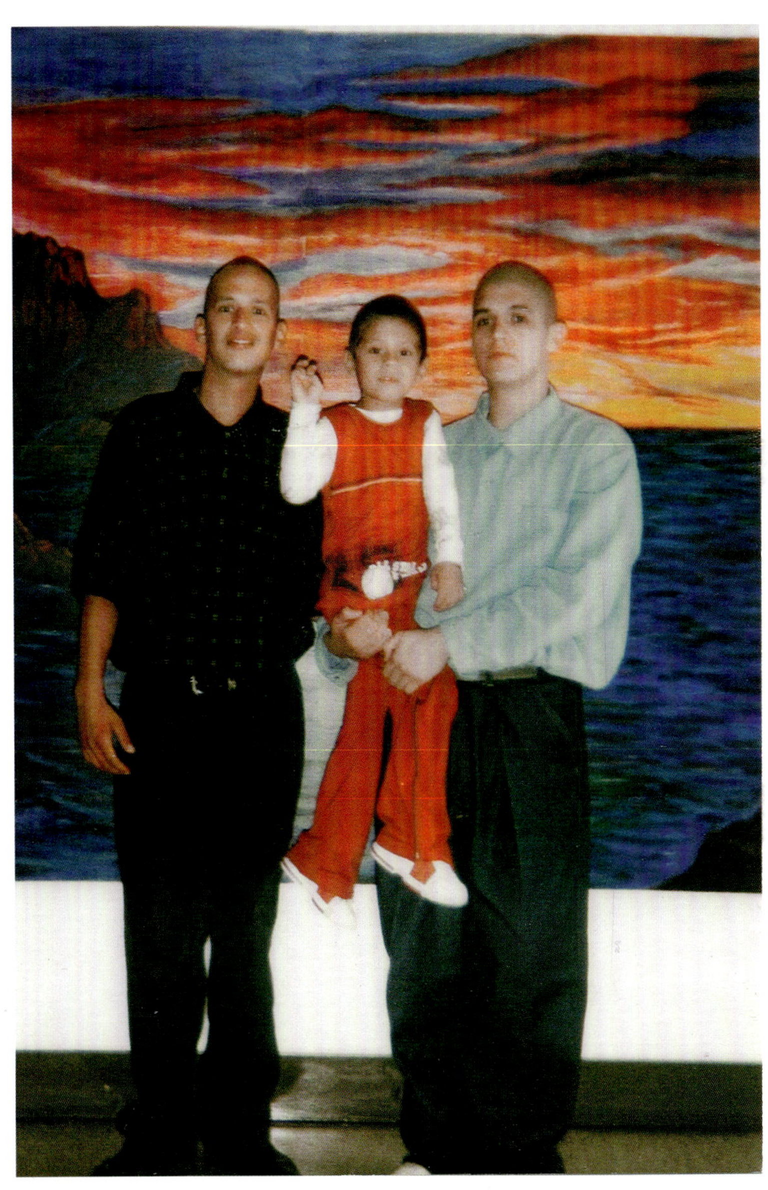

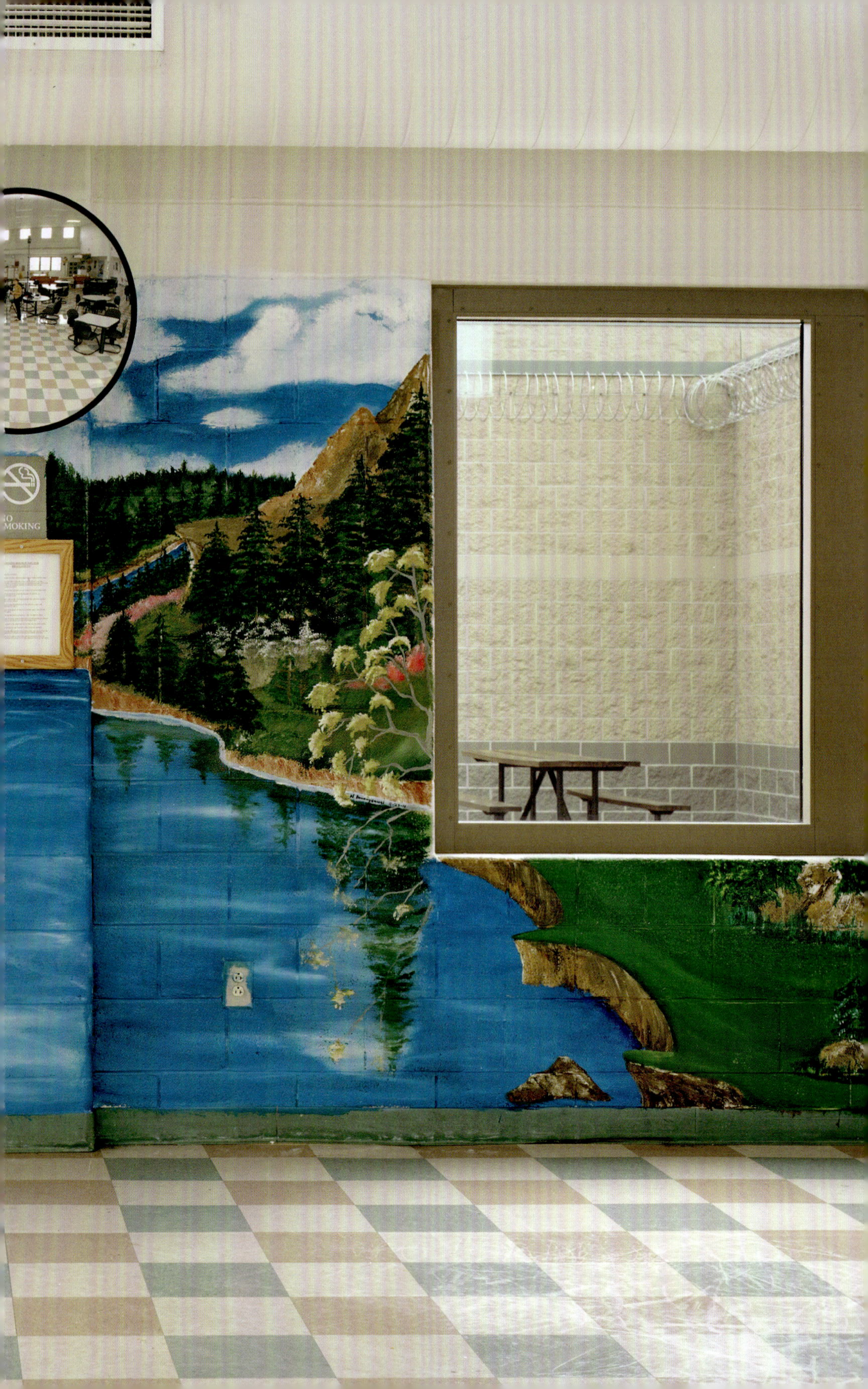

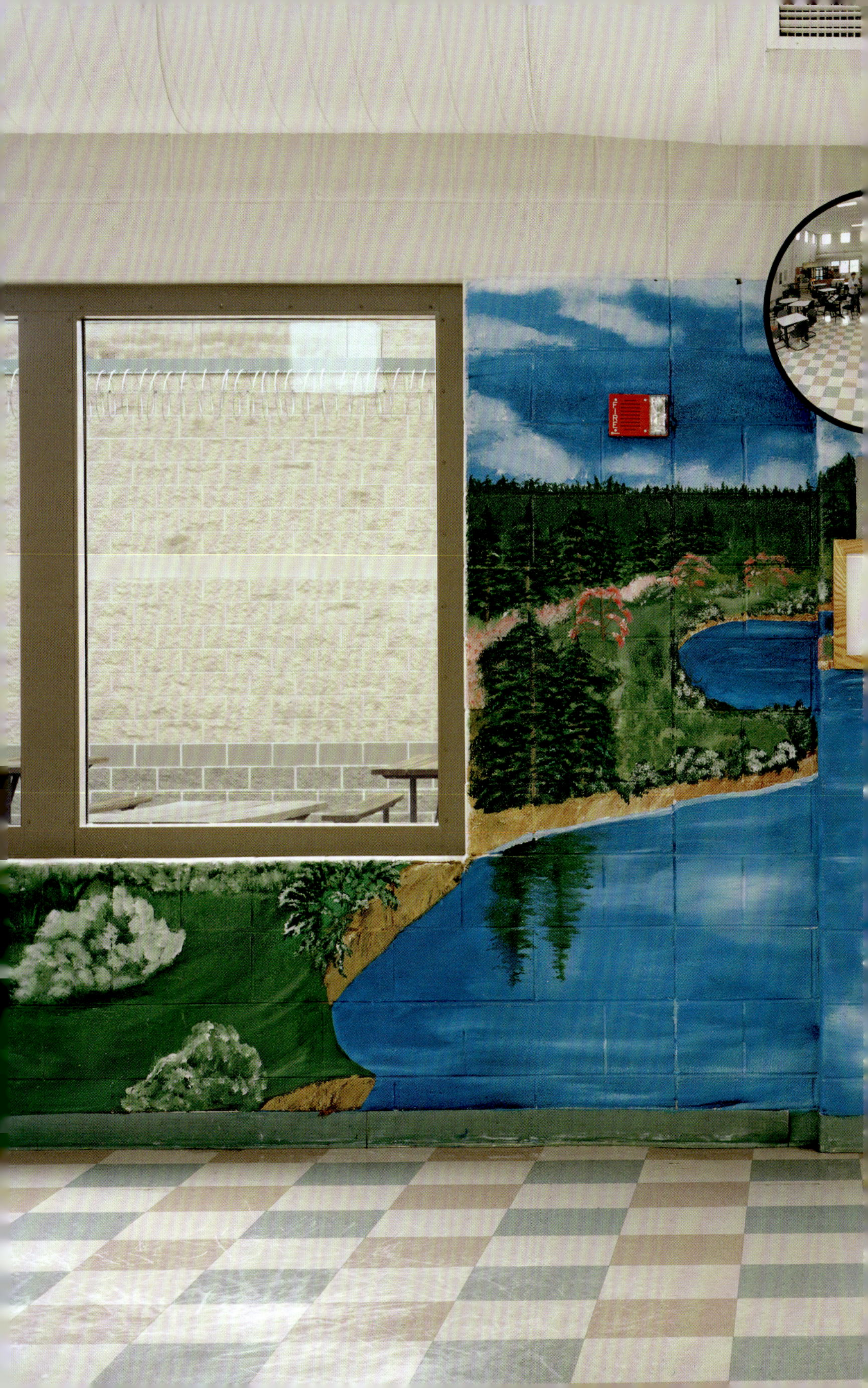

State Correctional Institution, Houtzdale, Pennsylvania

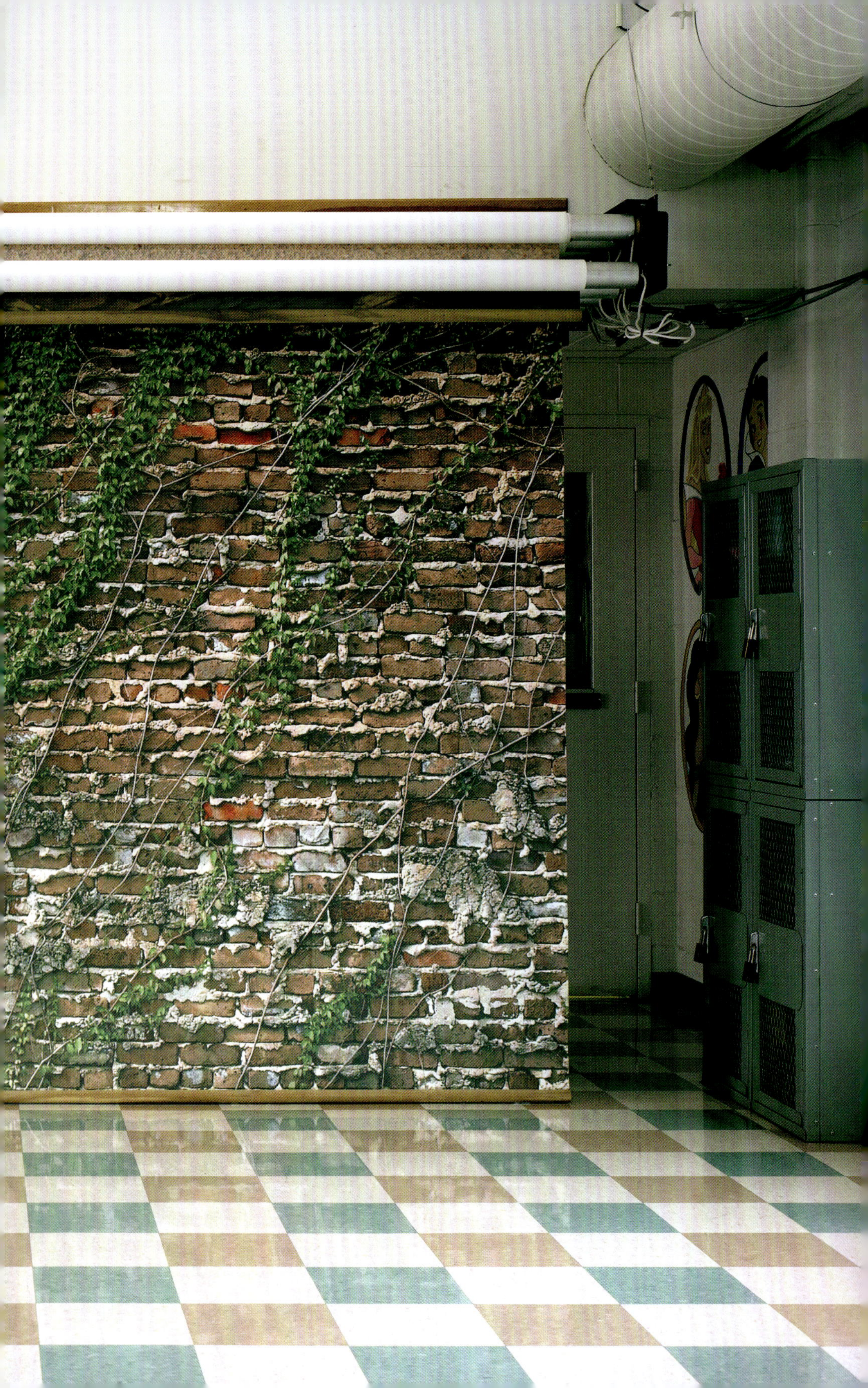

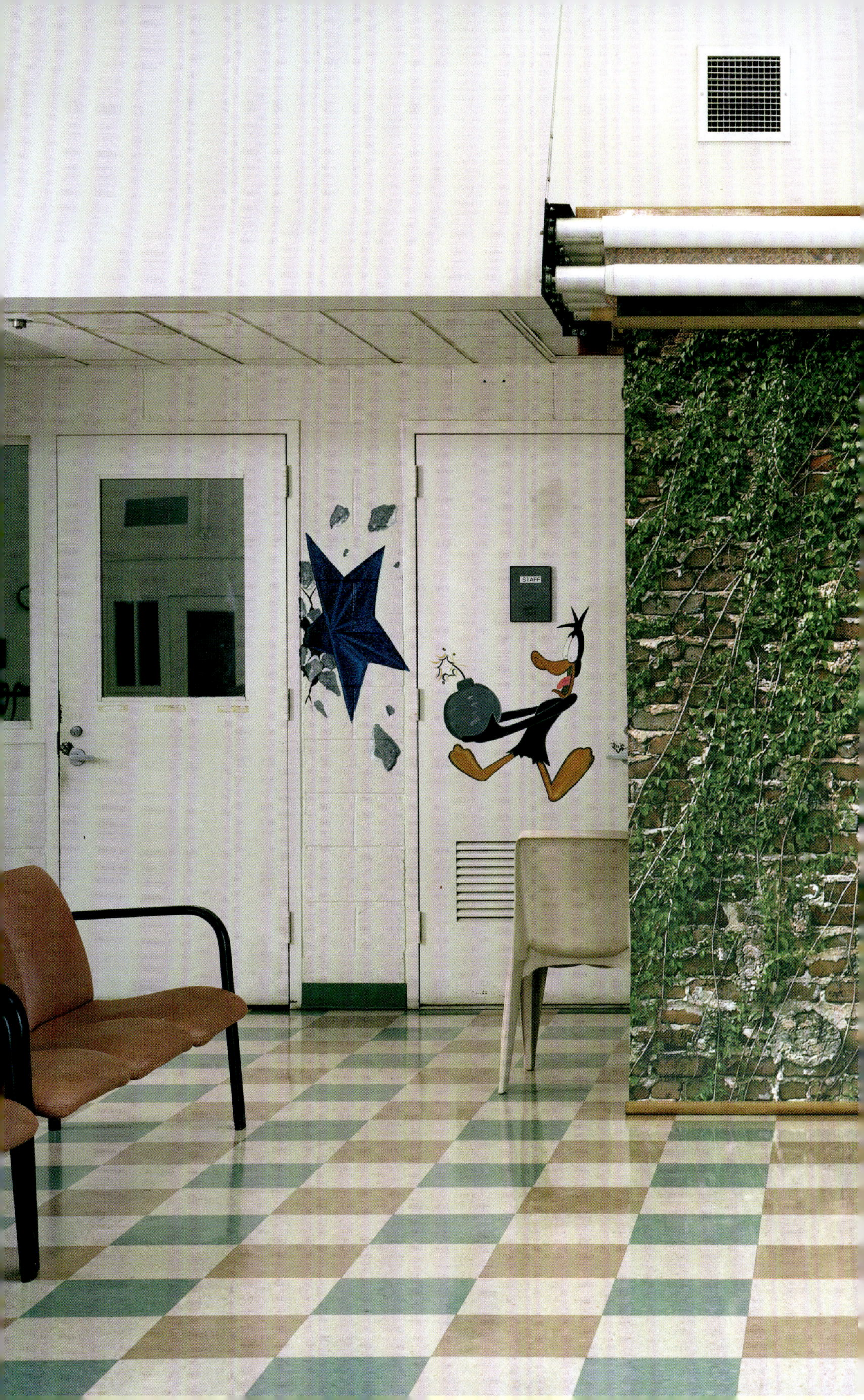

STAFF

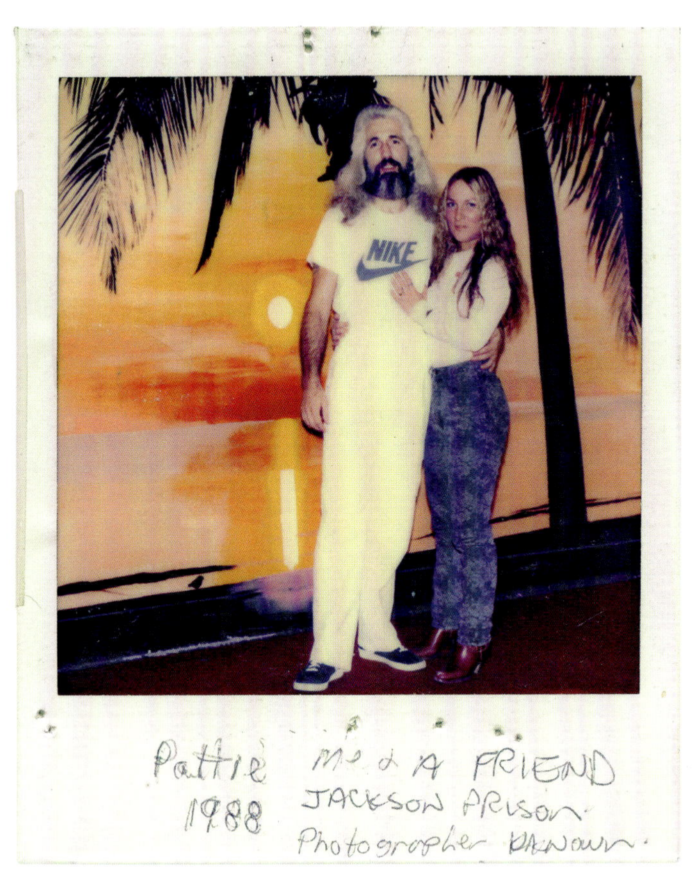

David Wells, Jackson Prison, Michigan

June 14, 2009

"Lana"

Well, I thought that I would get busy, and answer your letter while I'm just sitting here. I was a little surprised to hear from you, but glad that you wrote back.

At Jackson prison, through most of the 80s, I ran a big color photo lab. Occasionally, I did take pictures in the visiting room, but usually I was too busy shooting, developing, and printing 35mm film. I had a big processing machine and mini-printer machine to do the pictures.

The mini-printer uses big rolls of photo printing paper. I used to run the place like a photo-mat. I supplied five other prisons with 35mm cameras so that they could run photo lines at there prisons. Our inmate benefit fund used to pay for everything I ordered. The last few years I was running the lab they gave me a budget of $87,000 a year to run the lab. They would send me the exposed film from the other prisons with the picture orders the guys wanted. I would develop the film, print the pictures, then send them back to them. I made good money for a prison job, plus I had other good perks with the job.

Over the years, I have sent hundreds of pictures out to family. Some of the negatives dated back to the late 40s and 50s. Then, of course, pictures from the 70s and 80s. I even have pictures from the 1981 prison riot when I was at Jackson Prison. They made me send them out a few years back when I was at MacComb Correctional Facility. I had them for 25 years until some new female correctional officer decided that I shouldn't have them, so I sent them home. Yes, the visiting room photos are taken by inmates. Nowadays they use digital cameras for prison photos.

No, I don't do any photography anymore, but I will get back into it when I get out.

How many years did you visit your brother? Is he still in the prison system? Nowadays I believe the big reason so many people are paying attention to prison systems is because of the cost to

keep so many men and women in prison! In fact, I am hoping
to get a parole hearing and a public hearing within the year.
My commutation papers have been in front of the parole board
since the end of September 2008. Usually, within the month they
have turned me down. So who knows what they are thinking.

It is a good thing that you're doing. More people should care about
what is happening with our prison system. Most people do not
care, until it affects their loved ones. It's not to say that we should
not be punished for crimes. But treating people badly and making
them do large amounts of time in prisons does not make good
better people. They create monsters. In this state, most guys
do a lot of time for minor crimes. For 50,000 inmates in this prison
system, they actually spend over two billion dollars a year. That
is about $40,000 a year for each of us. They would be better off
just spending some of that money on a college education for most
of these guys. The better education people have, the less chance
they will end up in prisons.

I think I will sign off this letter for now, so I can get it out to you.
Bye for now, but take care of yourself.

In the Spirit of Freedom.

David

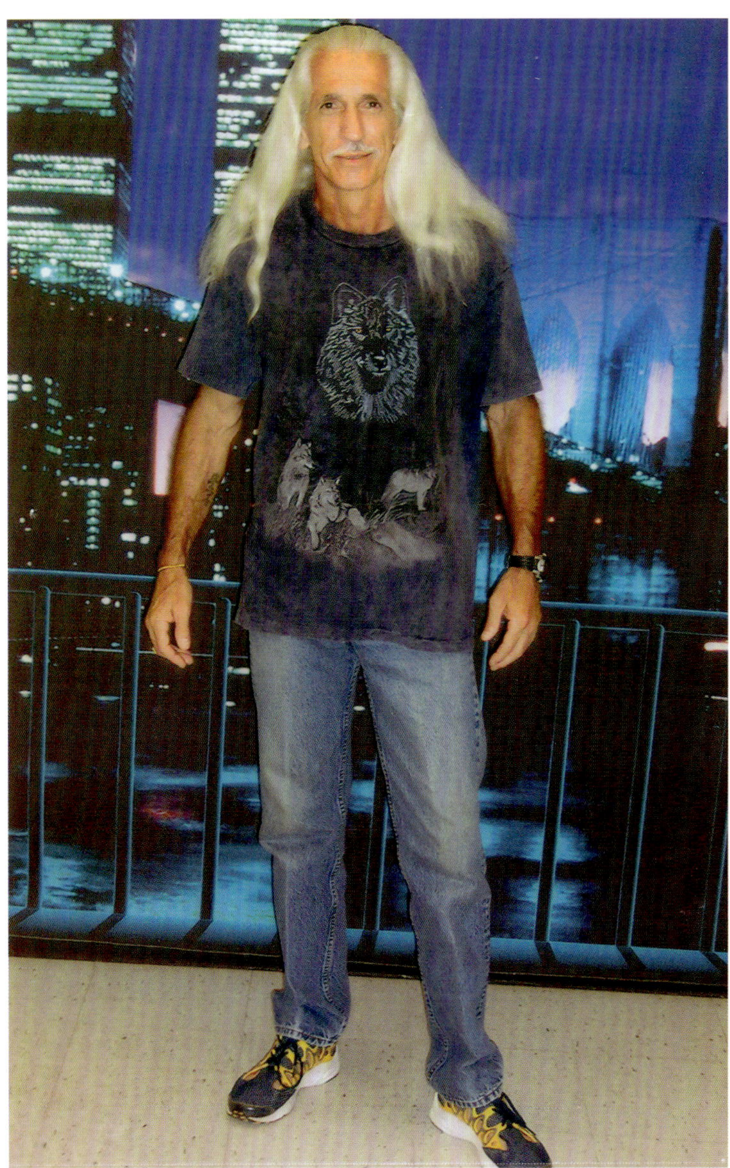

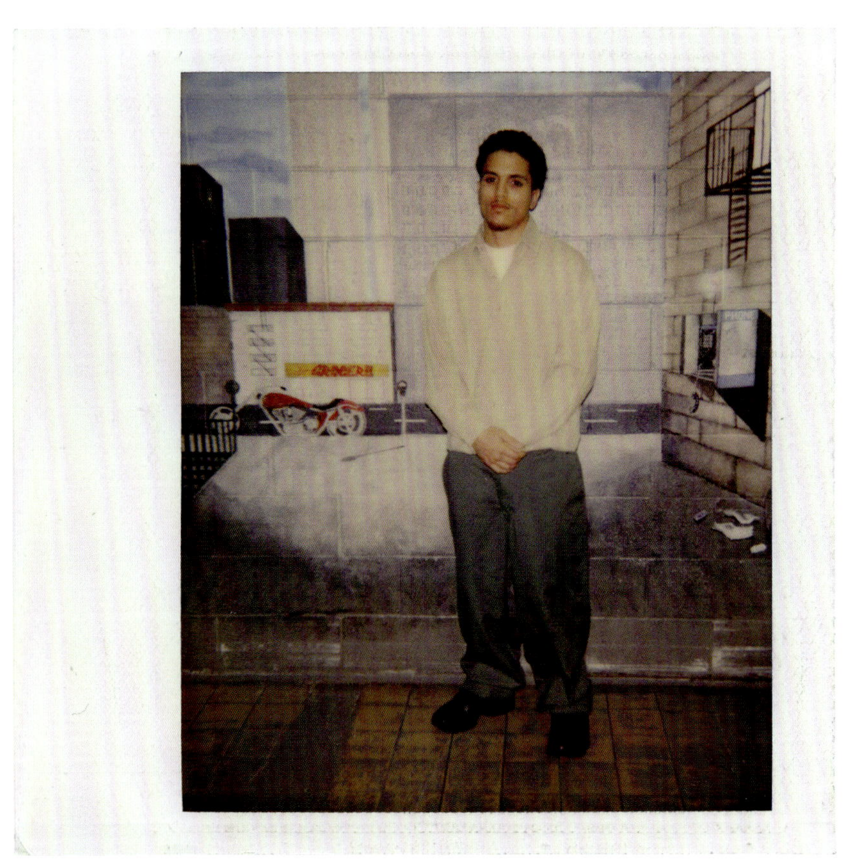

Anonymous

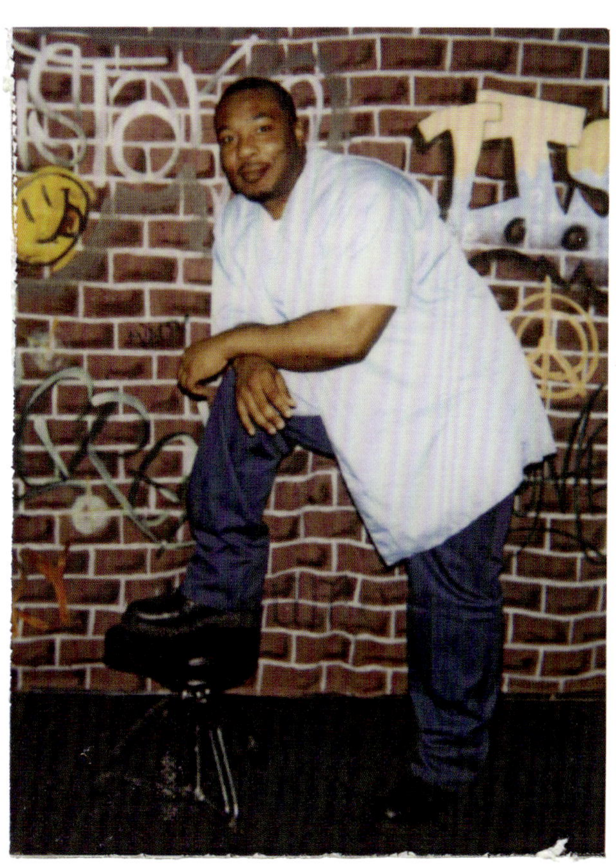

Kyren Oliver, Danville Correctional
Center, Danville, Illinois

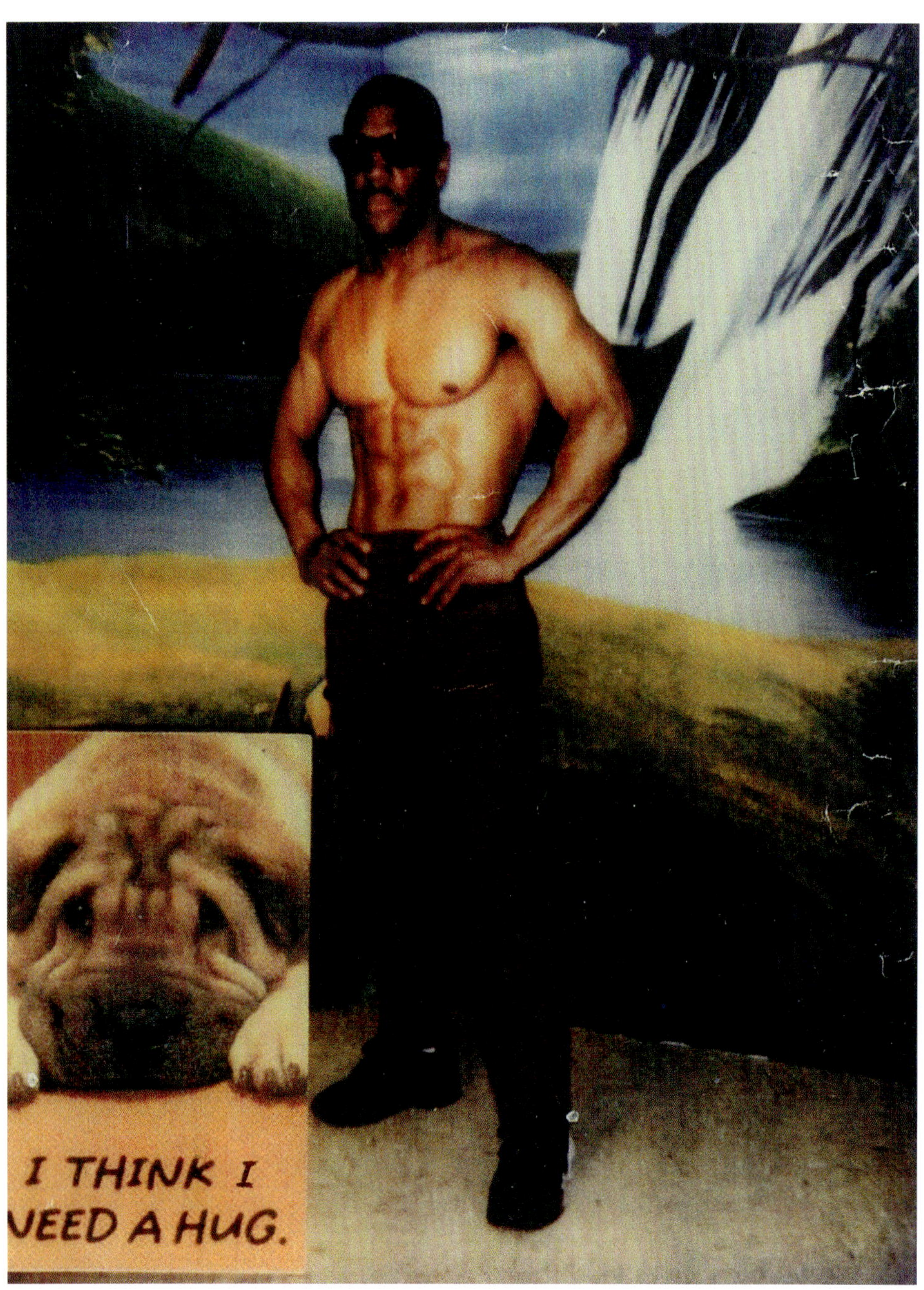

Juan Matias, Upstate Correctional
Facility, Malone, New York

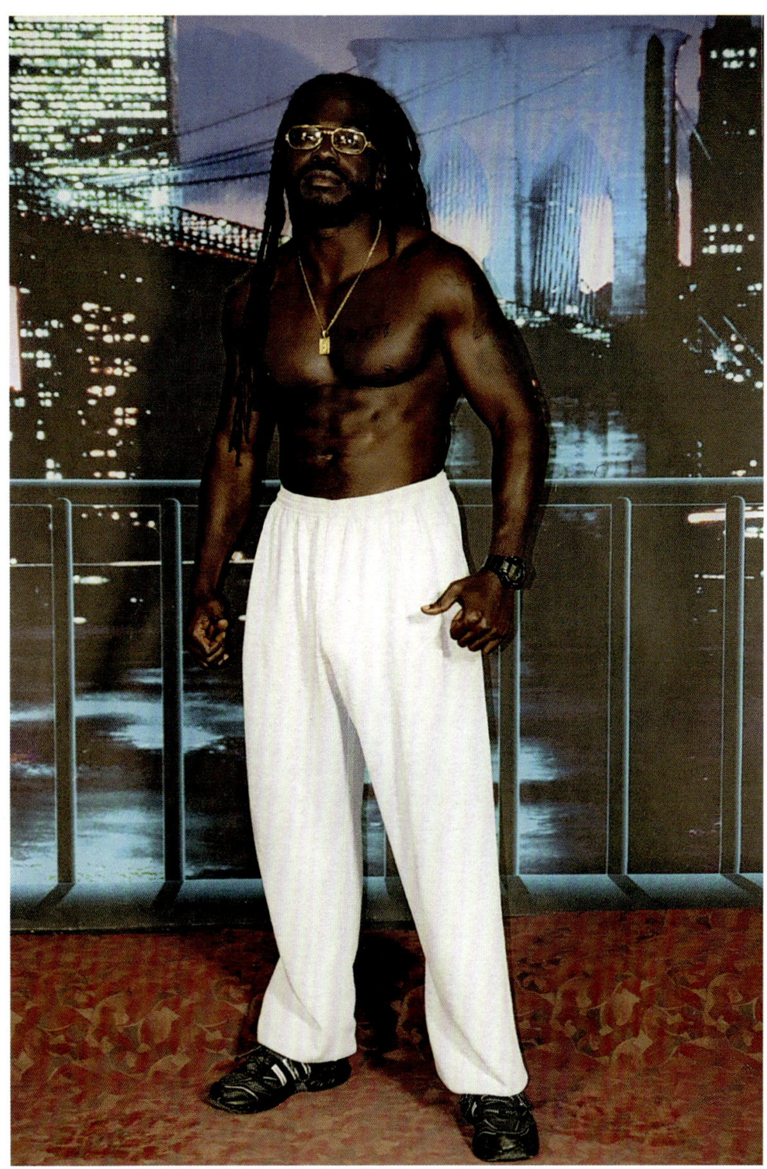

Momolu Stewert, Federal Correctional
Complex, Coleman, Florida

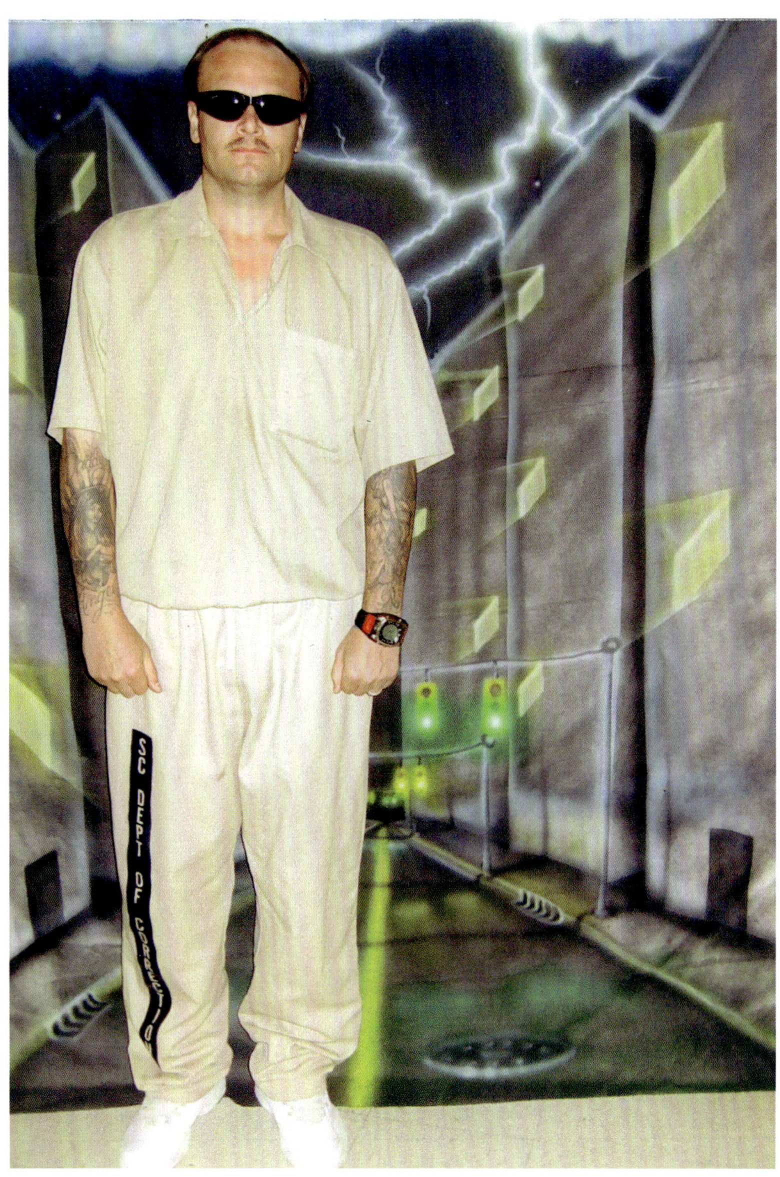

Adam Bickham, Lee Correctional
Institution, Bishopville, South Carolina

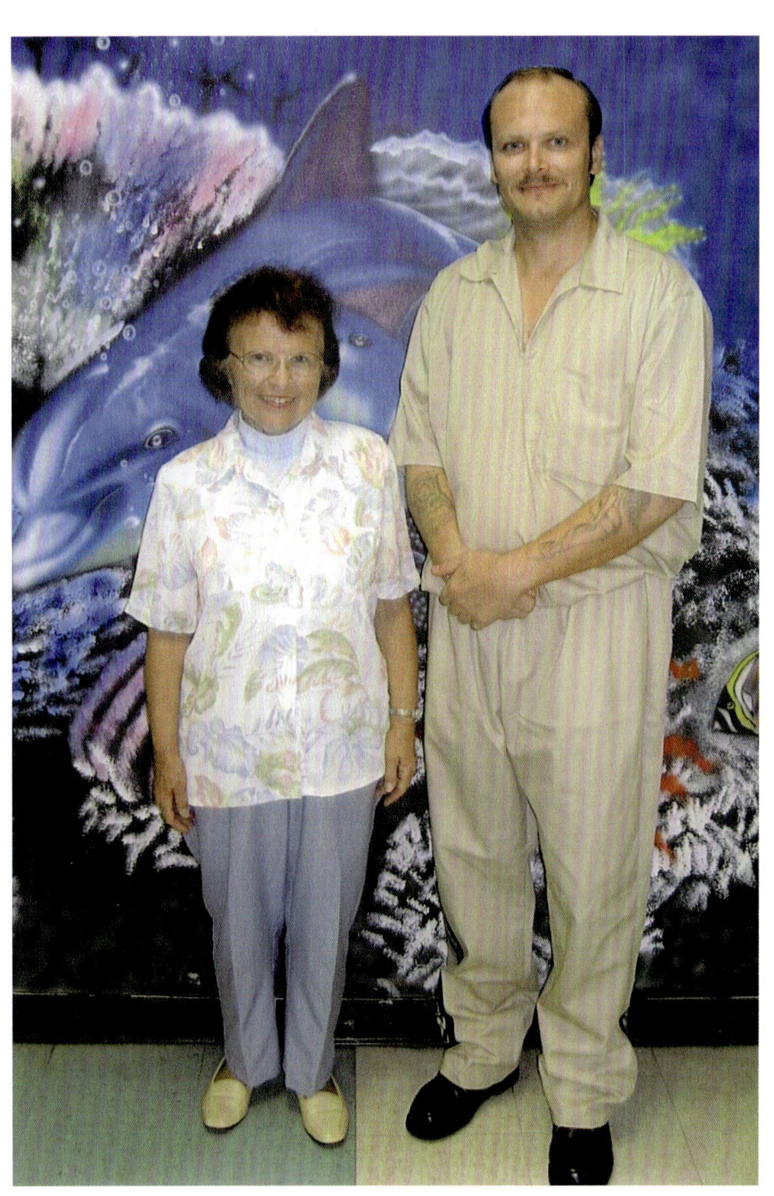

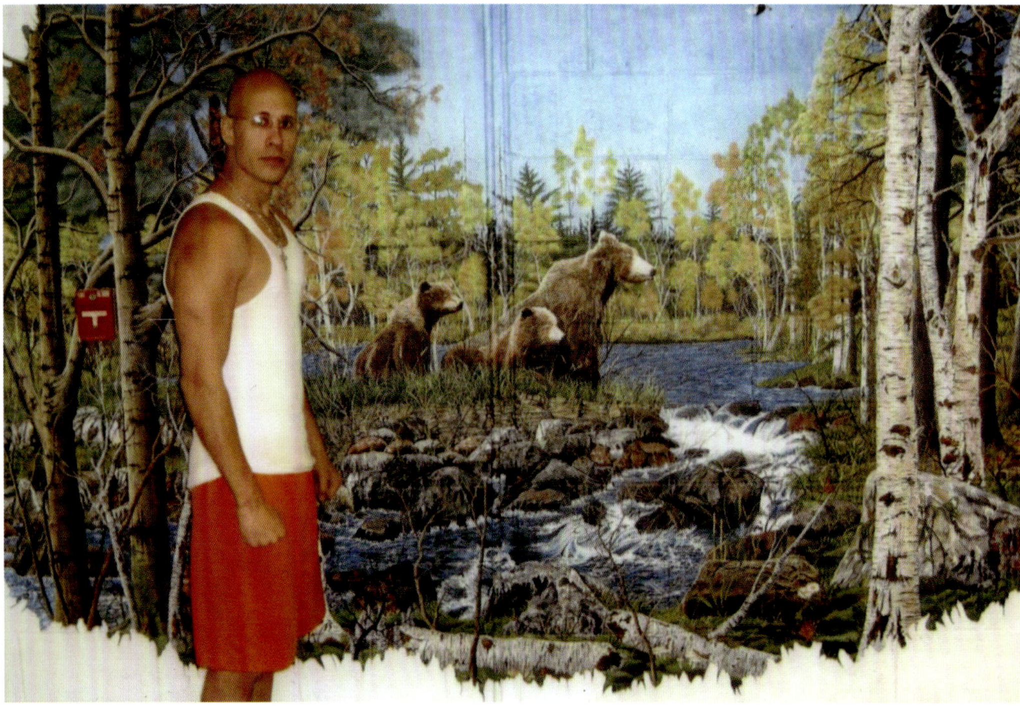

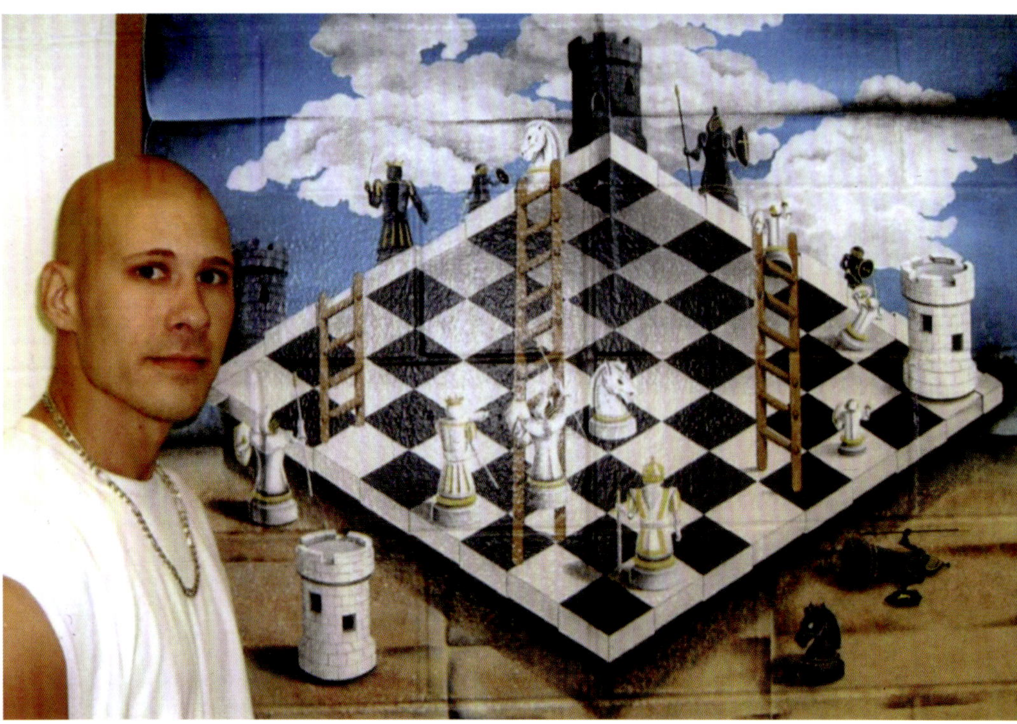

Adam Litwin, Boyer Road Correctional Facility, Carson City, Michigan

April 8, 2009

Hello! It was nice to hear from you. From the brief description you gave me, we have similar life experiences. I have a little sister who is now 19 and in college in Ohio. Unfortunately, I have been gone since she was six years old. However, I have always made it a point to be a positive male figure in her life, seeing as her father passed when she was five.

For personal reasons, I no longer paint or draw. However, I am enclosing three photos for you. The chess photo is a full length painting. I took the two photos one on either end because I thought it would be a cool idea to get the pictures cropped in together as if I was playing chess with myself. The name of the artist who painted the chess backdrop is Troy Reinstra #202107. Troy is the Director of a Christian Prison Ministry that he founded while incarcerated.

The third photo is done by Bahaa Shakir Kalasho #181993. It was done at Standish Max. Correctional Facility, the same with the other two photos. Bahaa Kalasho is the undisputed most talented artist in the M.D.O.C. It is so detailed that you literally have to walk up to the painting to catch all of the detail.

Unfortunately, I spent 11 years in maximum security and was not allowed contact visits, as I am now. Otherwise I would enclose a photo of myself and my sister.

My father has been in and out of prison my whole life. I myself have been locked up since I was 15 and have not been home since. I recently turned 29. I hope that your brother is now home and you two are able to build a better relationship. I know I'm looking forward to the same next year with my own sister and family.

I wish you luck Lee Lana.

As sure as,
The sun rises,

Adam

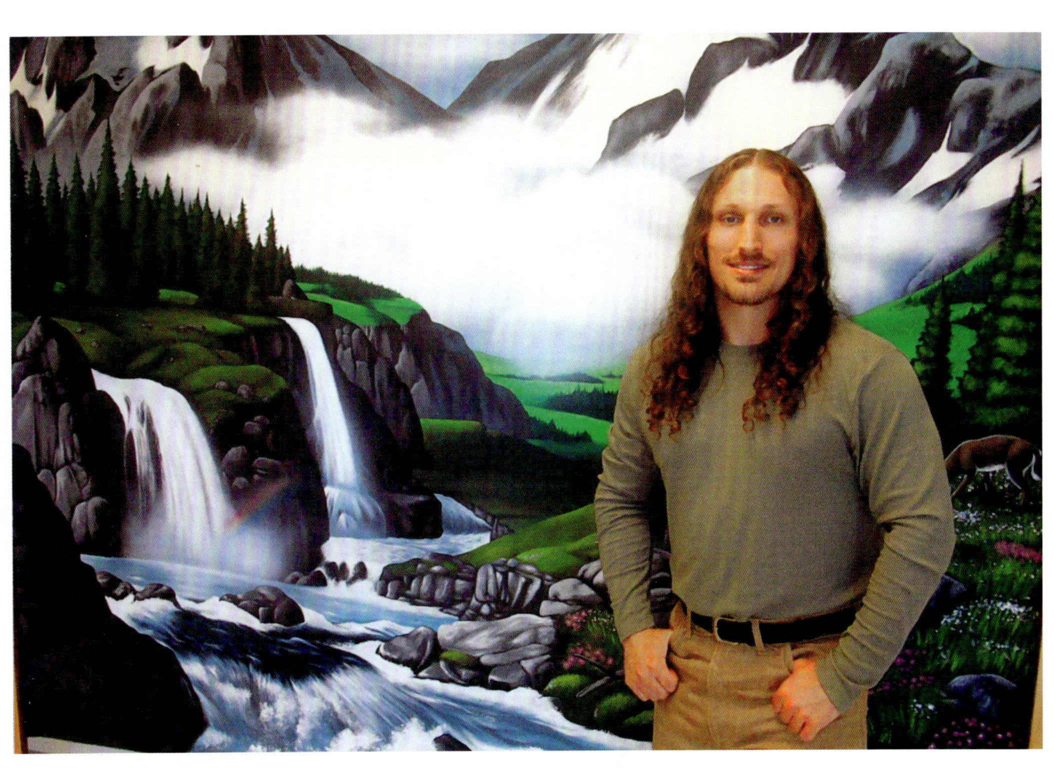

Ryan Muench, Stafford Creek Corrections
Center, Aberdeen, Washington

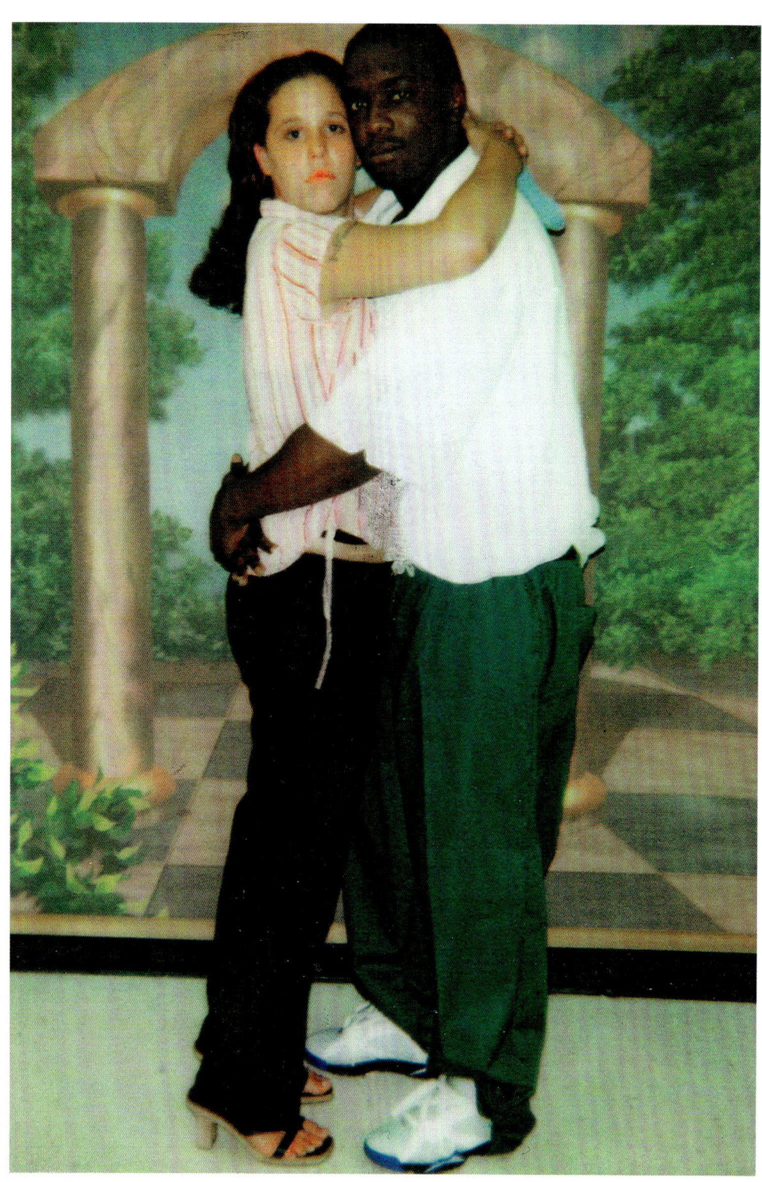

Joel Coleman, Auburn Correctional
Facility, Auburn, New York

State Correctional Institution, Graterford, Pennsylvania

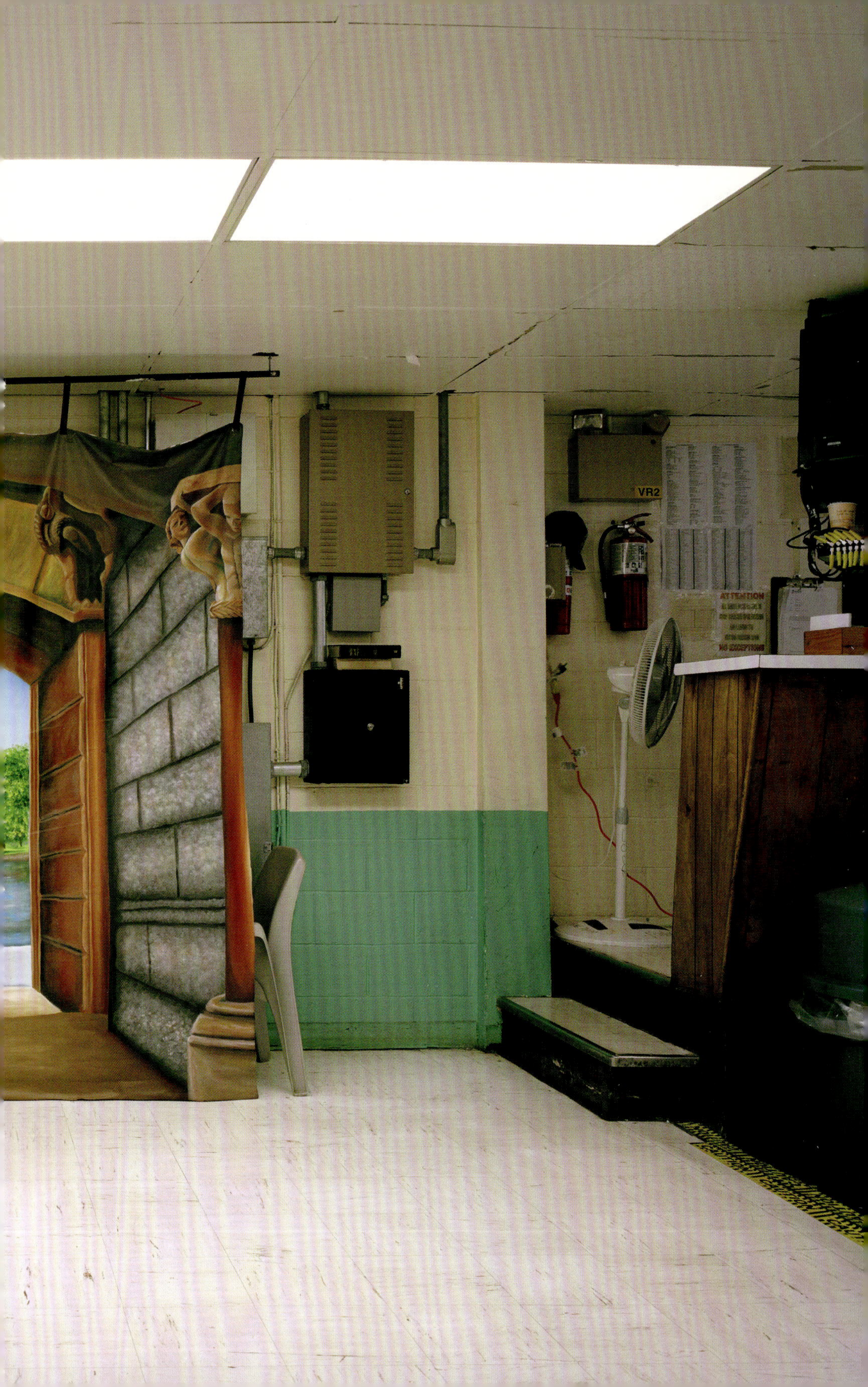

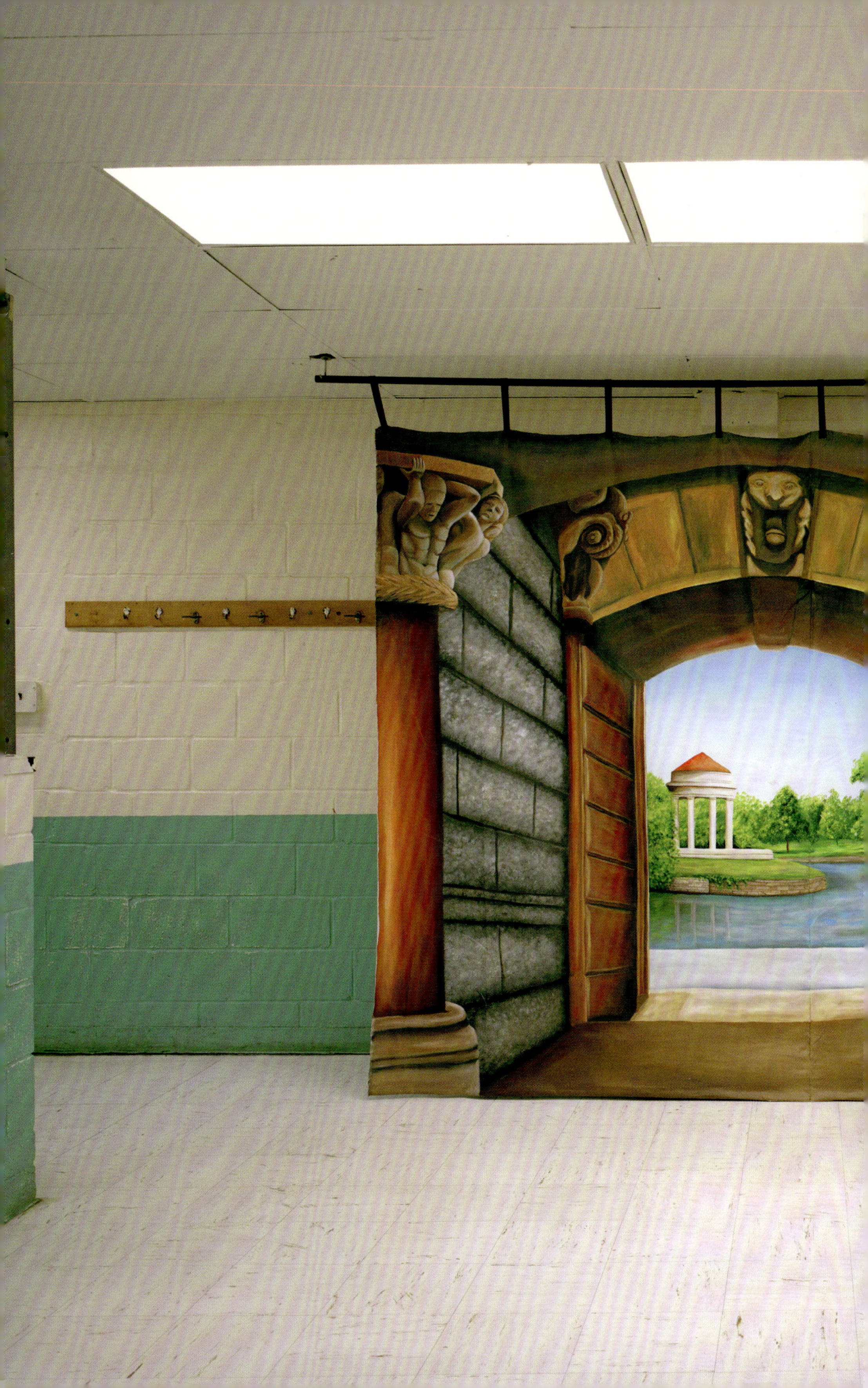

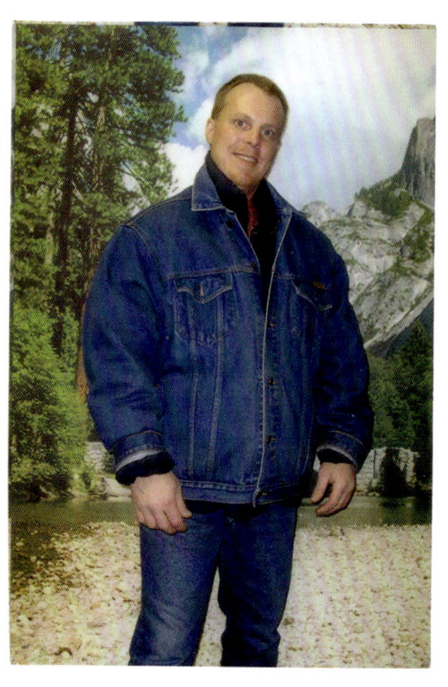 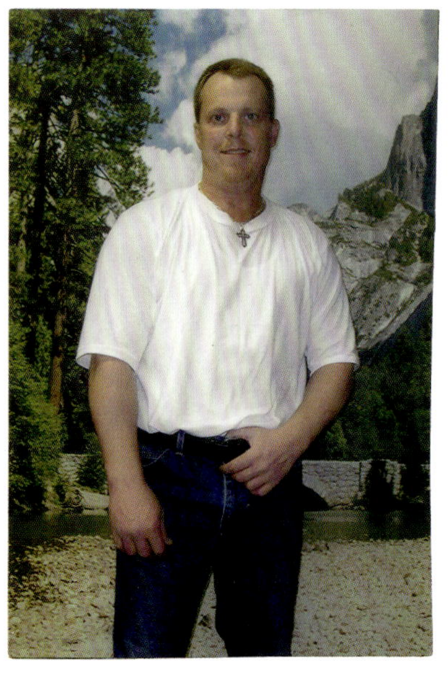

1)   5-28-08
will take some
new ones on my
BirthDay 5-28-09
And if you would
Like more Just
Let me Know.
          Your new
          Pen-PaL
          RogeR

2 my hAiR hAs
grown out Some.

Do these pictures
help you Any?

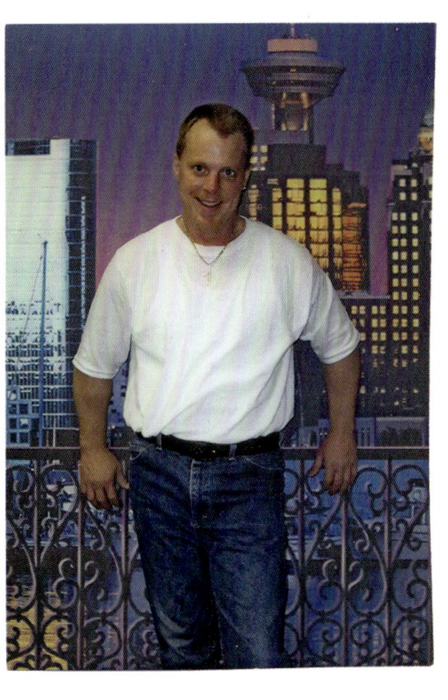 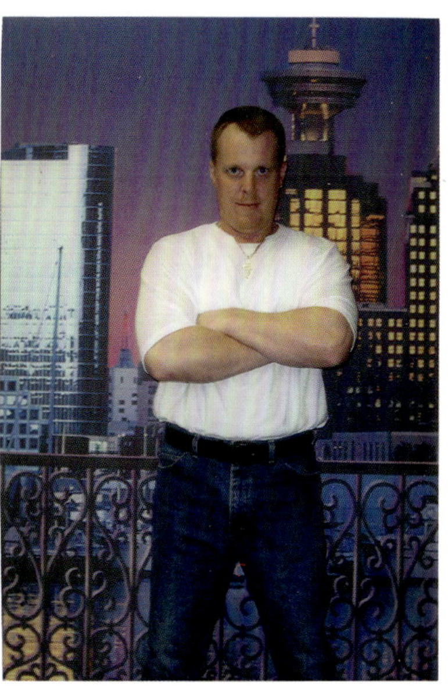

3) I hope so.
Let me know
how your painting
works out ok?

4) write back
soon. I would
Like that very
much!

Your new
Friend +
Pen Pan
Roger

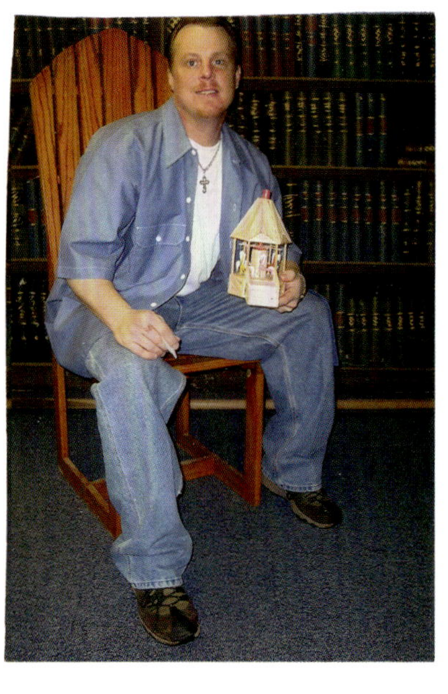

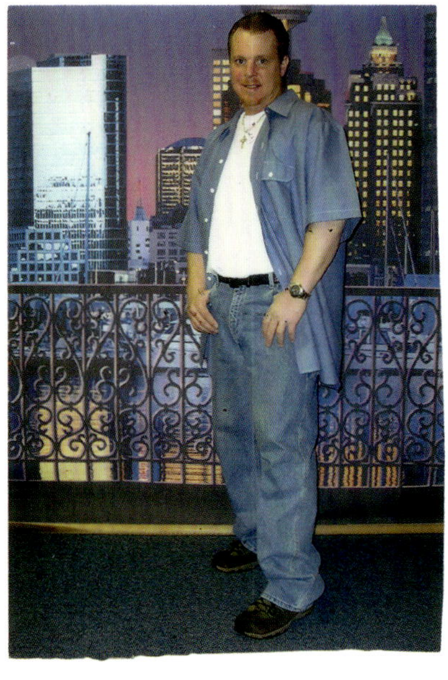

TO: Lee

This is A
new bAckground.
HoPe you LikE
It!

RogeR

TO: lee

Good Luck
on Your Book.

Always your
friend

Roger

July 1, 2009

Dear Lee,

Hello there. It's me again. I just got your letter that you sent out June 2, 2009. I was on a ride to Wayne County and I beat 11 out of 13 felonies that happened when I got shot and arrested September 27, 2004. So, I won court and now it's my time to get them in federal court for my lawsuit. I proved they shot me four times in the back for no reason. So, hopefully, I'll be set for life when I get out next year.

I bought another photo ticket because they have a new background in the booth. It's like a library or something. So when I go in for my hair-cut this week, I'll send you a new one. I got into a fight with five black guys in the county jail who were trying to take my breakfast. I got a nice scar under my left eye and a small one over it, as well. Oh well, can't keep my looks forever, right? It's what's in the inside that counts.

Nice picture you drew. Here's mine! (LOL)

Well, keep working hard and if you find me a pen pal, great. If you don't, I would love to hear from you from time to time, OK?

Sincerely Your Friend,

Roger

For the past 17 years 7 months I've
been incarcerated in federal prison on
drug conspiracy charges. I was given
a 27-year sentence, no drugs were
found upon my arrest. It was all based
on hearsay and to me the punishment
just didn't fit the crime. Stay away from
anyone who uses drugs or sell the stuff
because all the money in the world is
not worth being away from your children
for all the years the feds will give you.

People need to know that in all
actuality you don't have to be caught
with drugs to get a 30 year or life
sentence. Conspiracy is a very hard
charge to beat especially if you take
it to trial and don't snitch on the people
in your midst.

Claudette Hubbard (left), Federal Prison
Camp, Dublin, CA

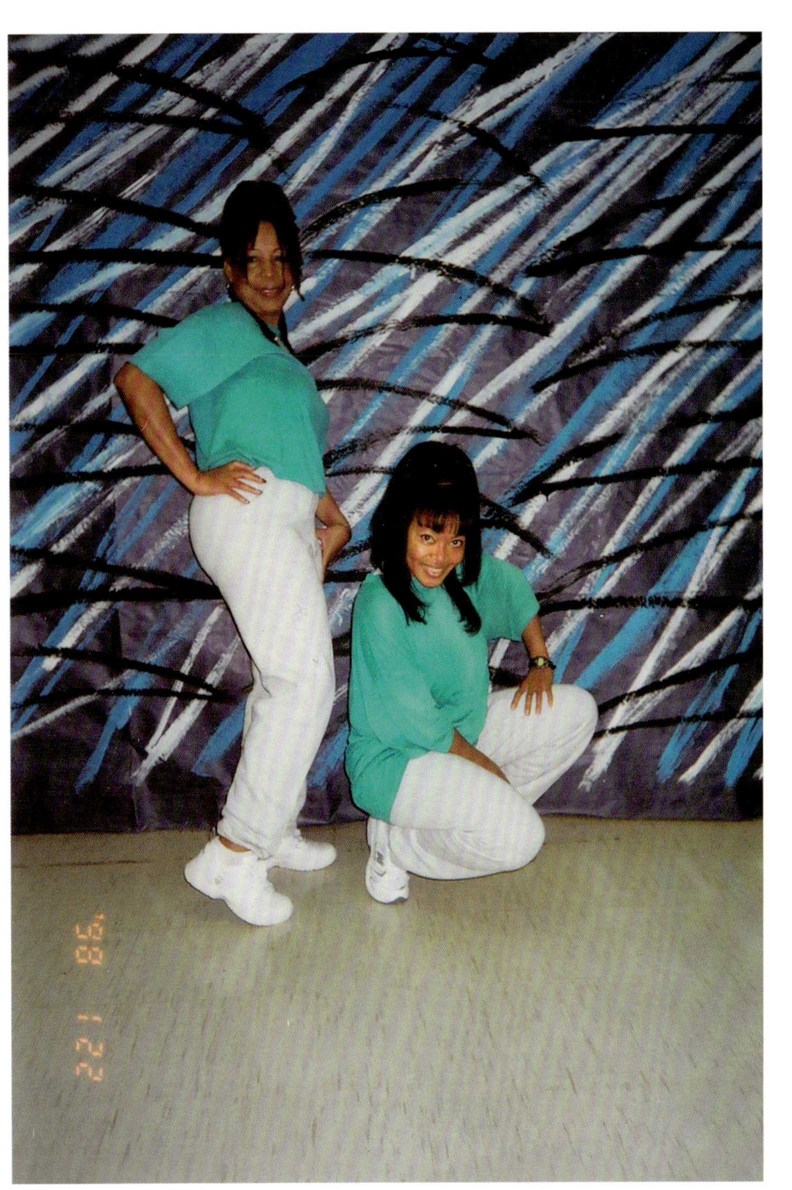

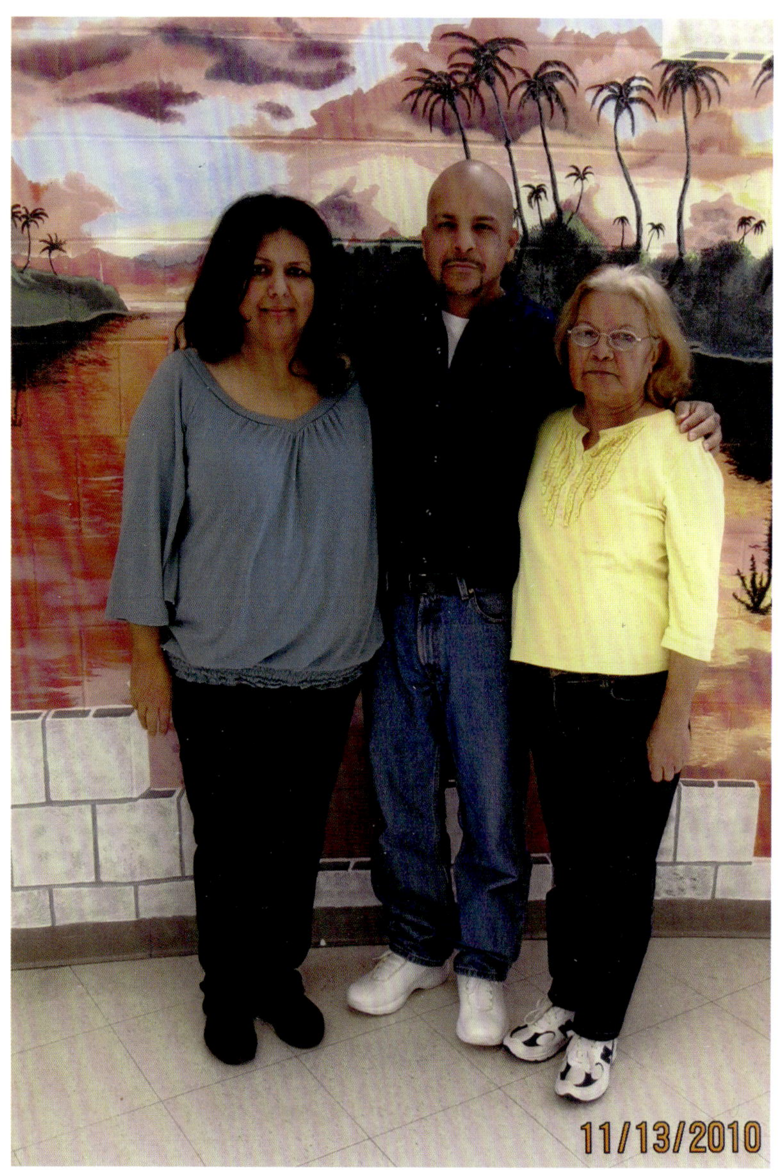

Ramon Cruz, Old Colony Correctional
Center, Bridgewater, Massachusetts

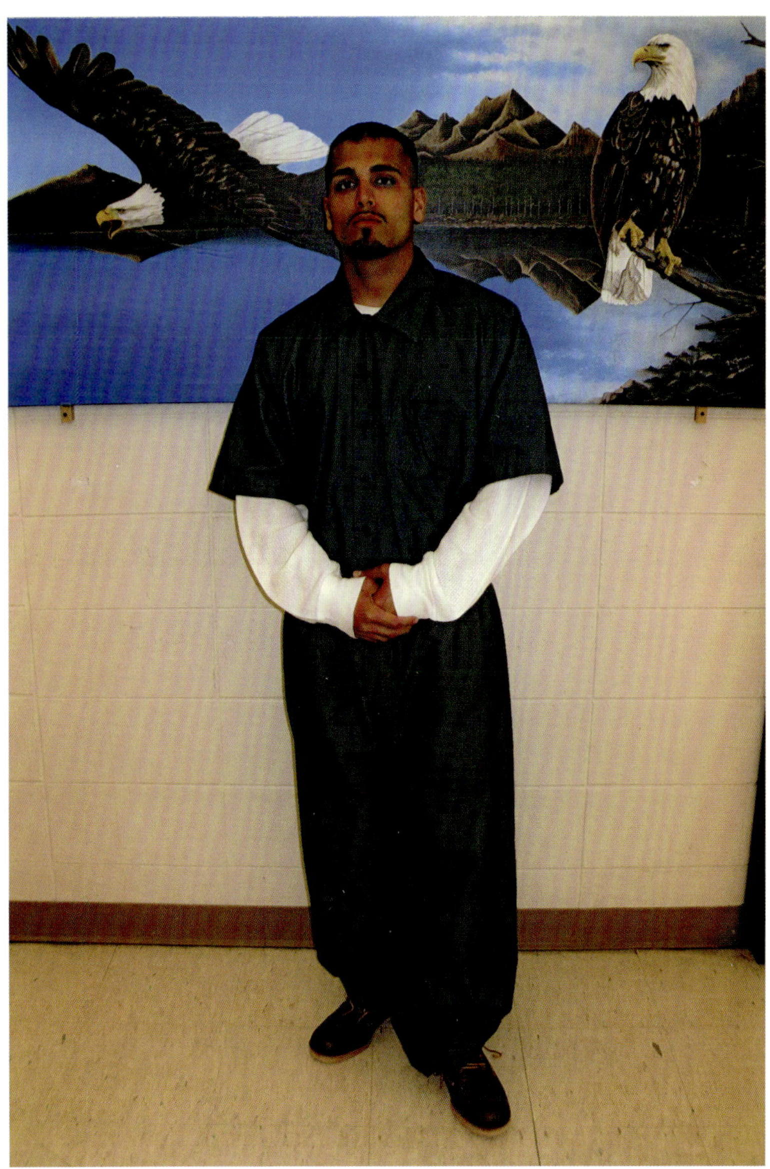

Usman Tariq, United States
Penitentiary, Leavenworth, Kansas

May 7, 2009

Dear Lee, Hello!

I'm not the person that you wrote. I'm Aaron Duchaine's cousin.
He wanted me to write you and send you this picture of me,
so you can see how I look. Let me introduce myself, My name
is Alonzo Salinas, I am 39 years old, Single, 6'3" in height, I'm an
understanding outgoing person. Been locked up for over 11 years
and I am ready to get out in 13 months. Be moving back to my
hometown Saginaw, Michigan. I plan to use my talent of making
greeting cards when I'm home, probably open up a card business.
Haven't made up my mind yet! The greeting cards I make here
are nice. I also write poems in each one of them, from birthdays,
to anniversary cards. Any card people want me to make for them,
I'll make. The business is good in here. So you say that your older
brother was in and out of prison, and you two took a lot of polaroid
pictures? I love taking pictures but it's very rare that I take
them because I don't have no one to send pictures to. So if you're
interested in writing me, I would like to hear from you. When you
write back, I'll tell you more about me. Send a picture.

Alonzo Salinas #'223118
Kinross Correctional Facility
16770 Watertower Drive
Kincheloe, MI. 49788

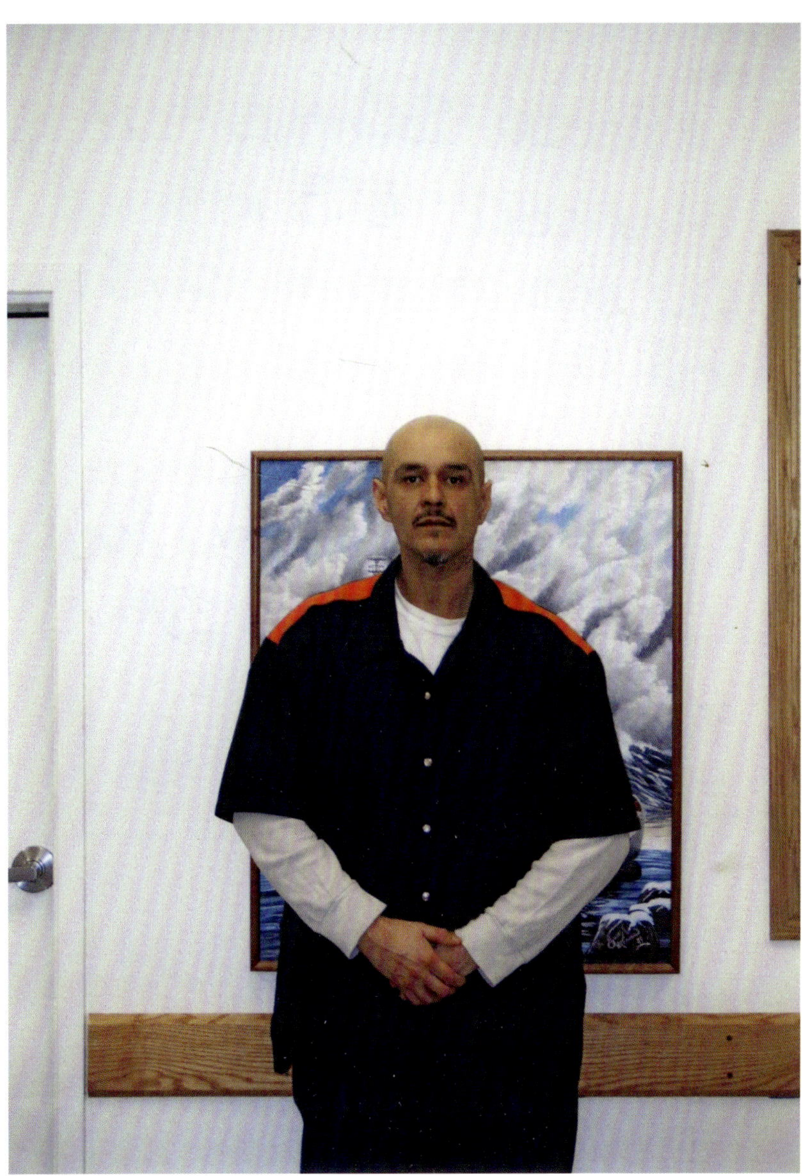

Alonzo Salinas, Kinross Correctional
Facility, Kincheloe, Michigan

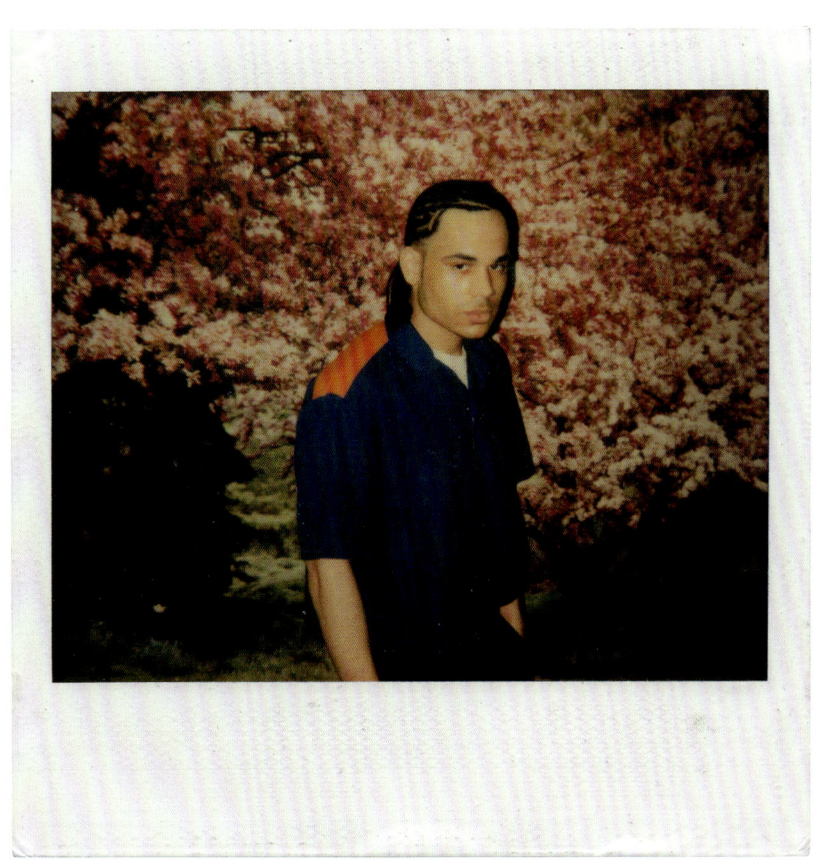

Anonymous, Ionia Maximum
Correctional Facility, Ionia, Michigan

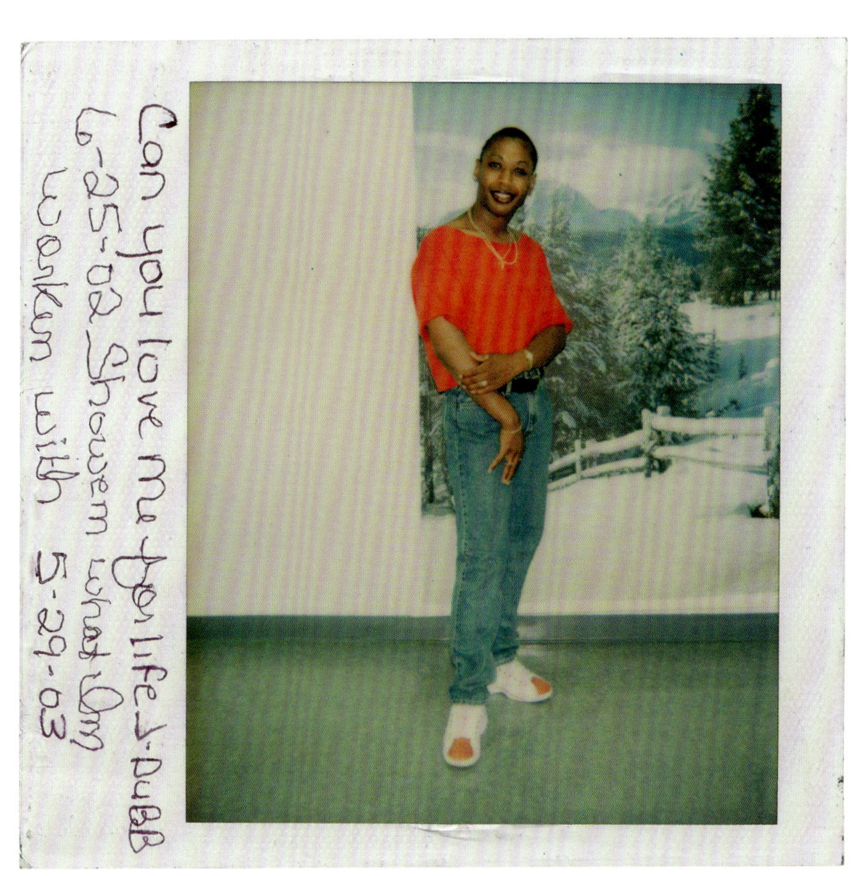

Anonymous, Ionia Maximum
Correctional Facility, Ionia, Michigan

I think the murals are supposed to
represent illusions. Even if I pretended
that I was someplace else, reality
would not let that moment last long.
I'm always aware of where I'm at.
The illusion serves as an escape for
some but for me, it is only a prop to
make me feel like I should be happy
in a place where everyday is sad.
I like being in front of the camera and
I like photography period. Nobody has
a camera in here and we can't take
pictures outside of the prison.

Antoine Ealy, Federal Correctional
Complex, Coleman, Florida

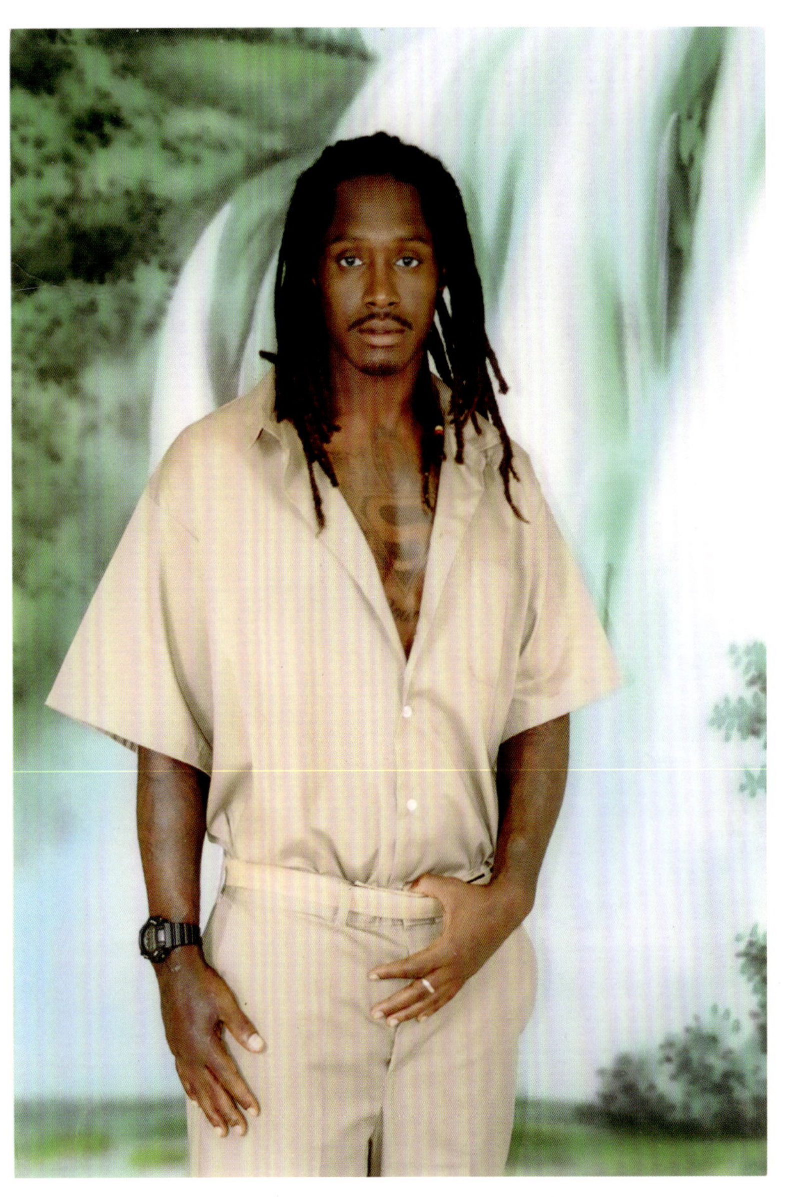

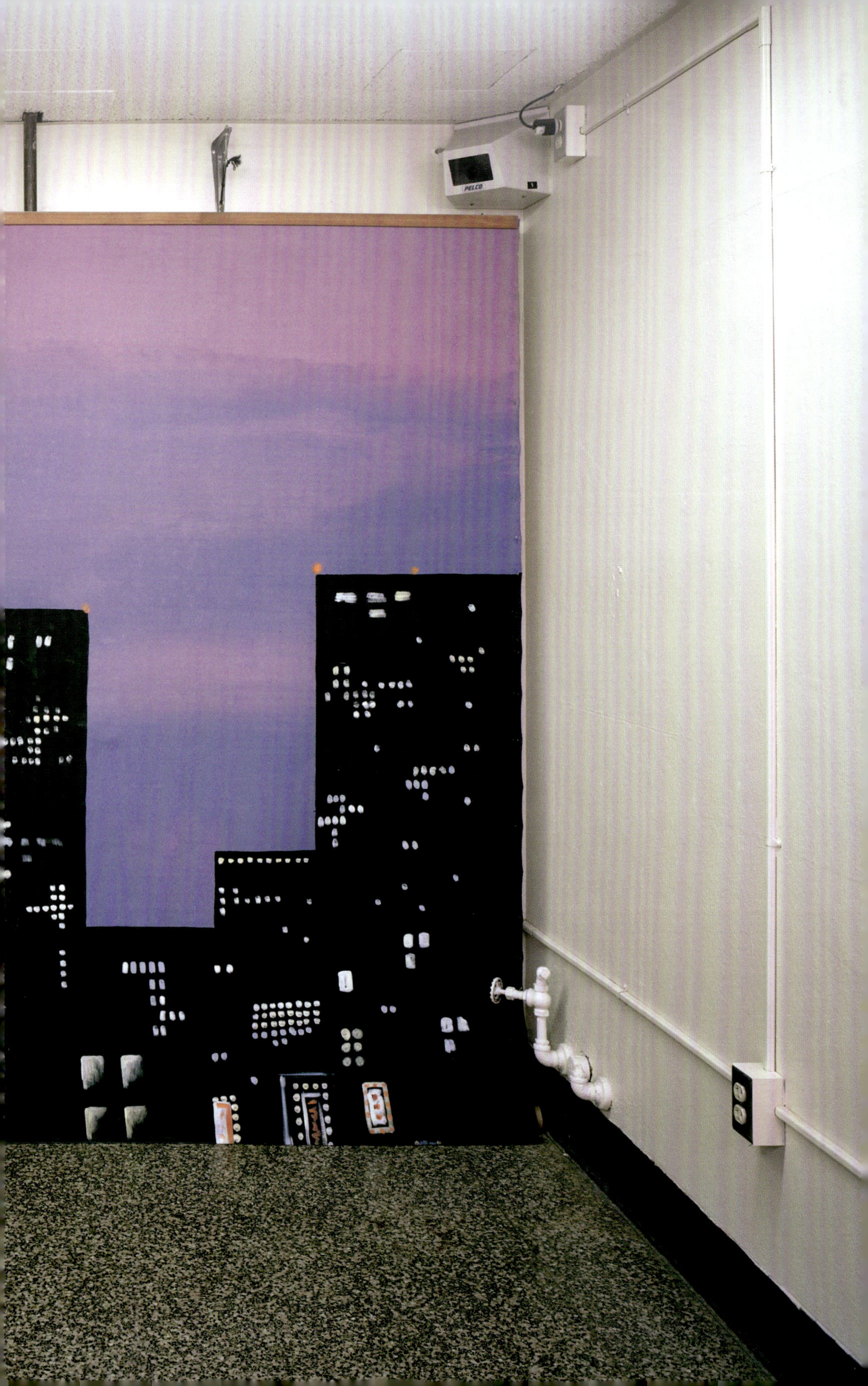

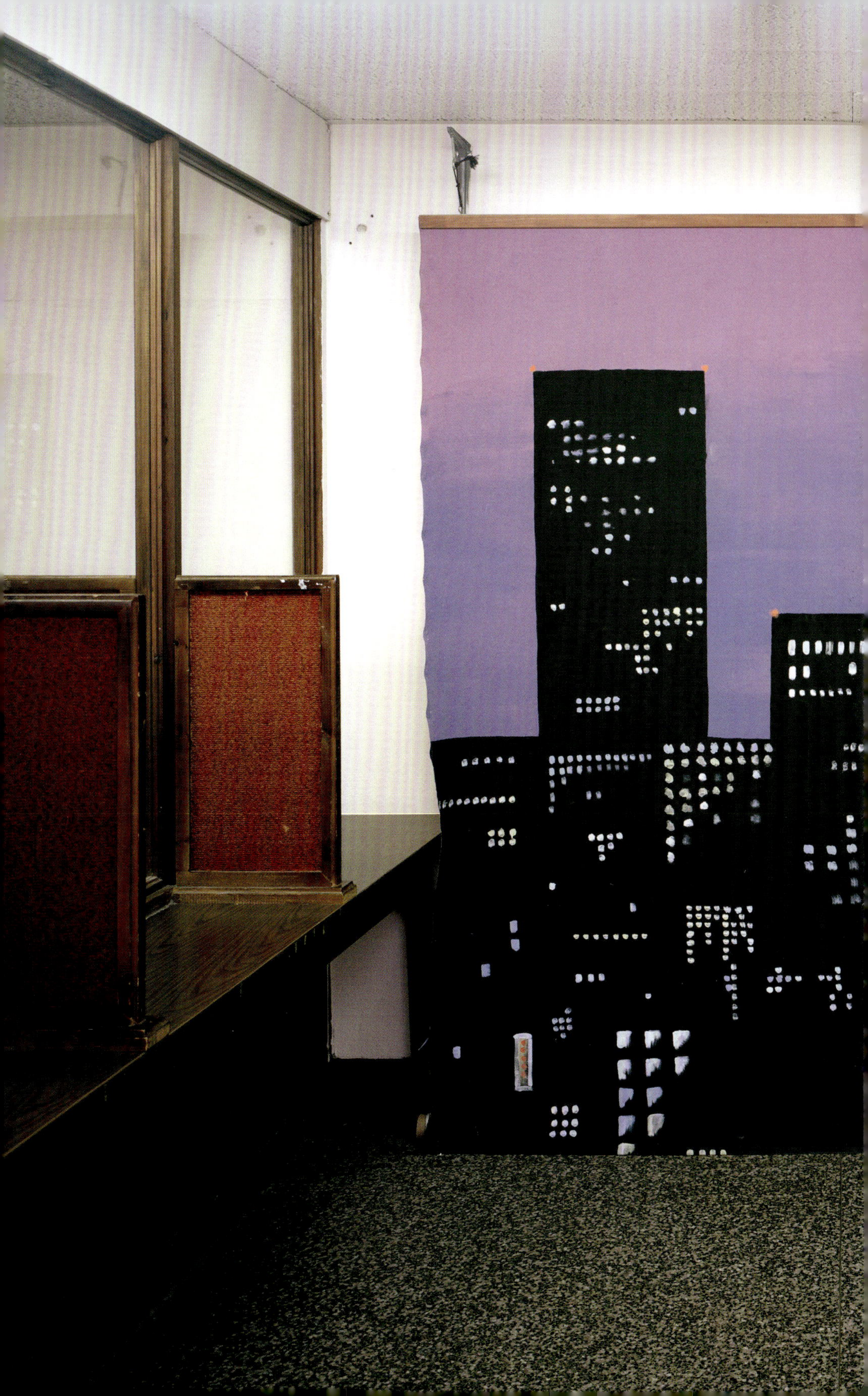

Auborn Correctional Facility, New York

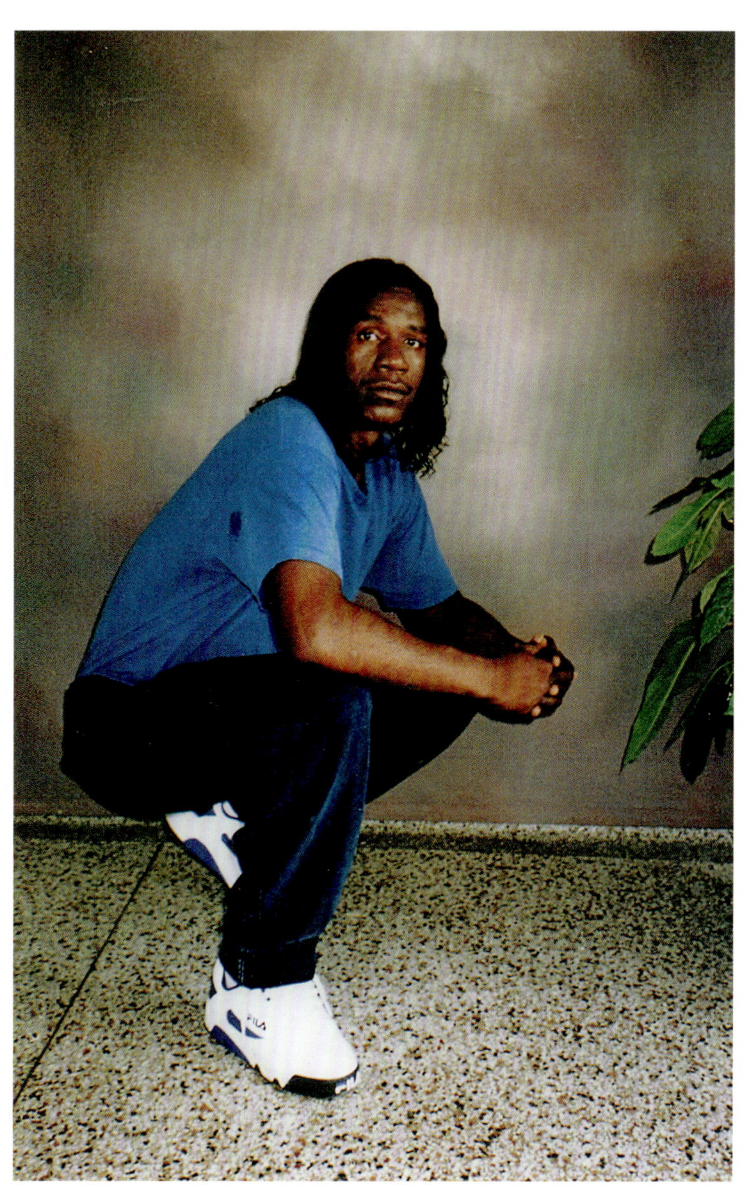

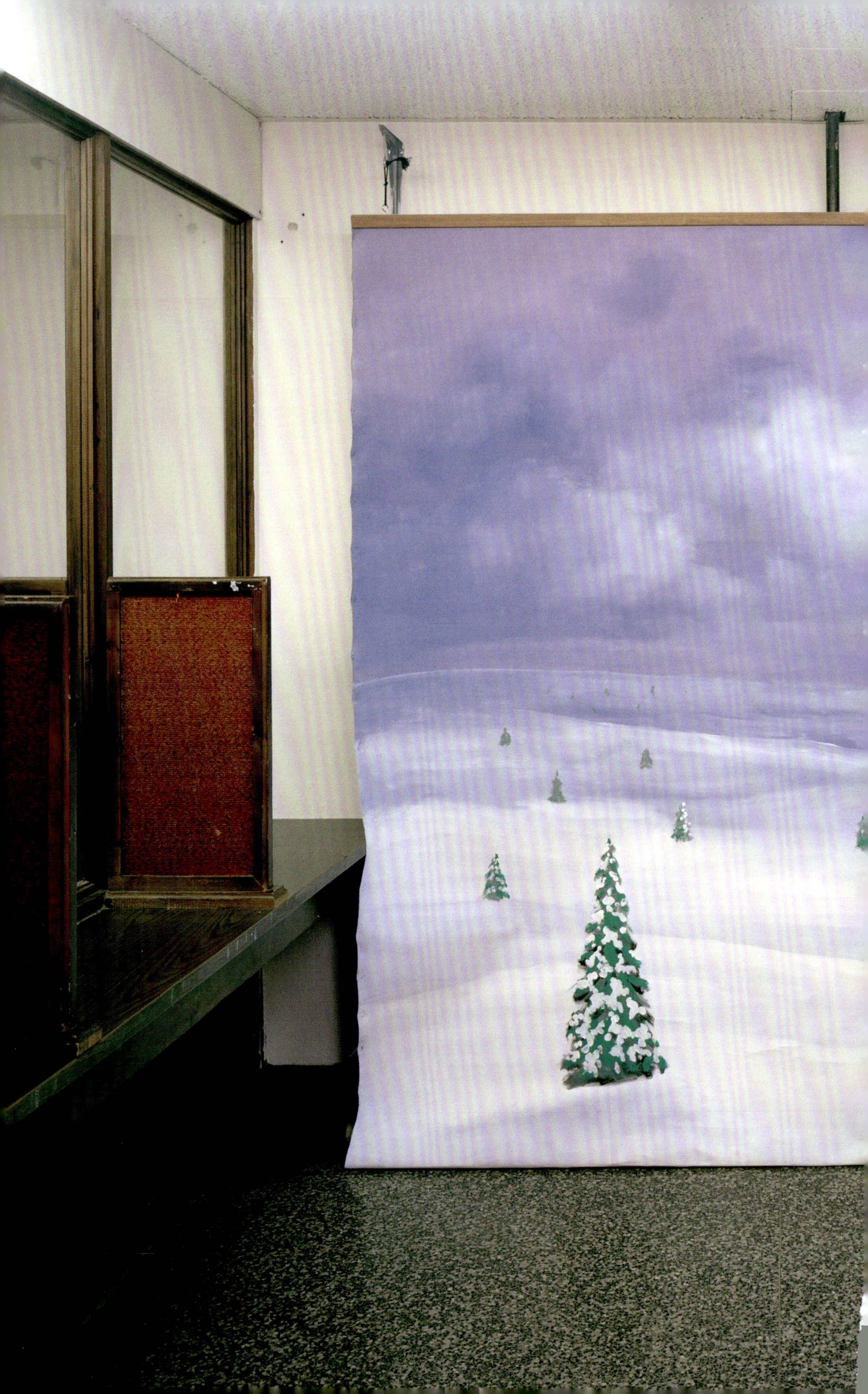

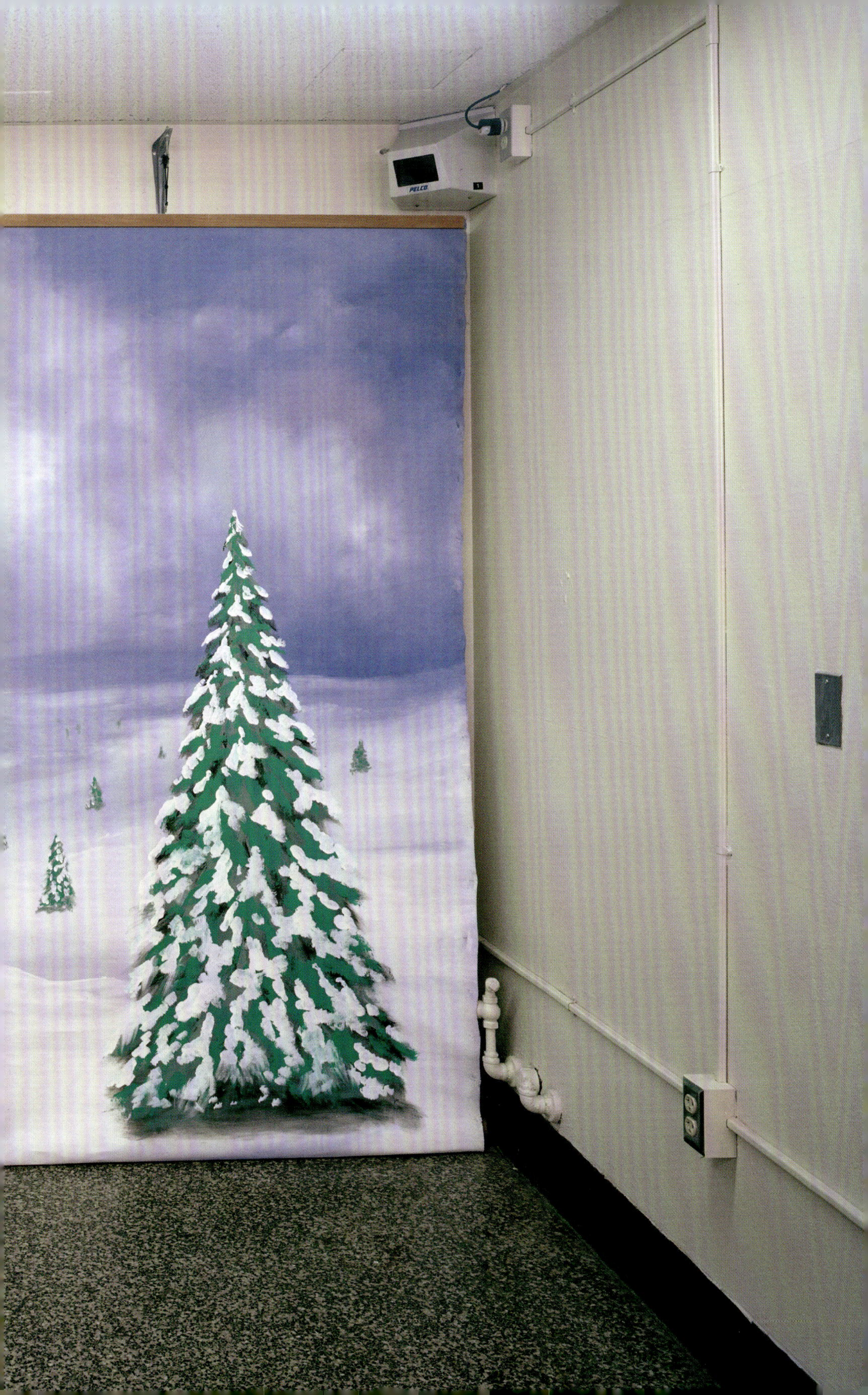

Greetings America,
When I struck a pose I was thinking,
how do I pose while incarcerated?
I definitely didn't want to smile, because
I didn't want people to think I was okay
with where I'm at. Basically I just took
pictures to let my loved ones know
I was alright.

Greg Chambers, Minnesota Correctional
Facility, Lino Lakes, Minnesota

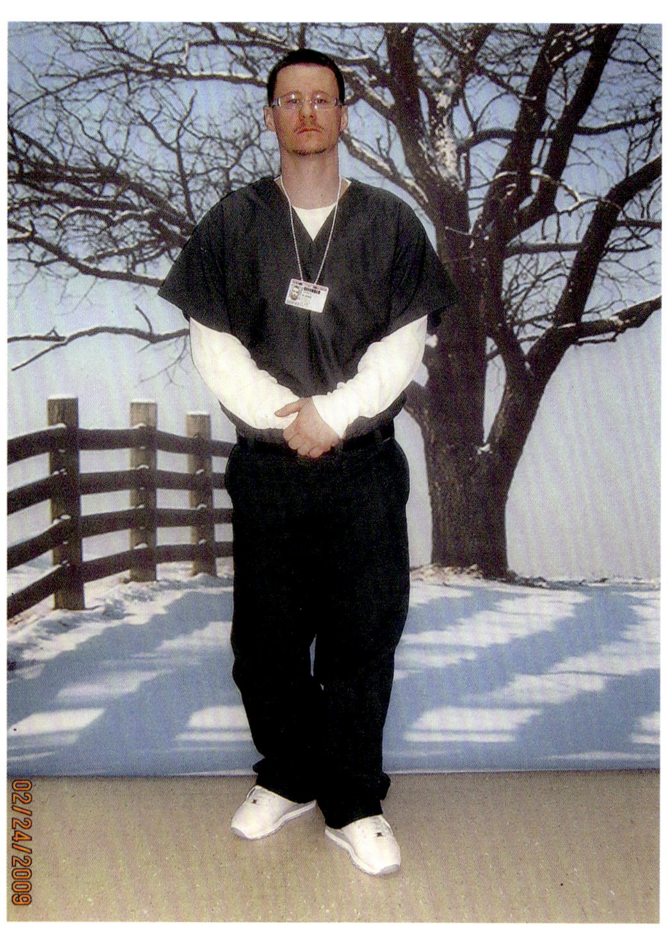

Anthony Kane, Columbia Correctional
Institution, Portage, Wisconsin

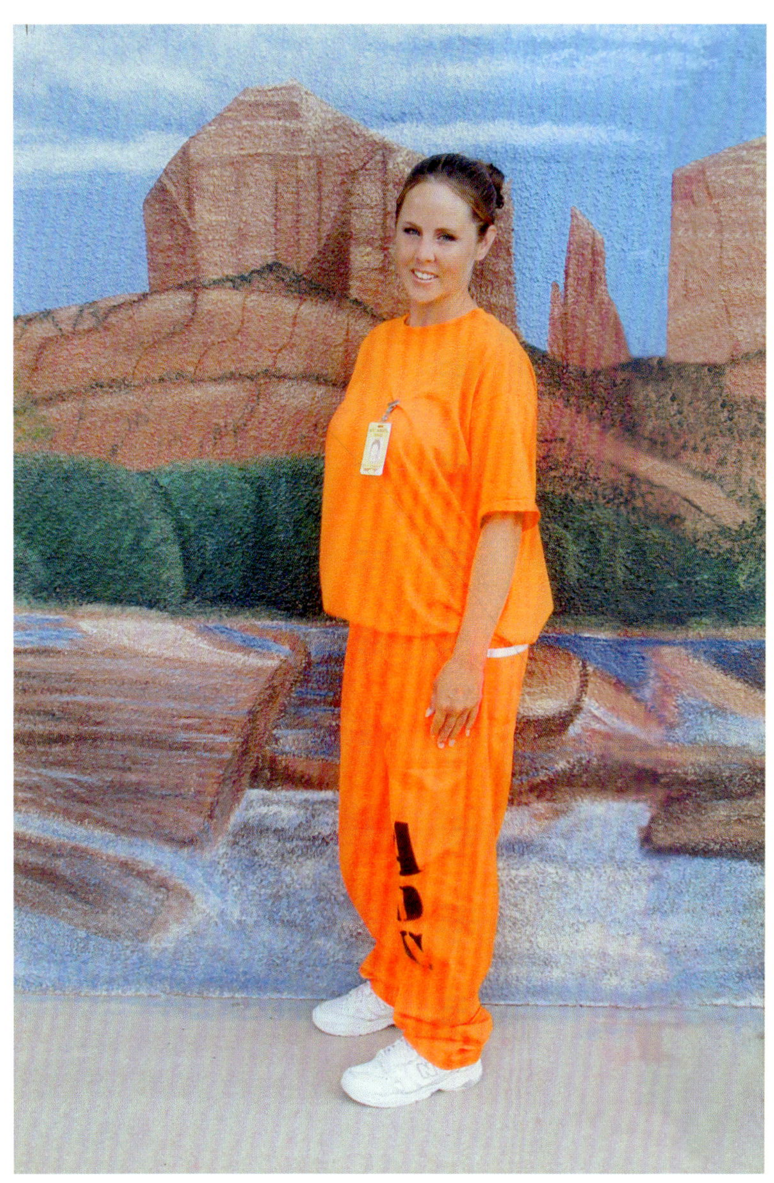

Manon Folkes, Arizona State Prison
Complex Perryville, Goodyear, Arizona

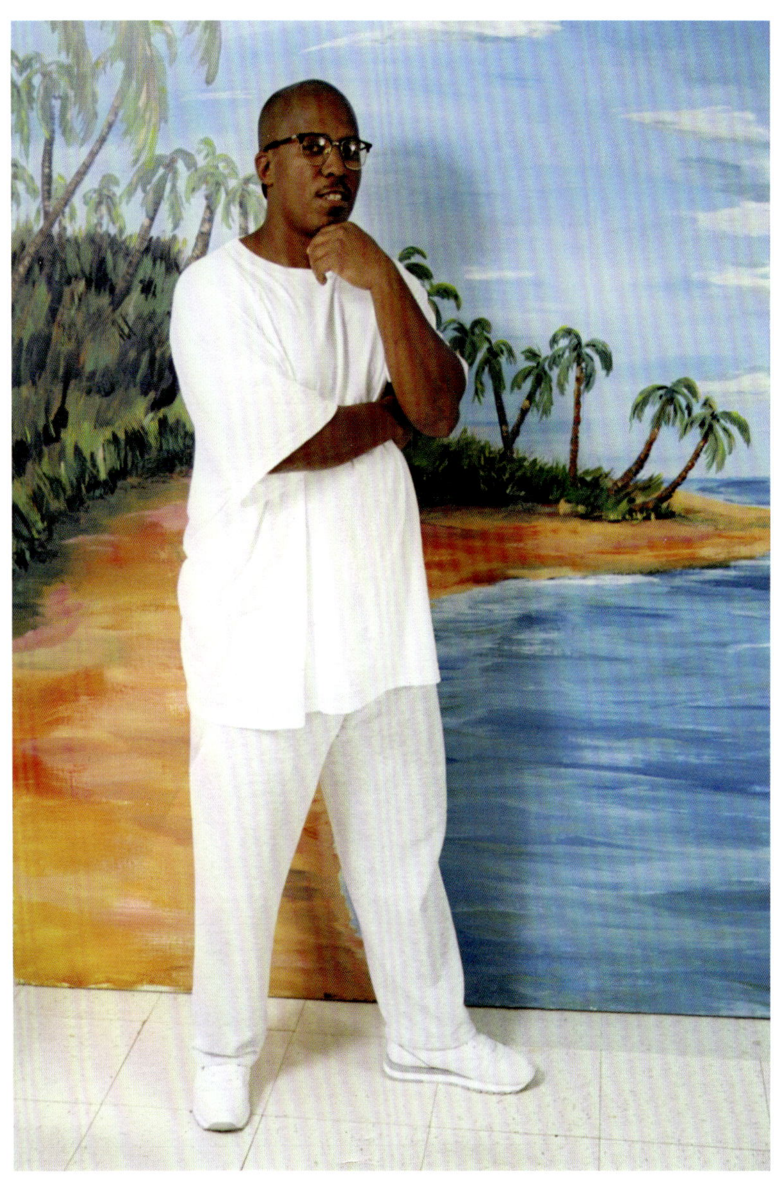

Robert RuffBey, United States
Penitentiary, Atlanta, Georgia

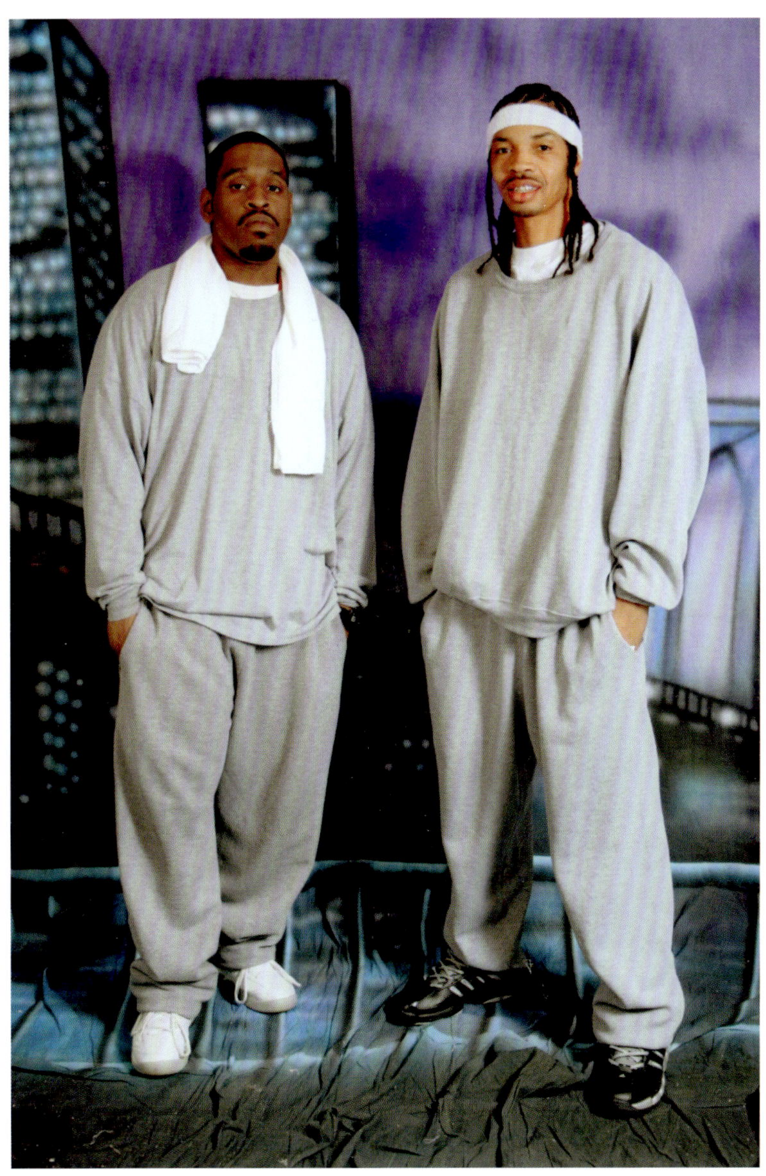

Kevin Jones (right), Unites States
Penitentiary, Atlanta, Georgia

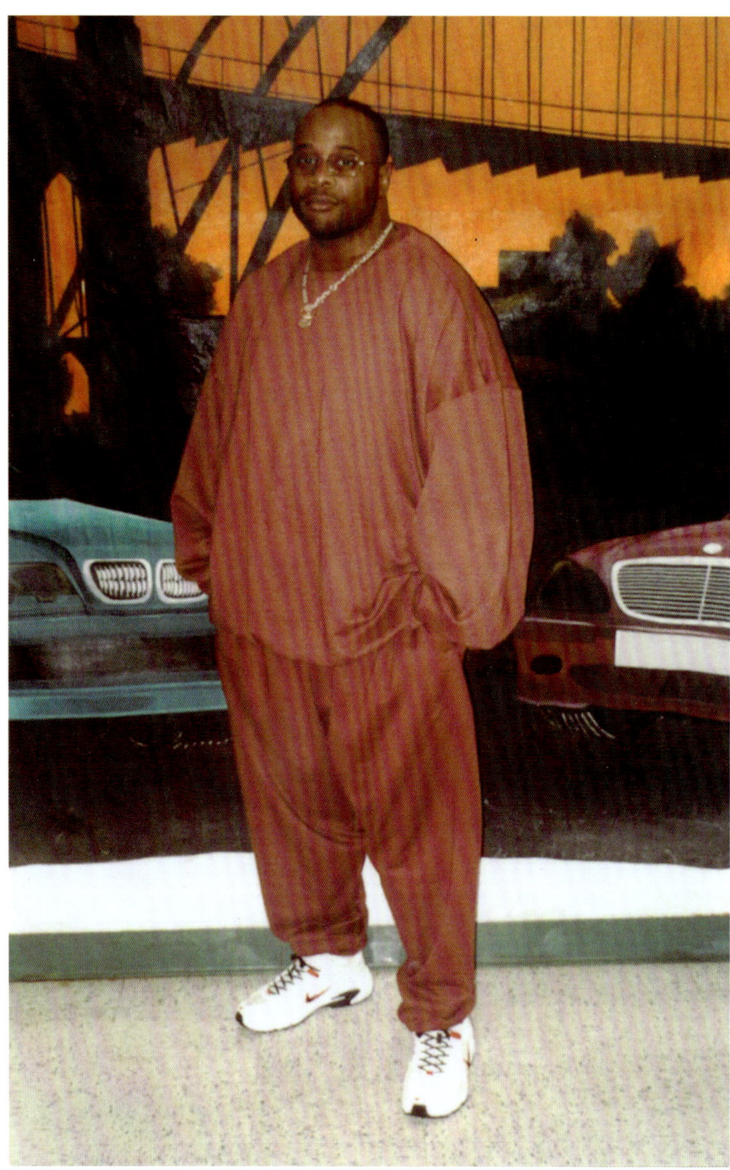

Jeffrey Goodwin, State Correctional
Institution, Dallas, Pennsylvania

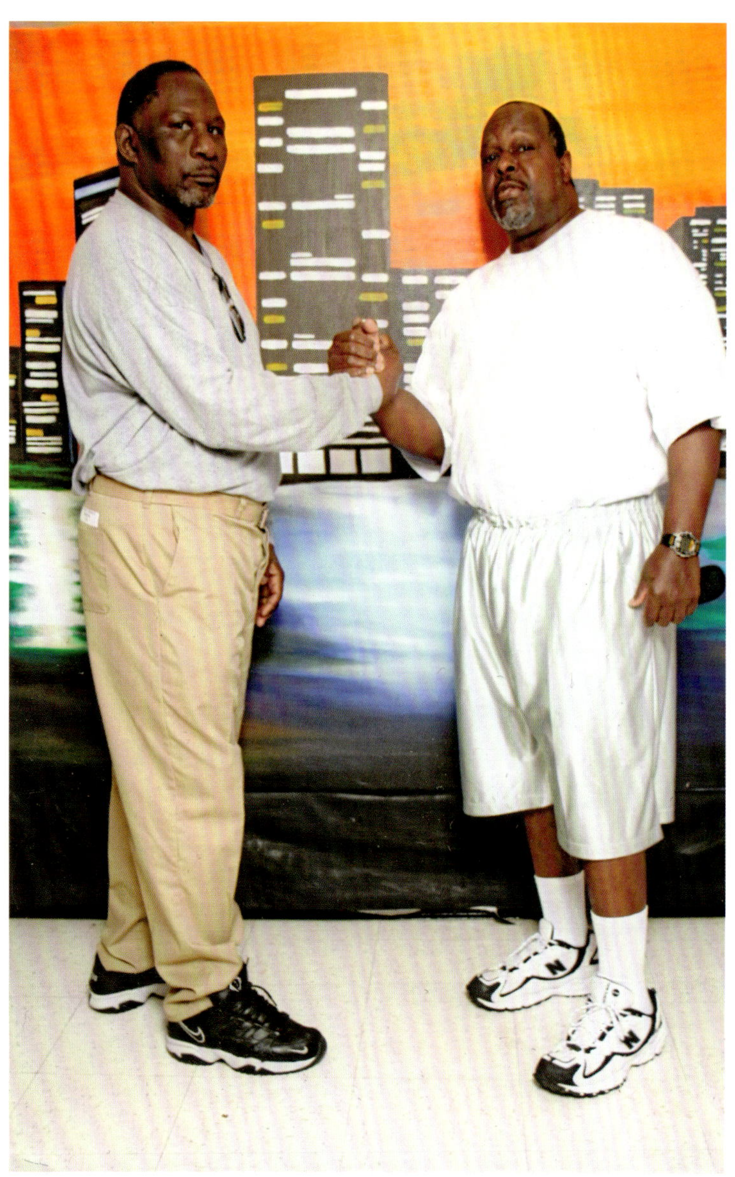

Norman Burgess (left), United States
Penitentiary, Atlanta, Georgia

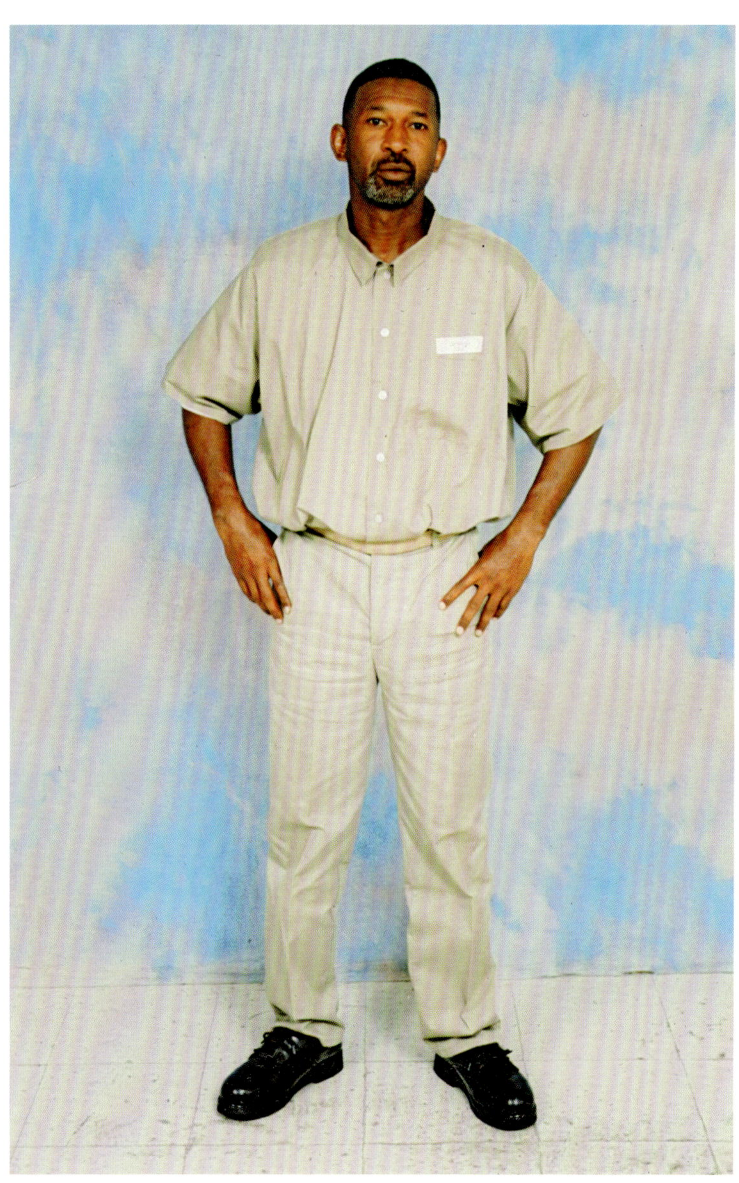

Steven Boyd, United States
Penitentiary, Atlanta, Georgia

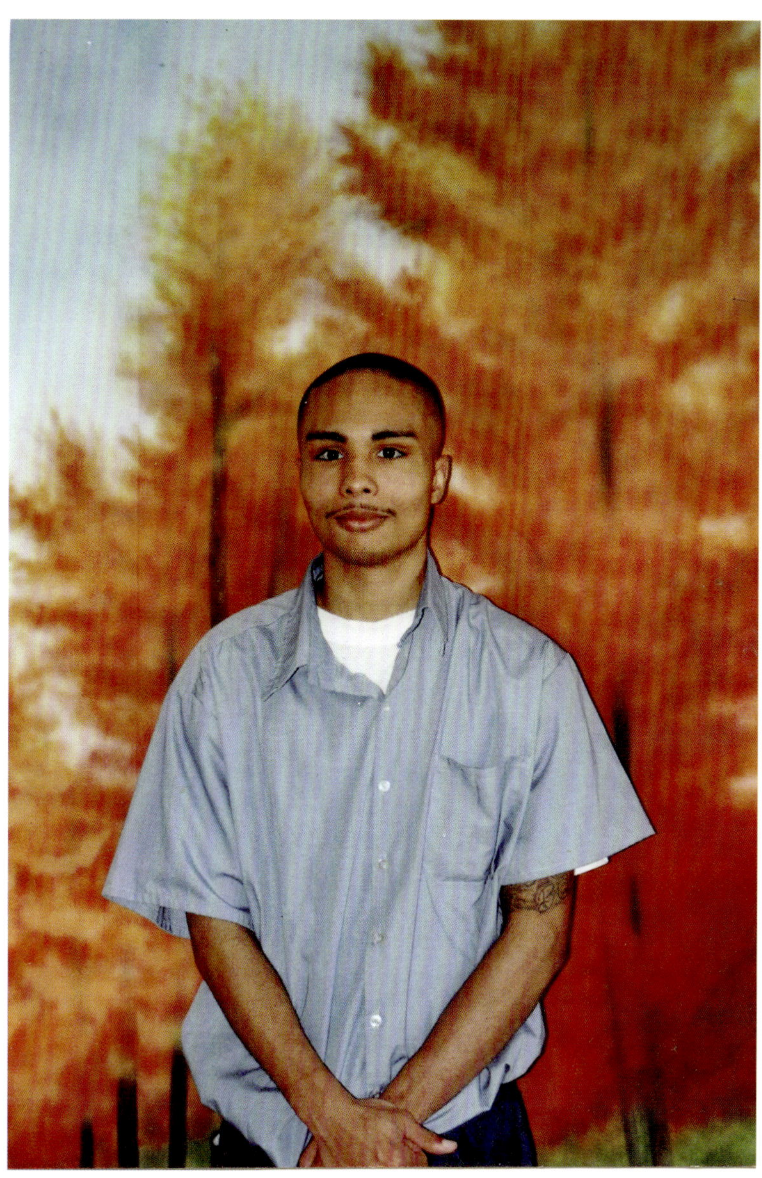

Brandon Gore, Southern Ohio
Correctional Facility, Lucasville, Ohio

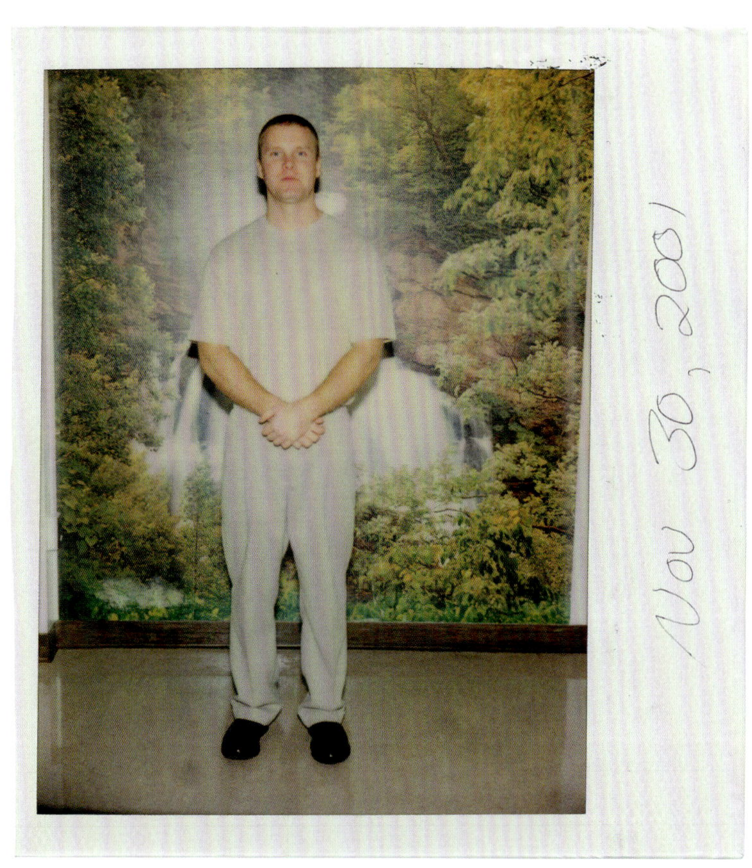

Bryan Seyka, Boyer Road Correctional
Facility, Carson City, Michigan

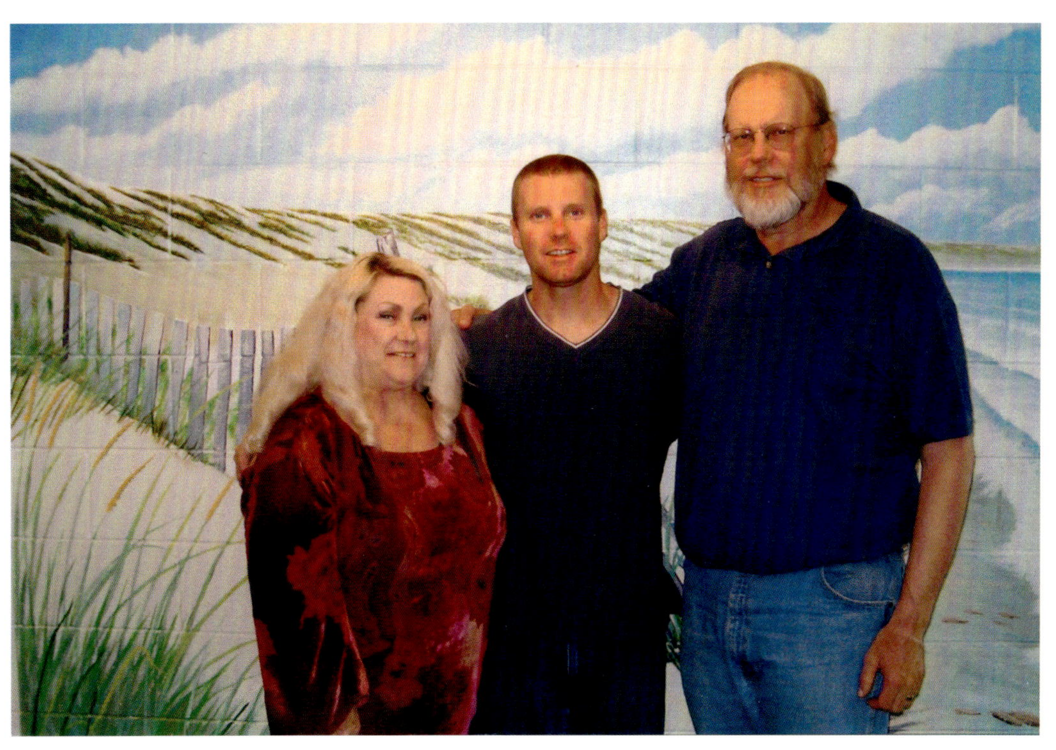

When this photo was taken, we were visiting our son Bryan, who was approximately one third of the way through his 25–50 year sentence for a bank robbery. This is a thought that always runs through my mind when having a photo taken in one of the prisons: Here we are, just a typical family enjoying each other's company; too bad that it is under these circumstances where we all feel somewhat captured.

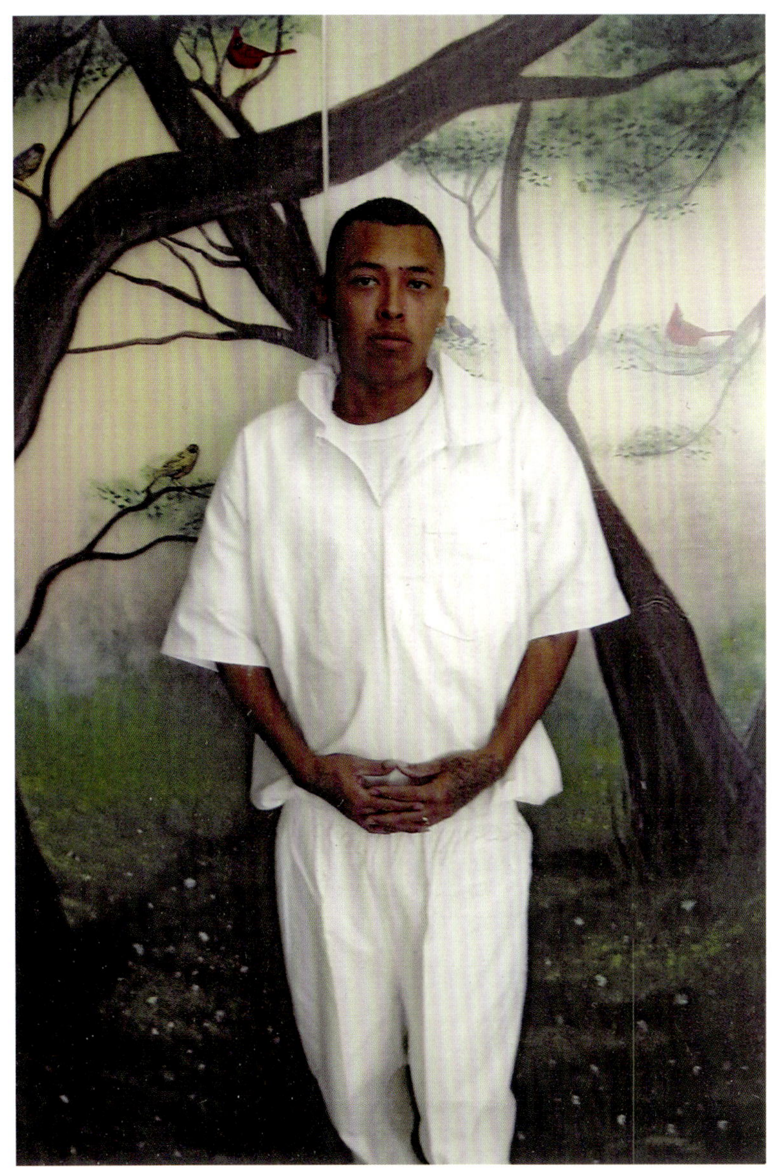

Brisio Pintor, Preston E. Smith Unit
Correctional Institution, Lamesa, Texas

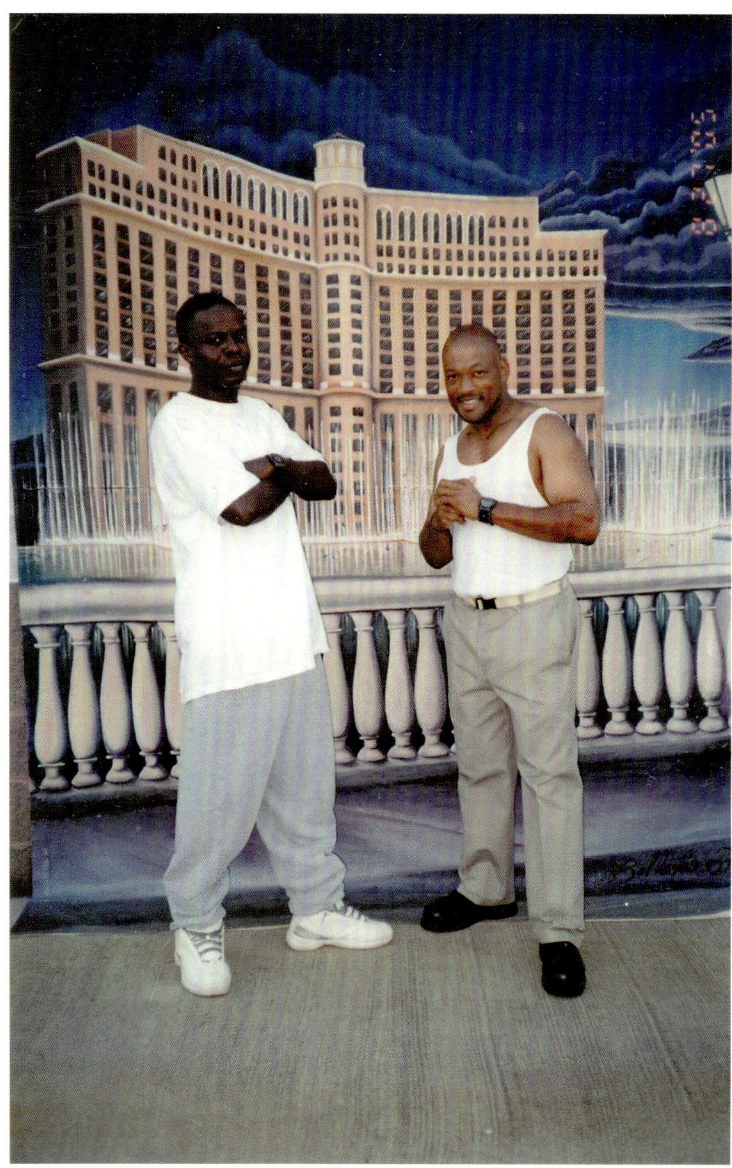

Anthony Gross (right), United States
Penitentiary, Marion, Illinois

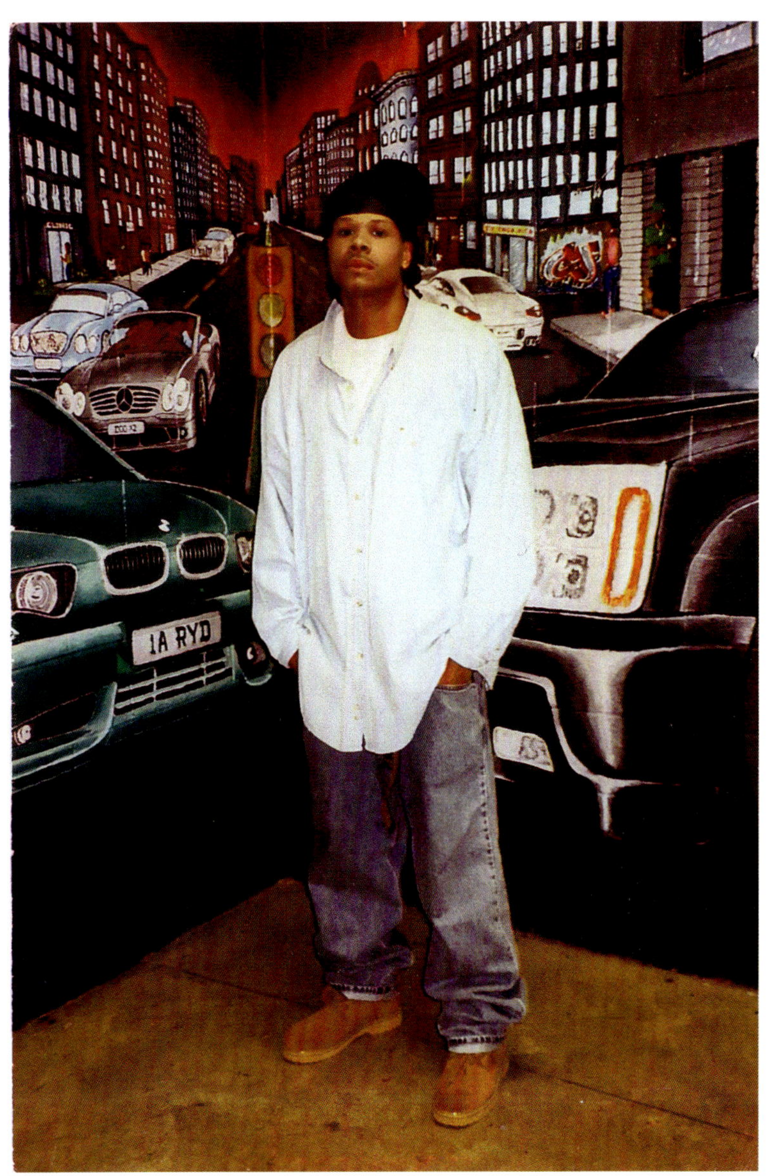

Dante Leese, Sussex I State Prison,
Waverly, Virginia

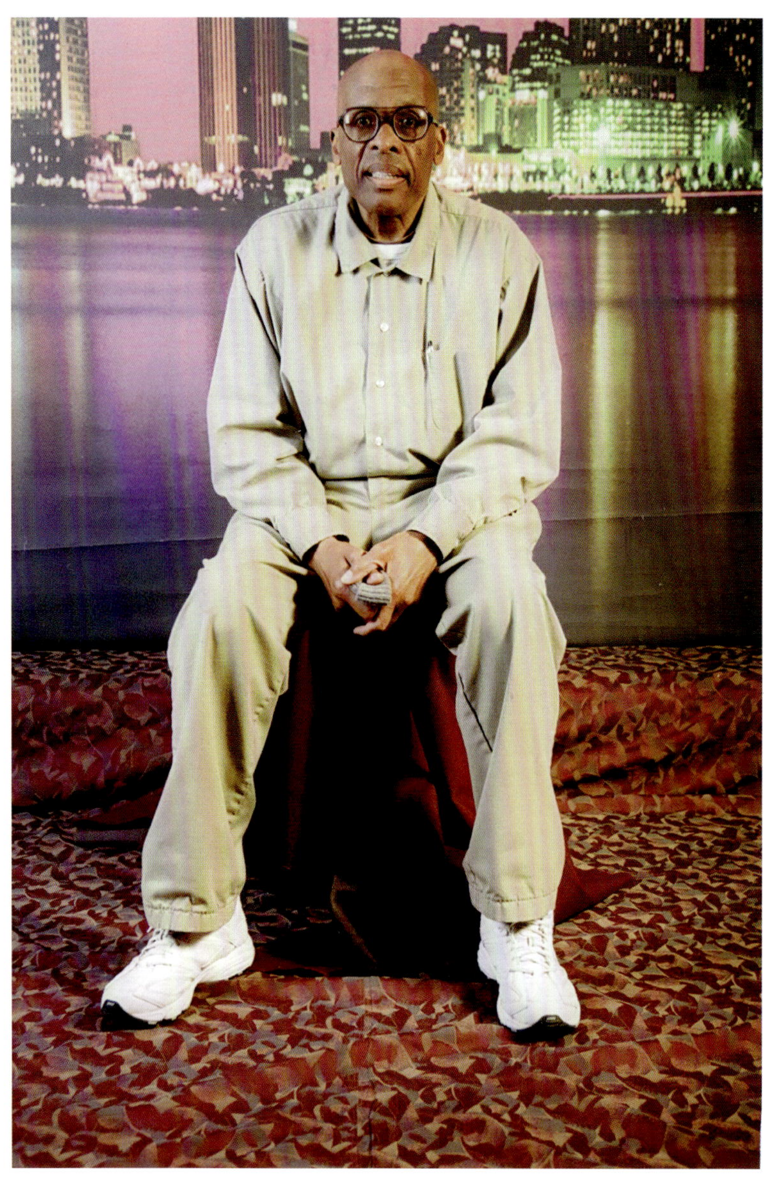

Reece C. Whiting Jr., Federal
Correctional Complex, Coleman, Florida

Gadsden Correctional Facility, Florida

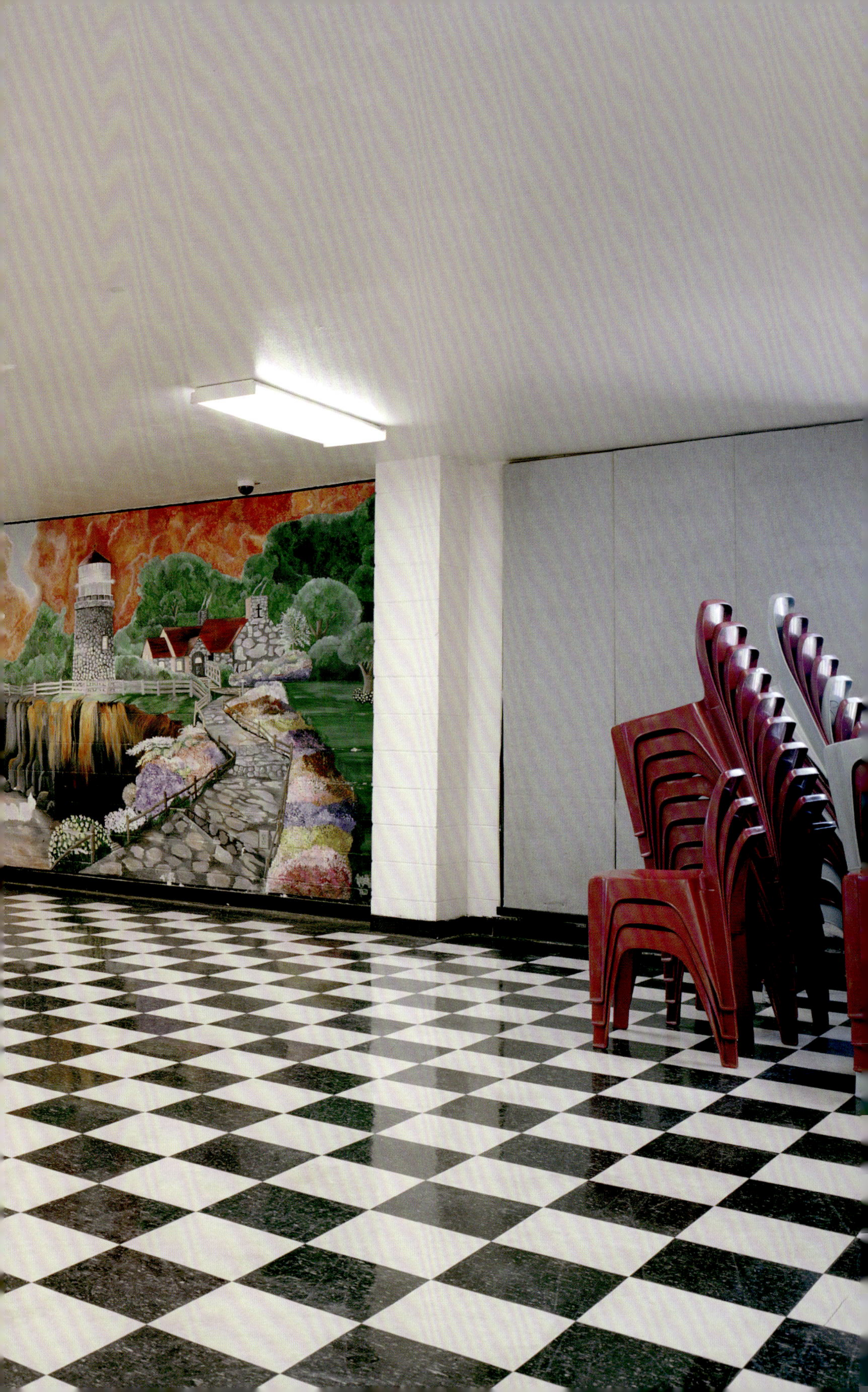

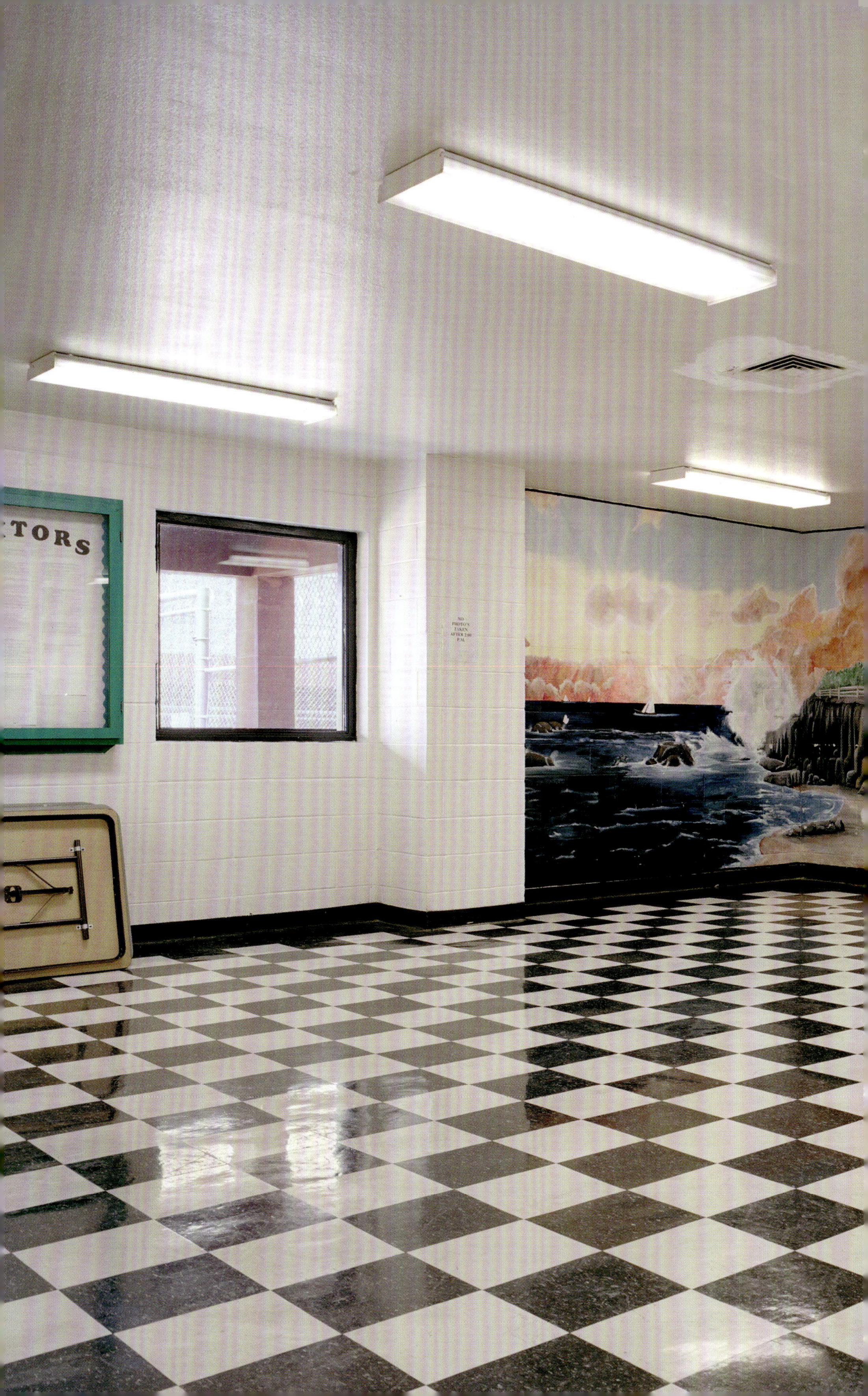

NO
PHOTOS
TAKEN
AFTER 2:00
P.M.

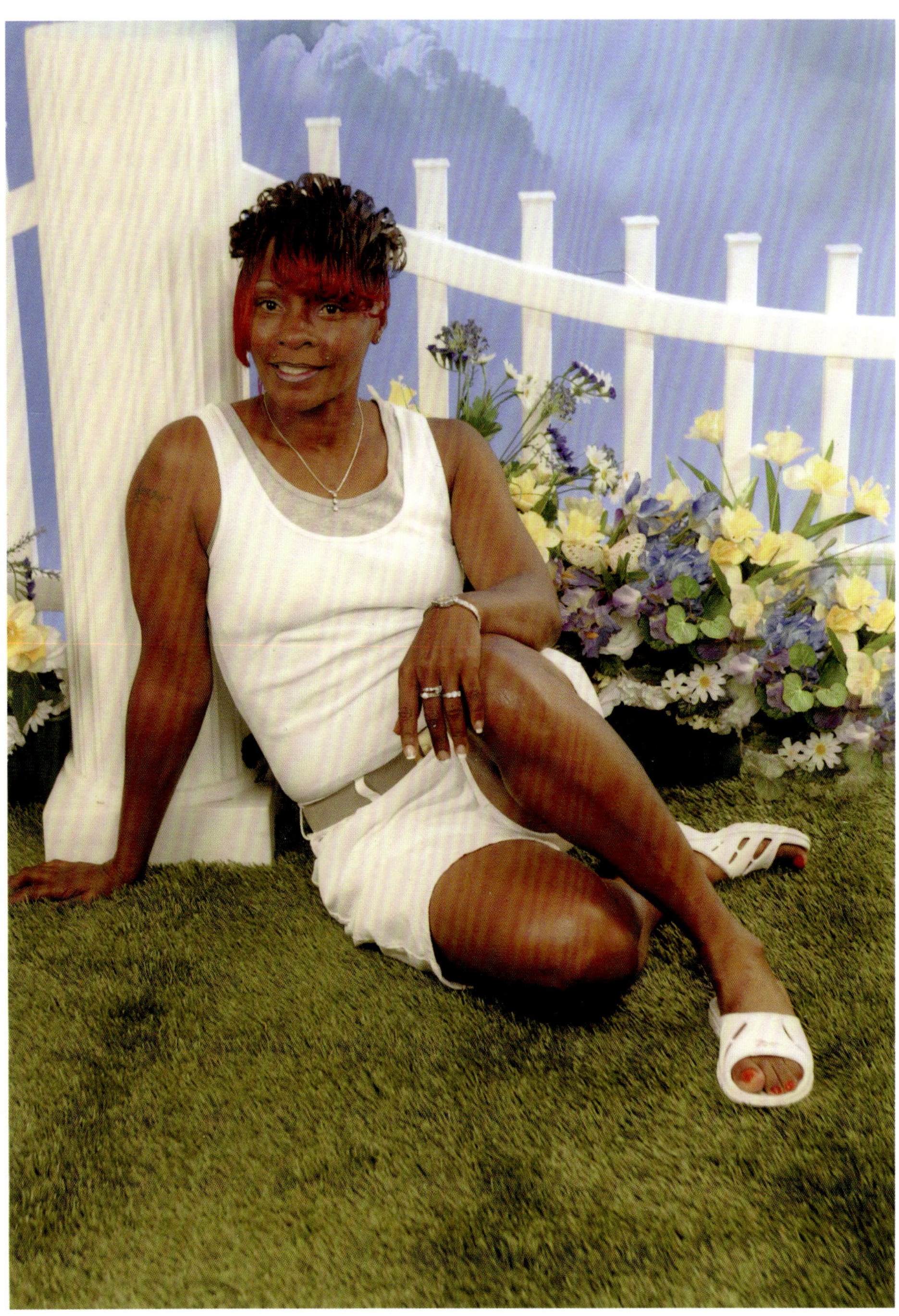

Victoria Williams, Valley State Prison
for Women, Chowchilla, California

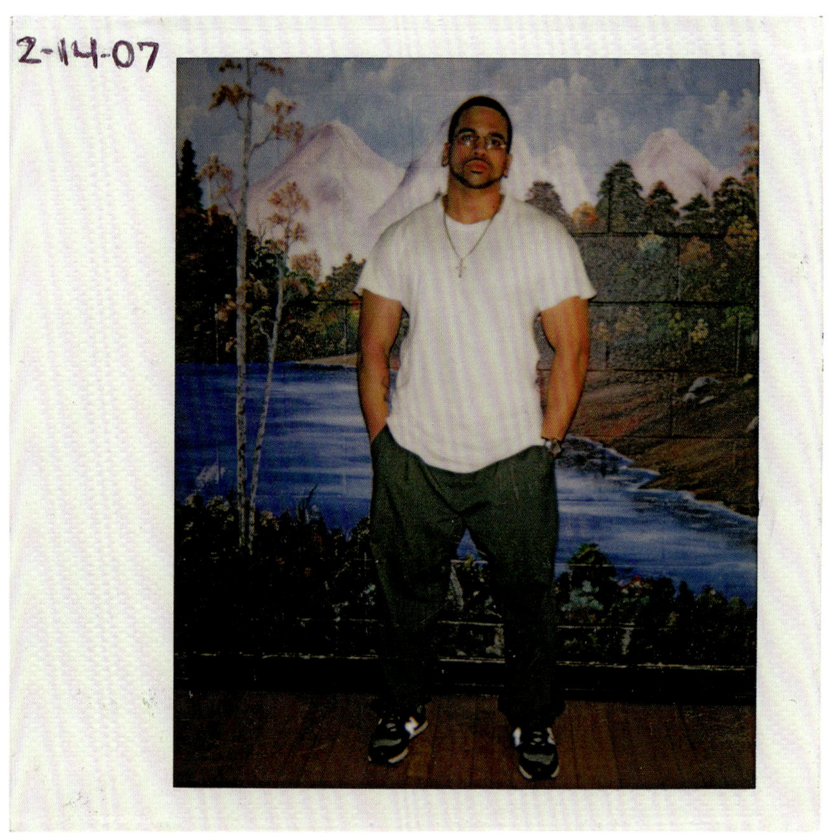

On the day this photo was taken I was
happy as I always am when my loved
ones come to visit. I was surprised
more than anything because I was not
expecting anyone to visit. I was new
to the facility where the picture was
taken. I felt at peace knowing that
I have family who will take a 24 hour
trip back and forth from New York City
to western New York to take me away
from the pain and suffering I endure
behind these walls especially with
having life without parole, for the six
hours the visit lasts for.

Vincent Moreno, Attica Correctional
Facility, Attica, New York

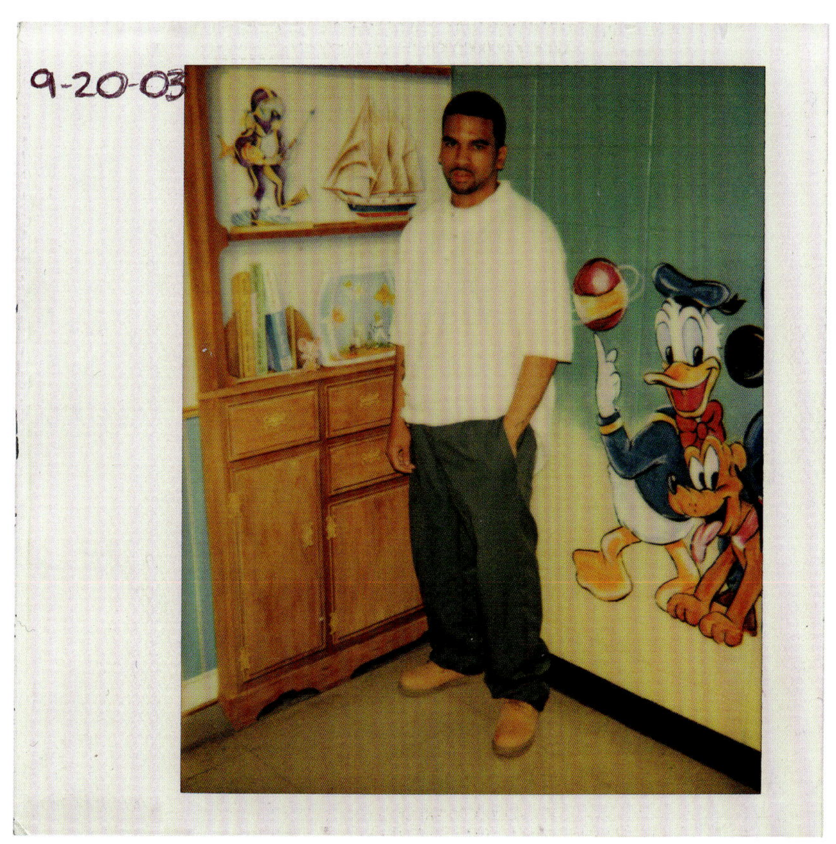
9-20-03

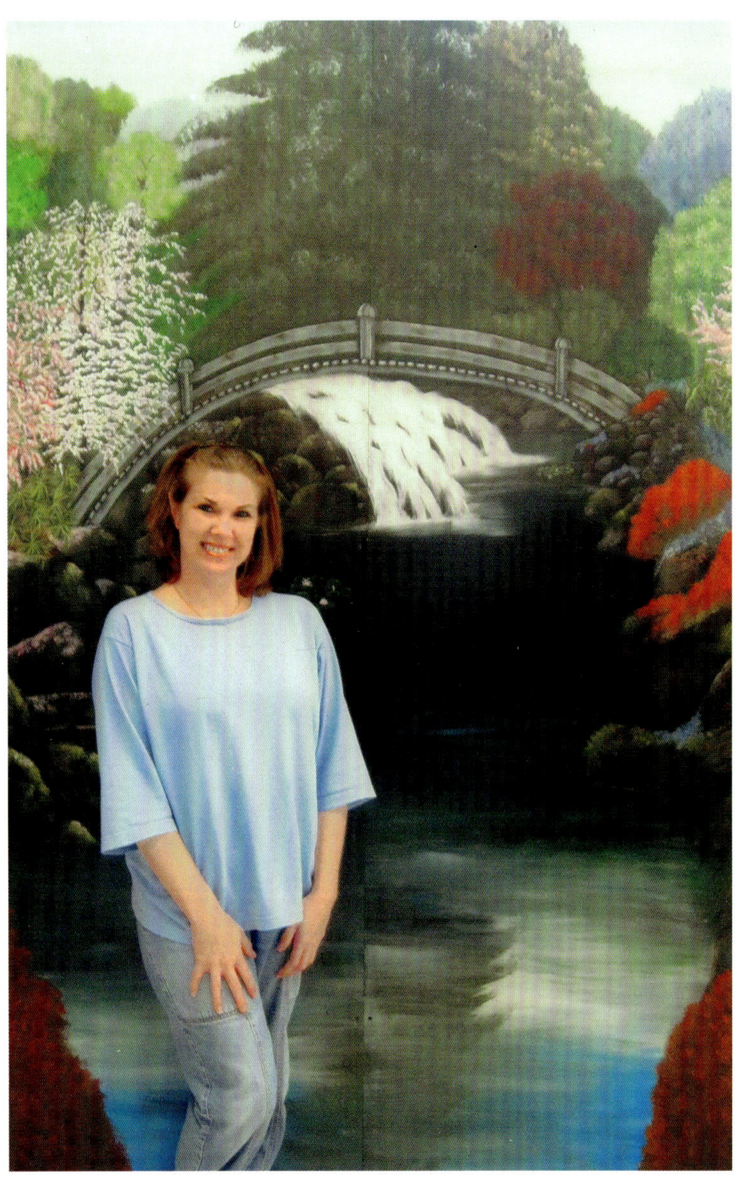

Kimberly Buntyn, Valley State Prison for
Women, Chowchilla, California

October 20, 2011

Hello Lee,

What a nice surprise to hear from you. I was just thinking about
you the other day. I was so glad to hear from you again. How are
you doing? I do hope that all is well with you and your boyfriend.

Well, I have another man in my life that I met off the internet.
He has come to visit me twice already. These last two weekends
in a row and I had a great time. He works in the movie and TV
industry. He's been in that for over 20 years. He works on all the
Adam Sandler movies, *The Closer*, *Two and a Half Men*, *CSI*, and
a couple other ones. He's been talking to my parents and, when
my son turns 18 in December, he is willing to go get him and bring
him on a visit. I am getting so excited. God is good.

They have good backgrounds, but I don't have any good makeup
on my property right now. As soon as I take a decent picture,
I will send one to you. Darn, I forgot the name of the book I was
in. What was it again? So, the holidays are coming up. What are
your great plans?

OK I'm going to go for now. I wish you happy holidays. Take care.

Your Friend,

Kimberly.

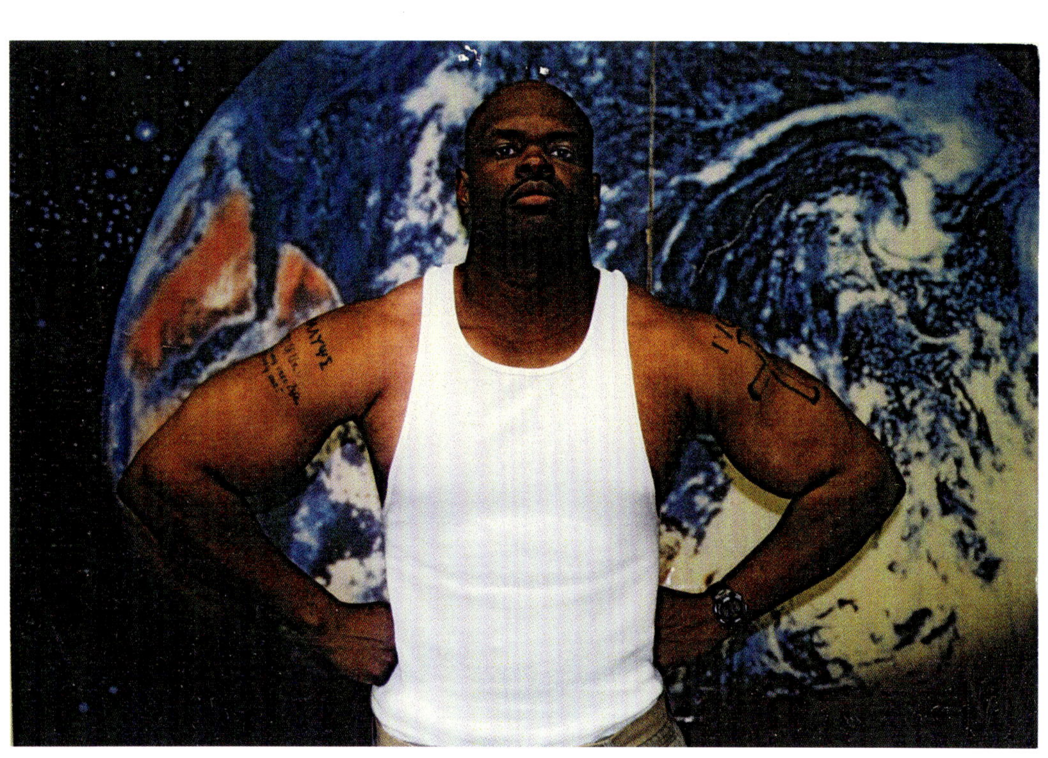

Michael Armstrong, Federal Correctional
Institution, Fort Dix, New Jersey

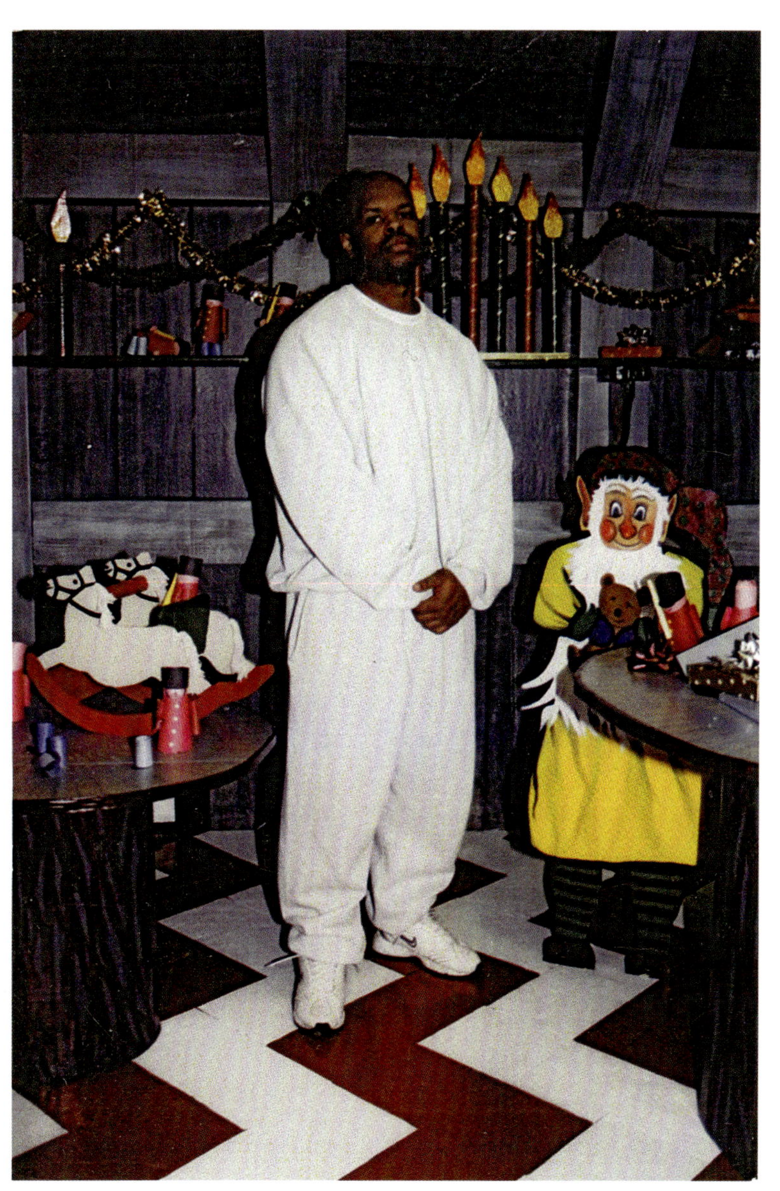

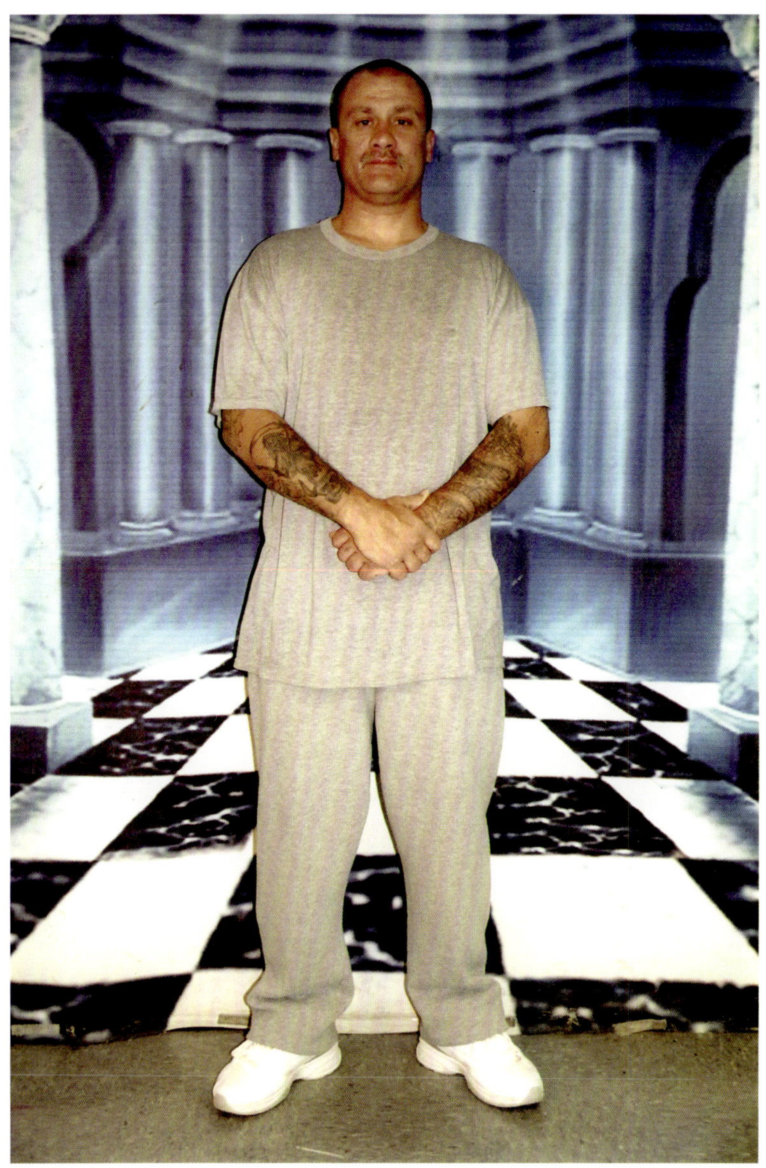

Roy King, Federal Correctional
Institution, Terre Haute, Indiana

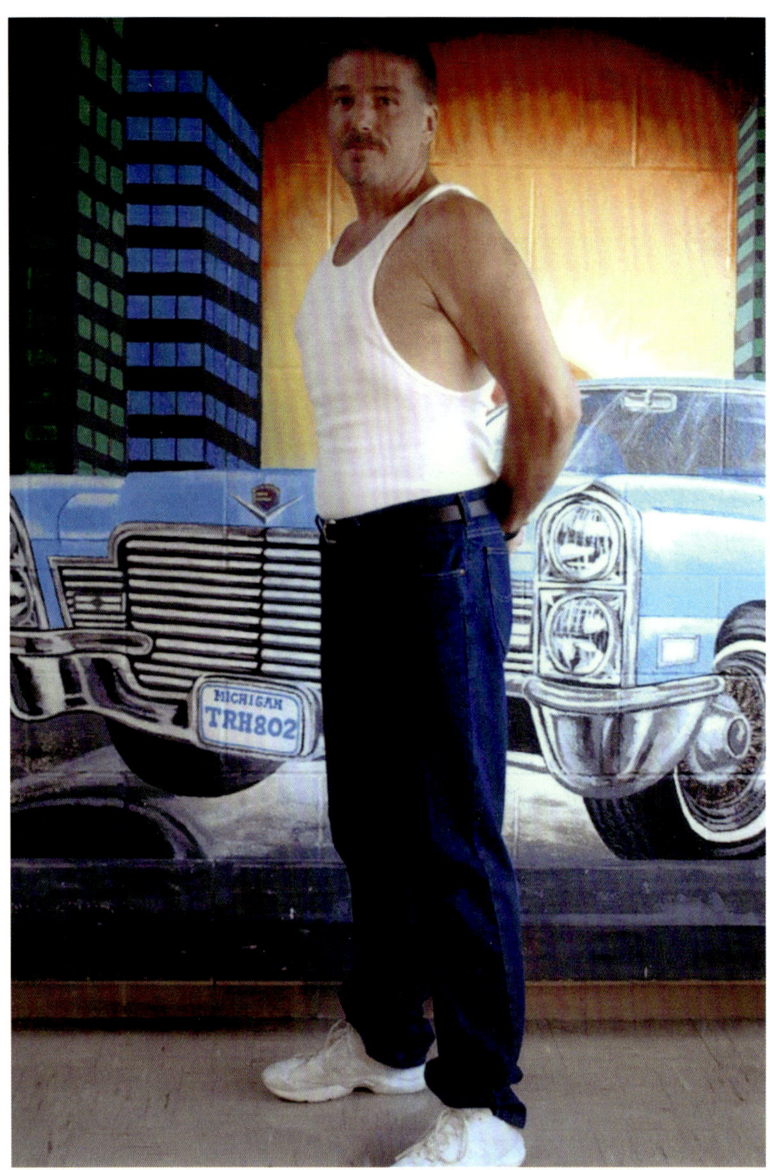

I had this photo taken so I could get
a webpage on friendsbeyondthewall.com,
a pen pal website for prisoners.

Chris Gollagher, Parr Highway
Correctional Facility, Adrian, Michigan

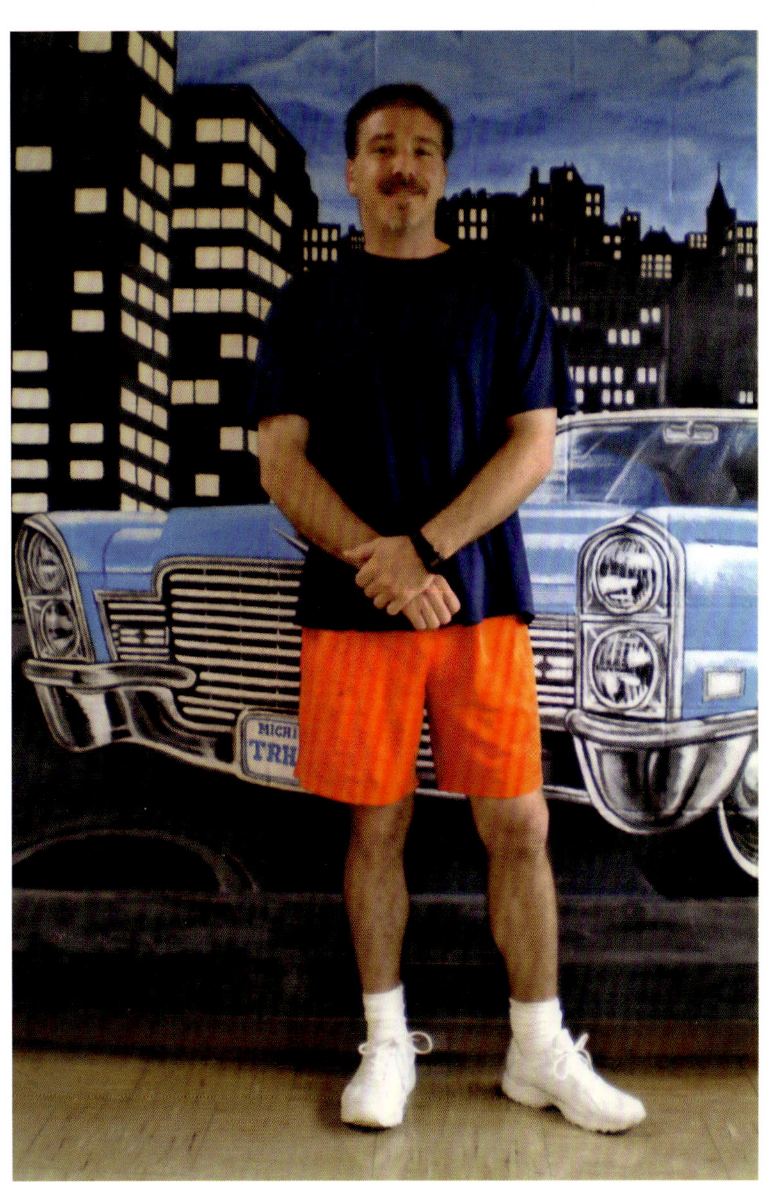

November 10, 2009

Dear Lee Lana,

It is very nice to hear from you. How are you? I really hope you are keeping up with the good work. I keep myself pretty busy also. I am the only certified physical trainer in this place so I am in charge of all the wellness classes. I am also a suicide companion. For some people, it's a lot harder than for others to be in a place like this. So sometimes there are a few guys who try to commit suicide and part of my job is to make sure that they don't do anything like that. I am also a college student. I am trying to get a degree in Psychology from Coastline Community College. It is very hard sometimes because I have a lot on my plate but every time I think of quitting, I think of my little girl, and that gives me the motivation to keep going. I have a beautiful little girl. Her name is Gracie Alina. She is five years old and she is the love of my life. It makes me sad to talk about my baby because I have not seen her in almost four years. Her mom refuses to answer my letters but I will never give up on my child. She means the world to me. She is the only proof that I have that I exist. I don't even know why I am telling you this because I don't know who you are but sometimes I just want somebody to know that I do have someone out there who I love more than anything else in this world. Anyhow! Guess what? I helped paint a new mural where the old one used to be. It's pretty cool. I am not a bad guy, I just made a mistake when I was younger and now I am paying for it. It is past midnight and I have a long day ahead of me tomorrow. I have to be up at 5 a.m. so this is it for now. Take care of yourself and your loved ones.

Sincerely,
Juan Carlos Ochoa

P.S. I like to be called Juan Carlos, or just Carlos

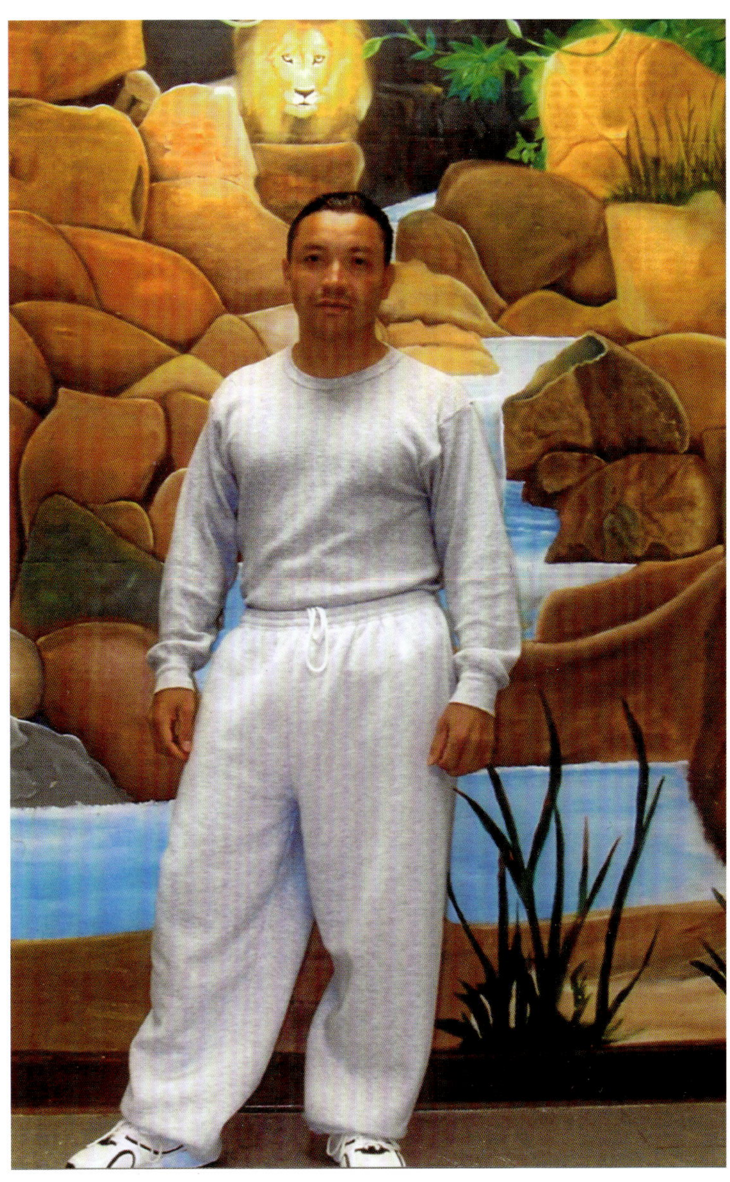

Juan Carlos Martinez Ochoa, Federal
Correctional Institution Victorville I,
Adelanto, California

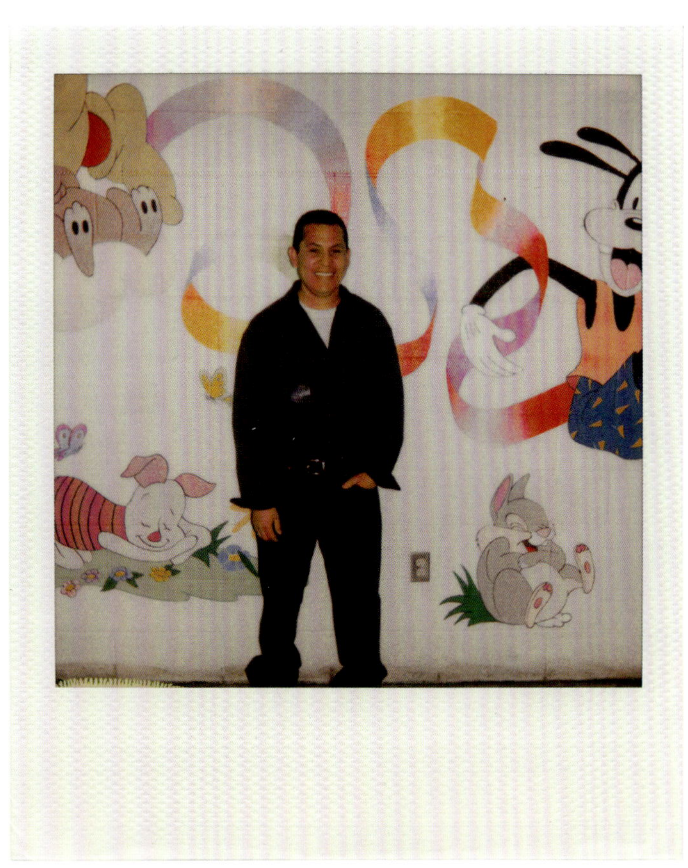

Rolando Espinoza, High Desert State
Prison, Indian Springs, Nevada

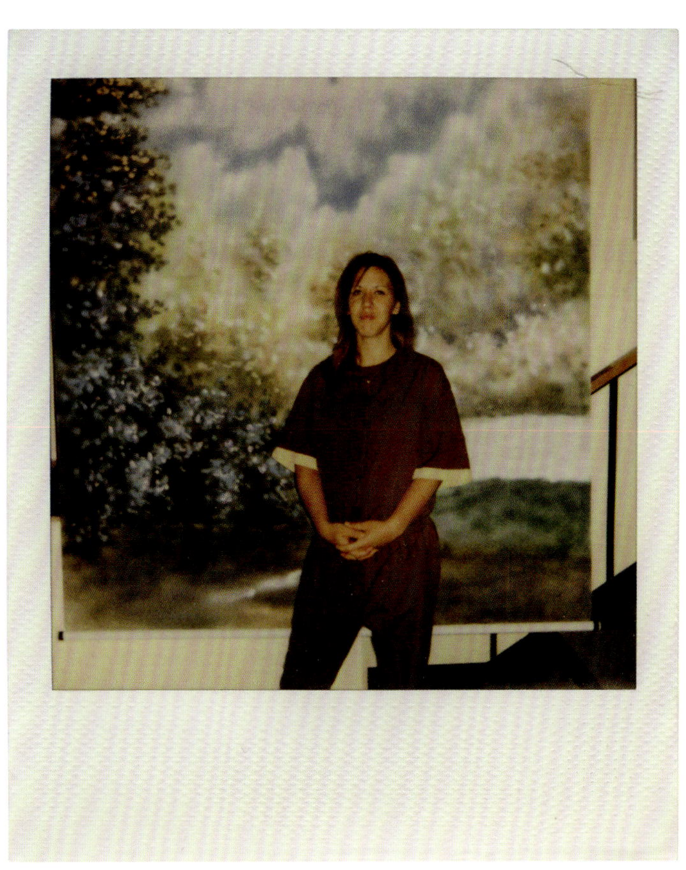

Randi Kopitsky, State Correctional
Institution, Muncy, Pennsylvania

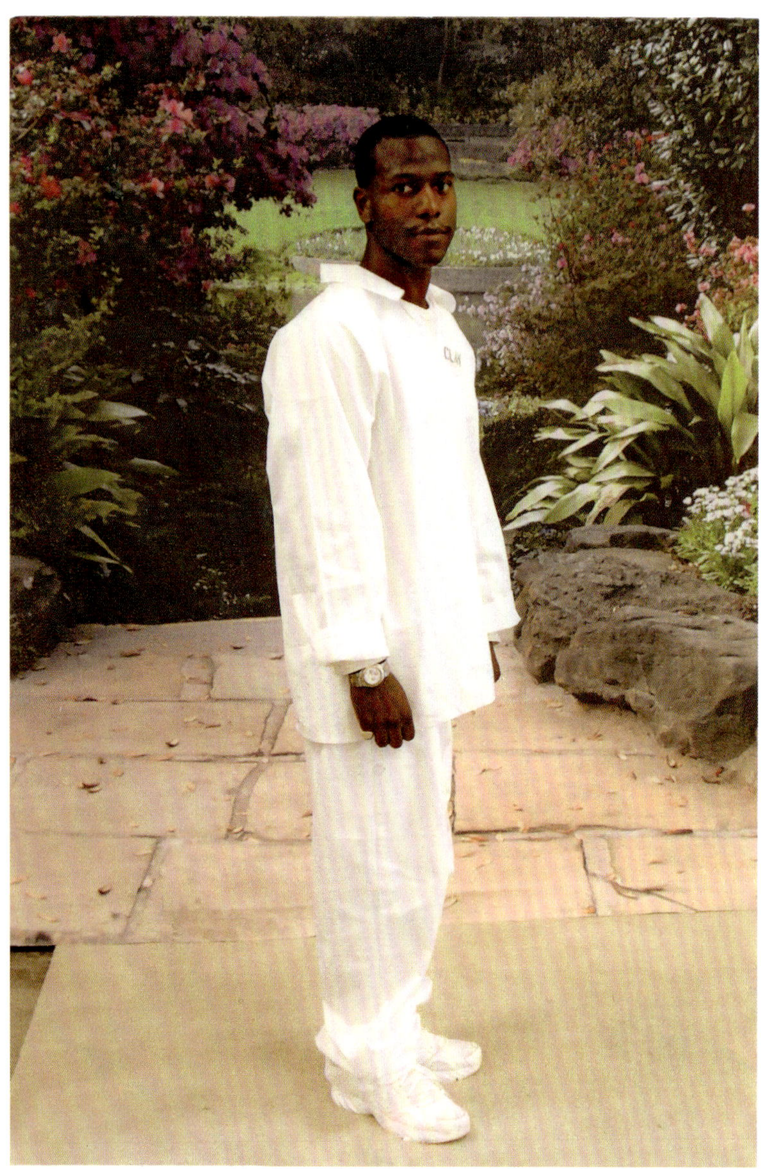

John Lee Clay, Varner Unit, Grady, Arkansas

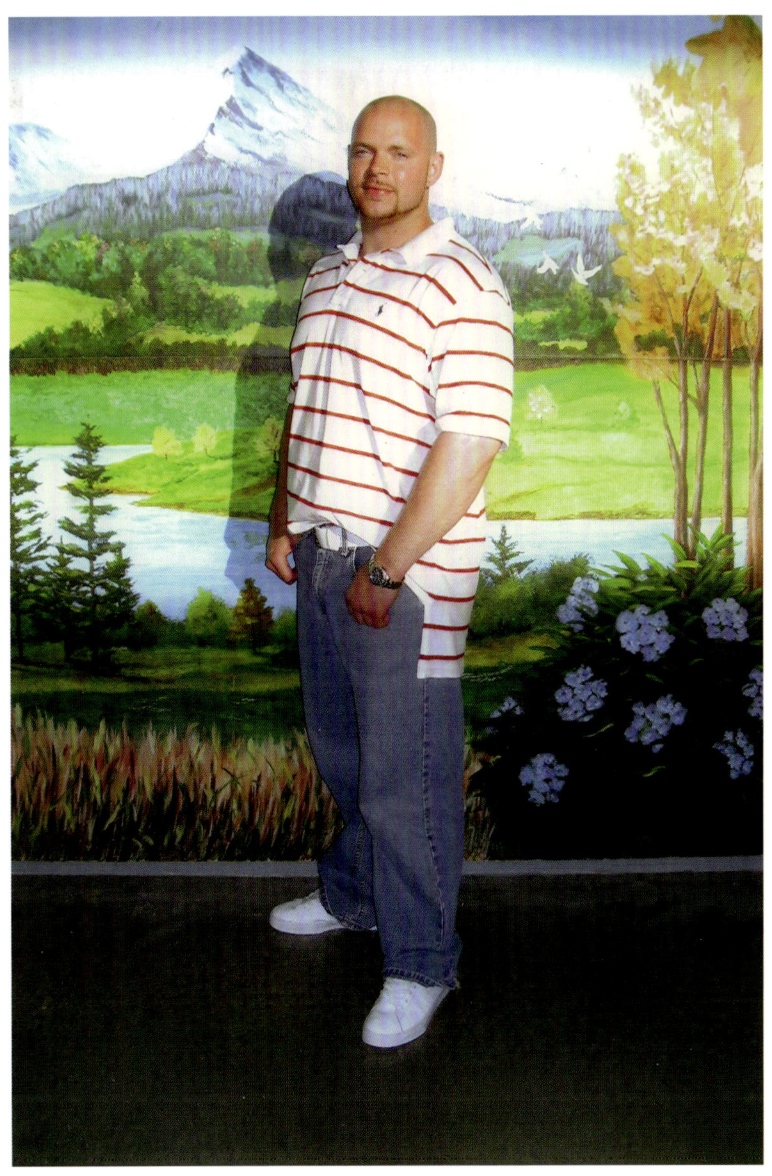

When I took this photo I was thinking about
being free. I felt like I was ready to go kick it,
hang out, or go to the waterfront and enjoy
the nice warm summer breeze and sunset.
But my reality is that I am locked up.

Tyler Miesse, Stafford Creek Corrections
Center, Aberdeen, Washington

November 2, 2009

Dear Ms Lee Lana,

This missive is to inform you that I received your letter along with the Release Agreement. Though I have filled out mine, I am sad to inform you that my visitor, (my Grandmother) has passed away.

Also I would like to inform you that tomorrow I will be going to another prison so look forward to my address change. Thank you.

Le'Jon Young.

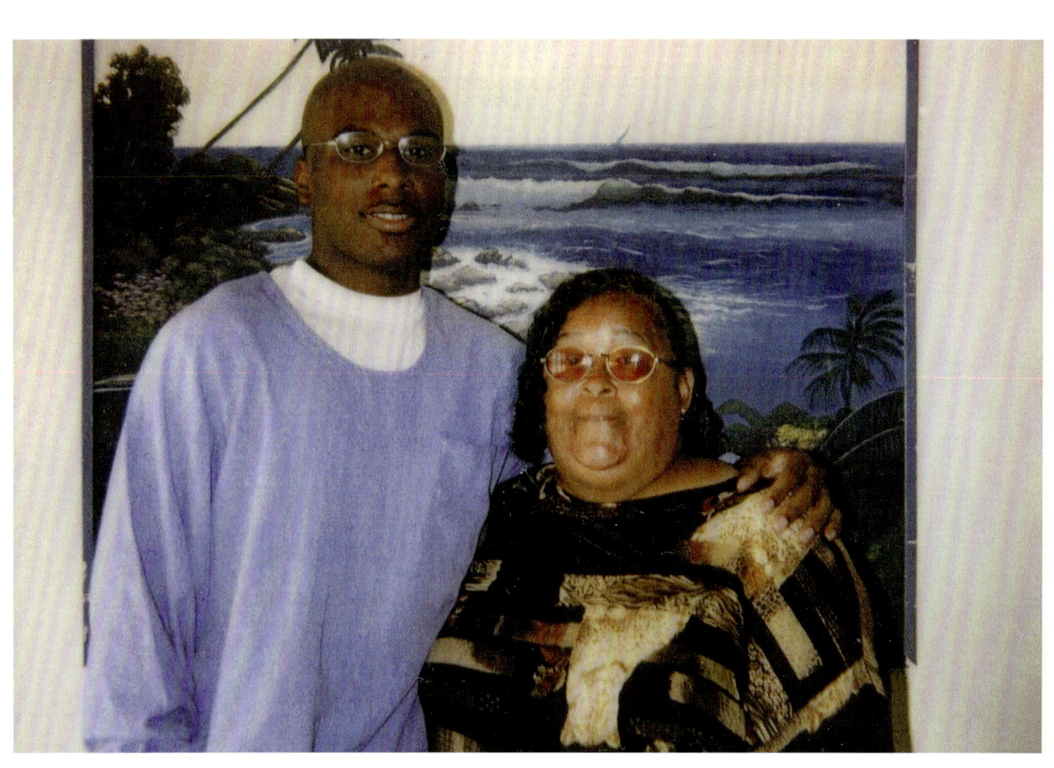

Le'Jon Young, California State Prison
Centinela, Imperial, California

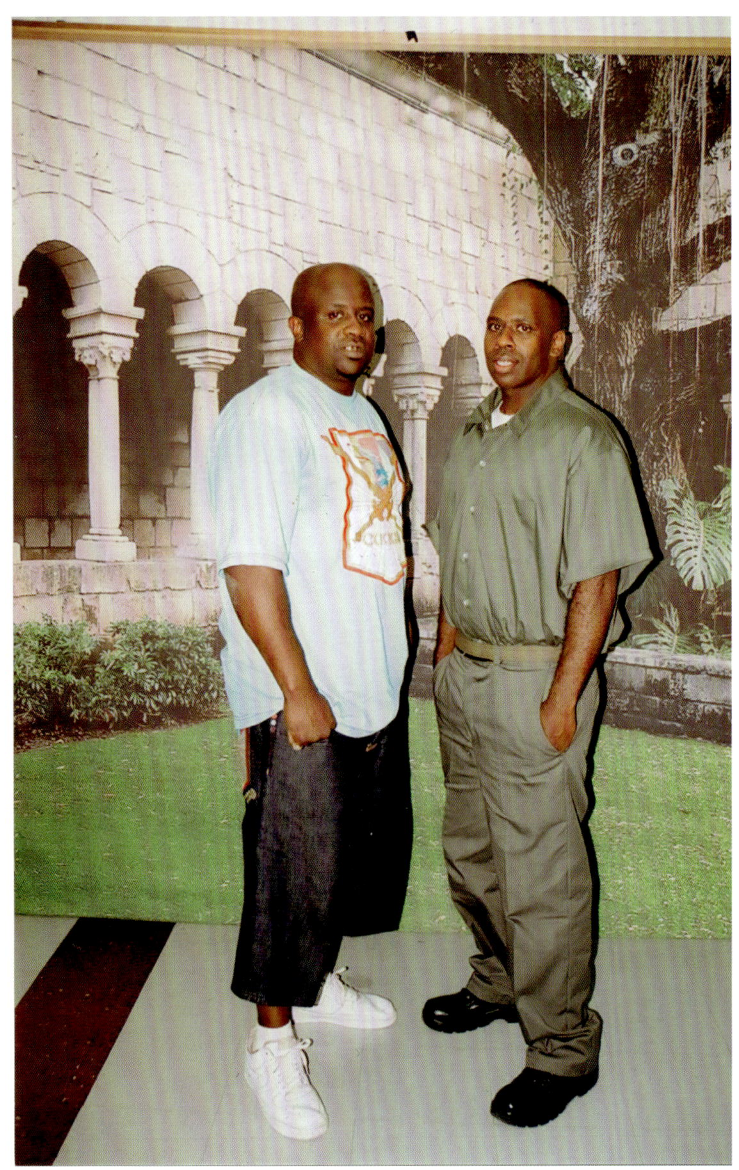

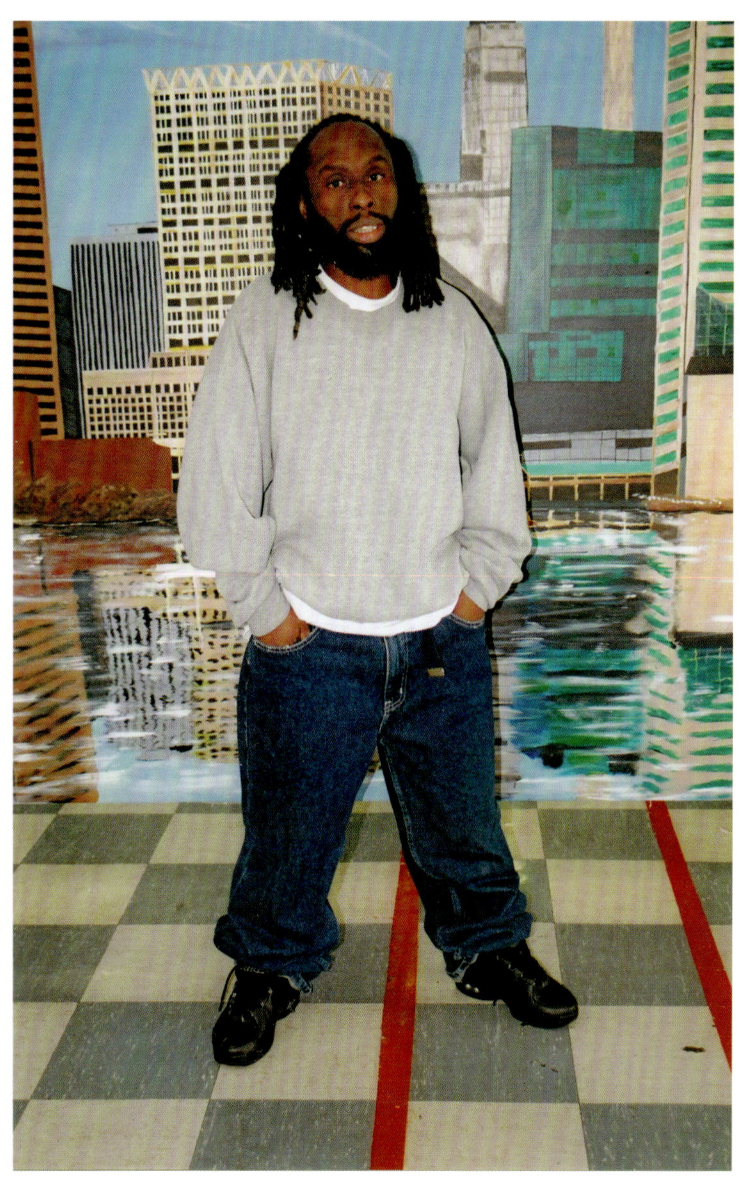

I only have a few words to say and
I mean them with all my heart and soul.
Now I will quote Dorothy in *The Wizard
of Oz*, 'There's No Place Like Home.'

Raymond Jones, Maryland Correctional
Institution, Hagerstown, Maryland

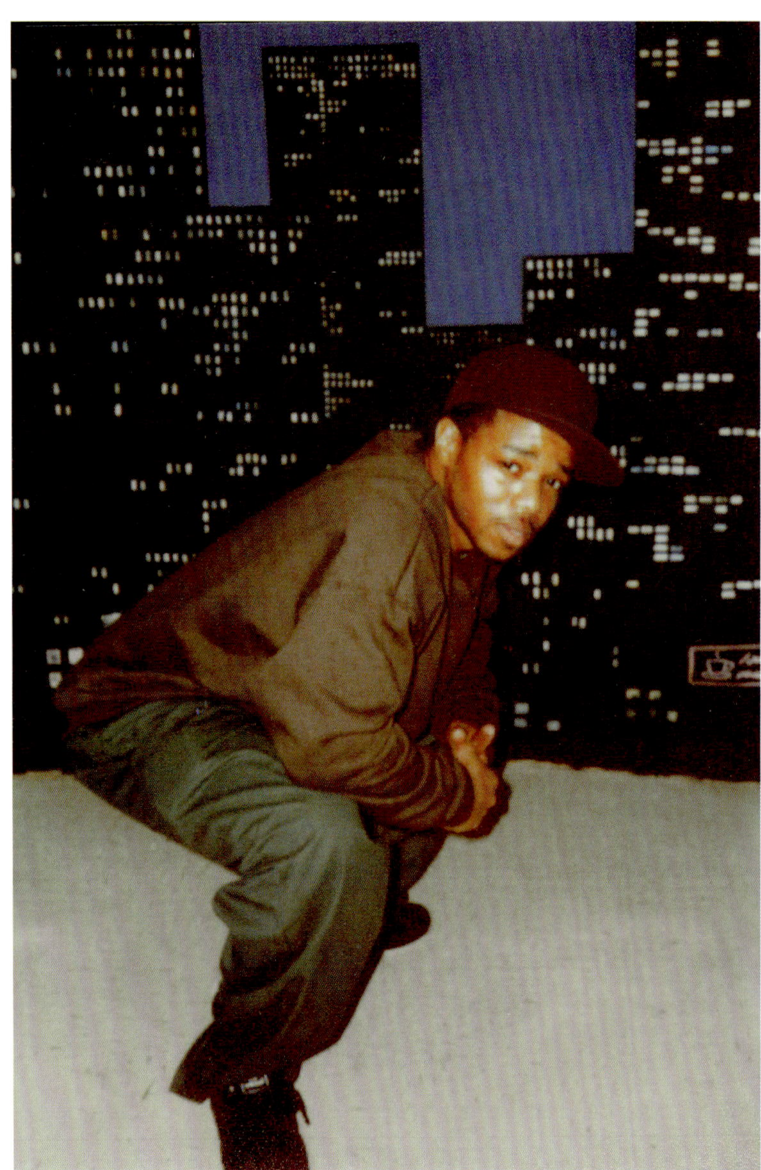

James Bazemore, Auburn Correctional
Facility, Auburn, New York

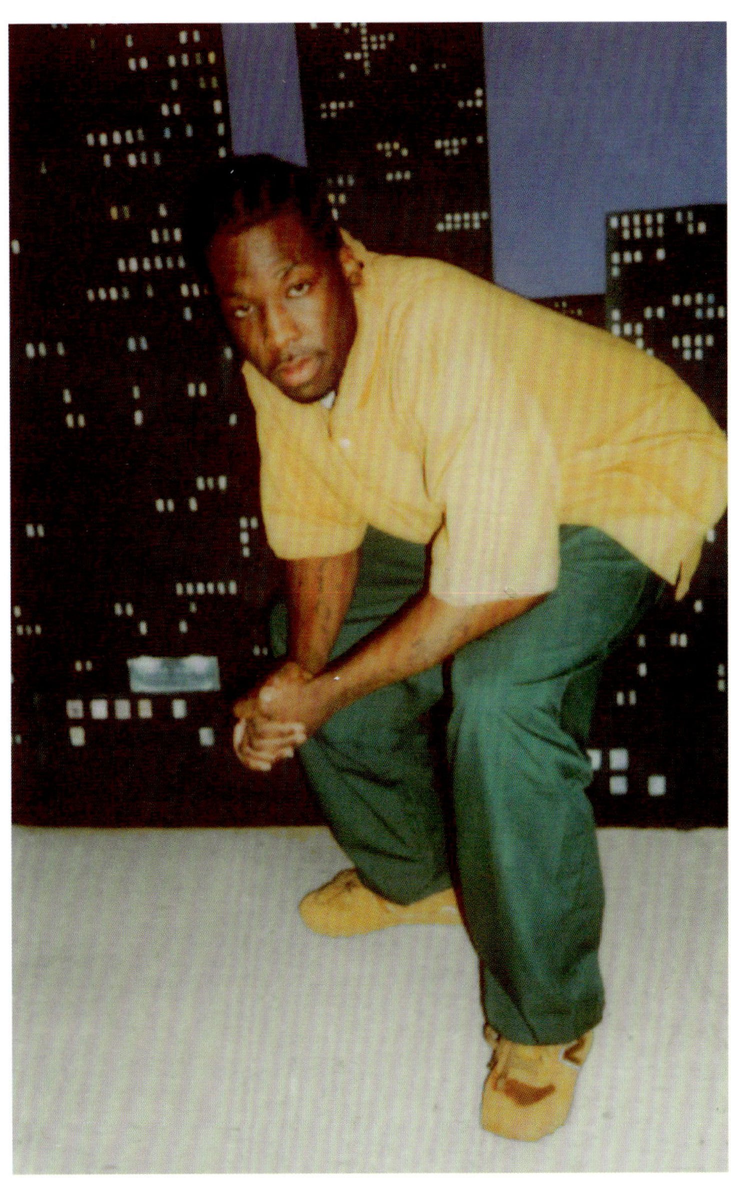

Rahmel Emmanuel, Auburn Correctional
Facility, Auburn, New York

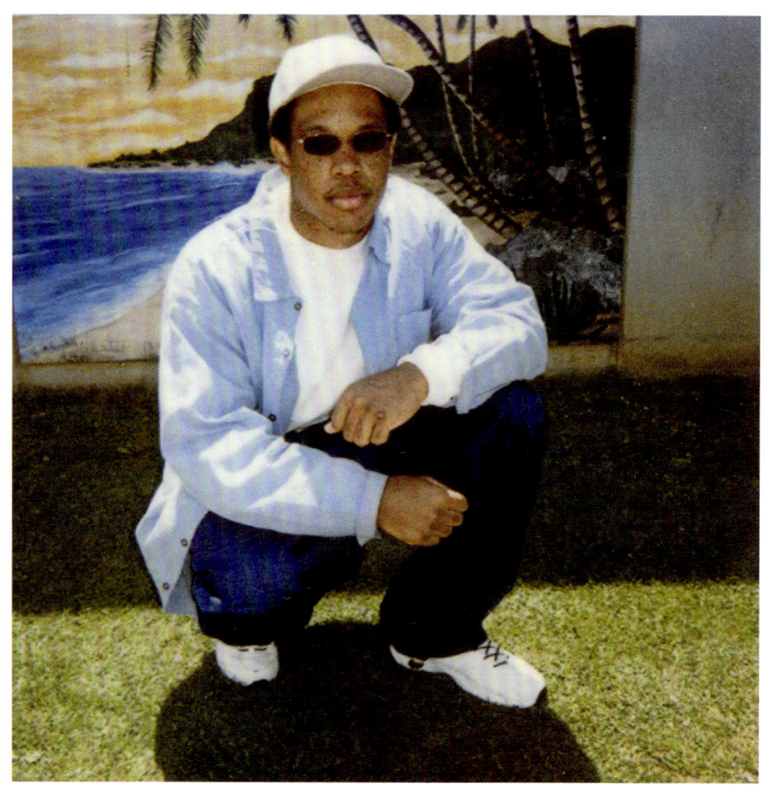

I parole next year, so I am preparing
for my future on the outside. This is
gonna probably be one of the biggest
moments of my life, getting out after
12 years of imprisonment. I came in at
17 years old and I will be leaving at 29.
A lot has changed in the world since
1998. However, I am ready to get out
and move on with my life and put this
all behind me.

Jason Brown, Pelican Bay State Prison,
Crescent City, California

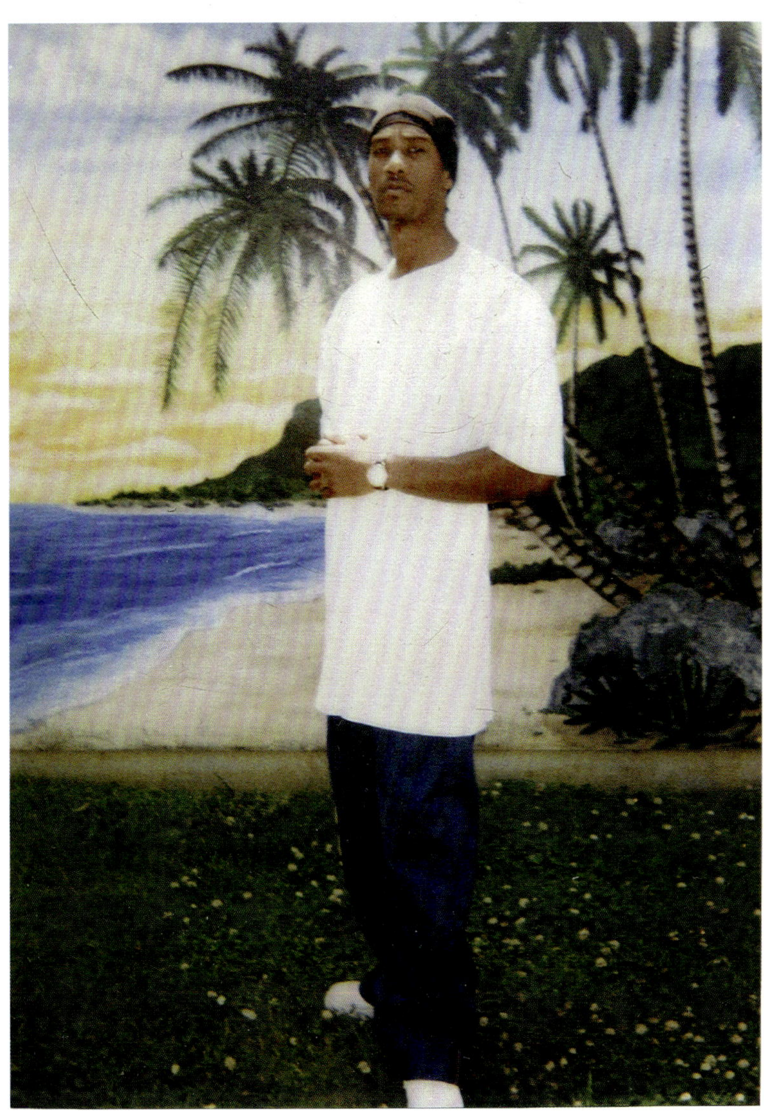

Marcus Bonds, Pelican Bay State
Prison, Crescent City, California

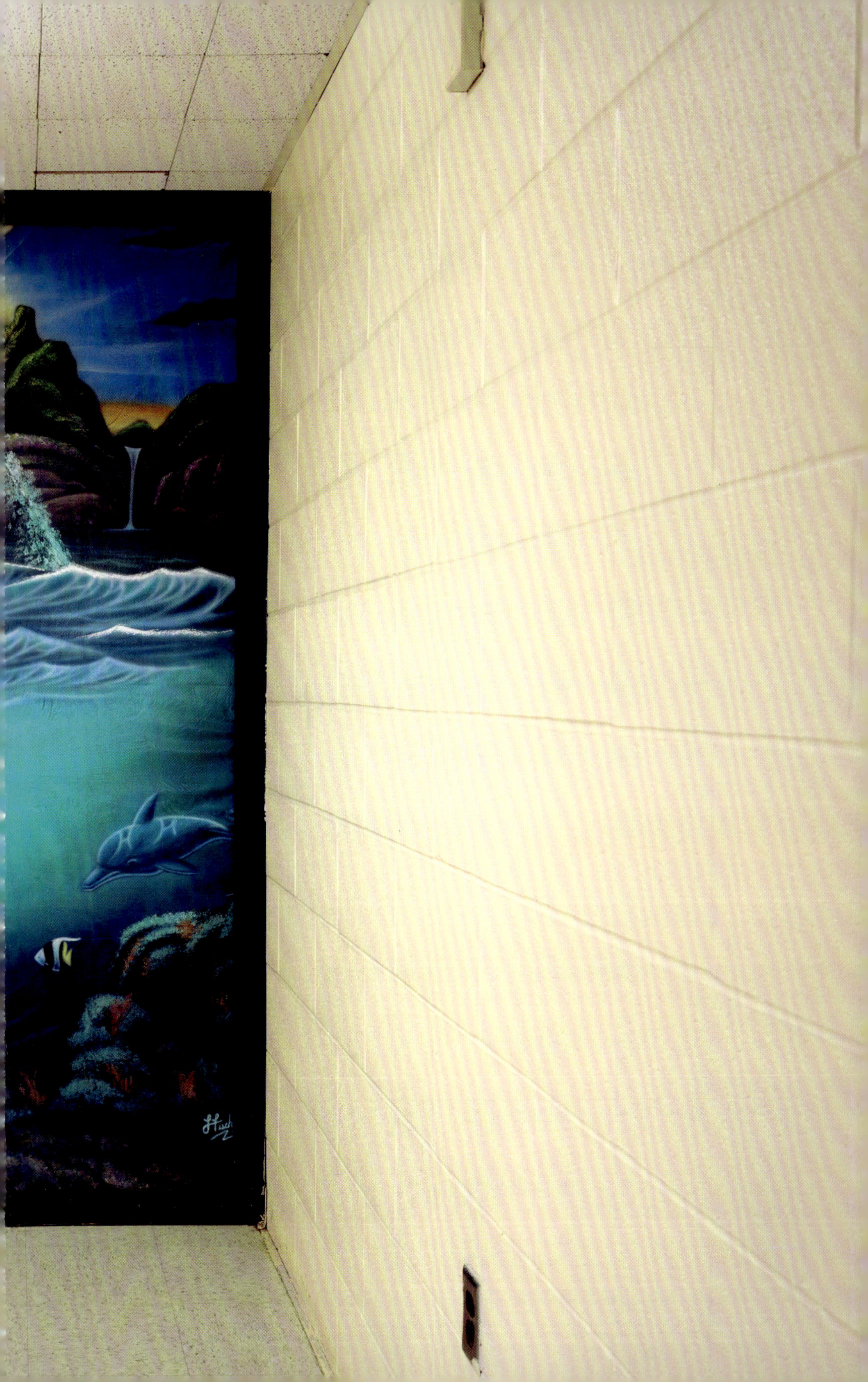

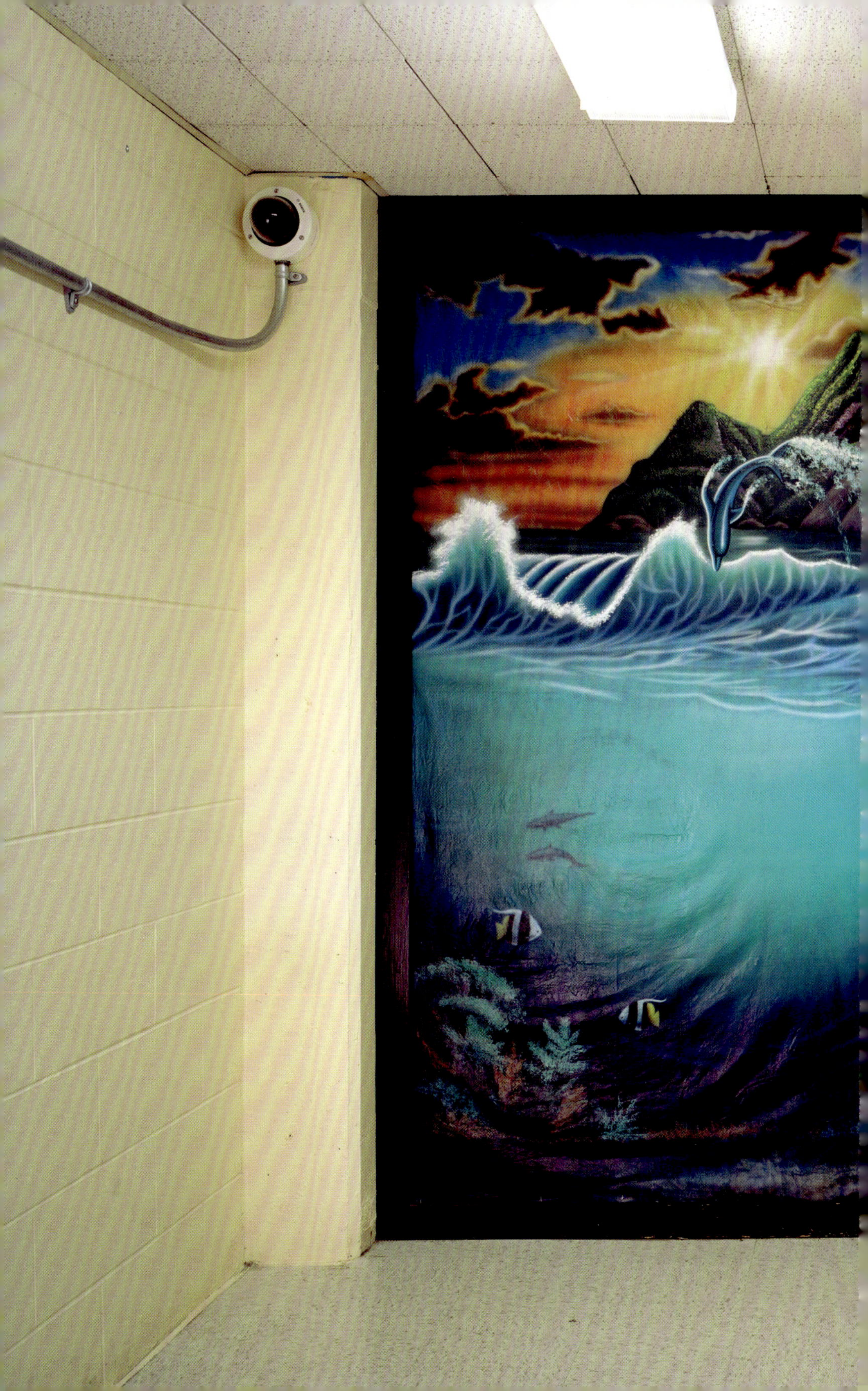

Shawangunk Correctional Facility, New York

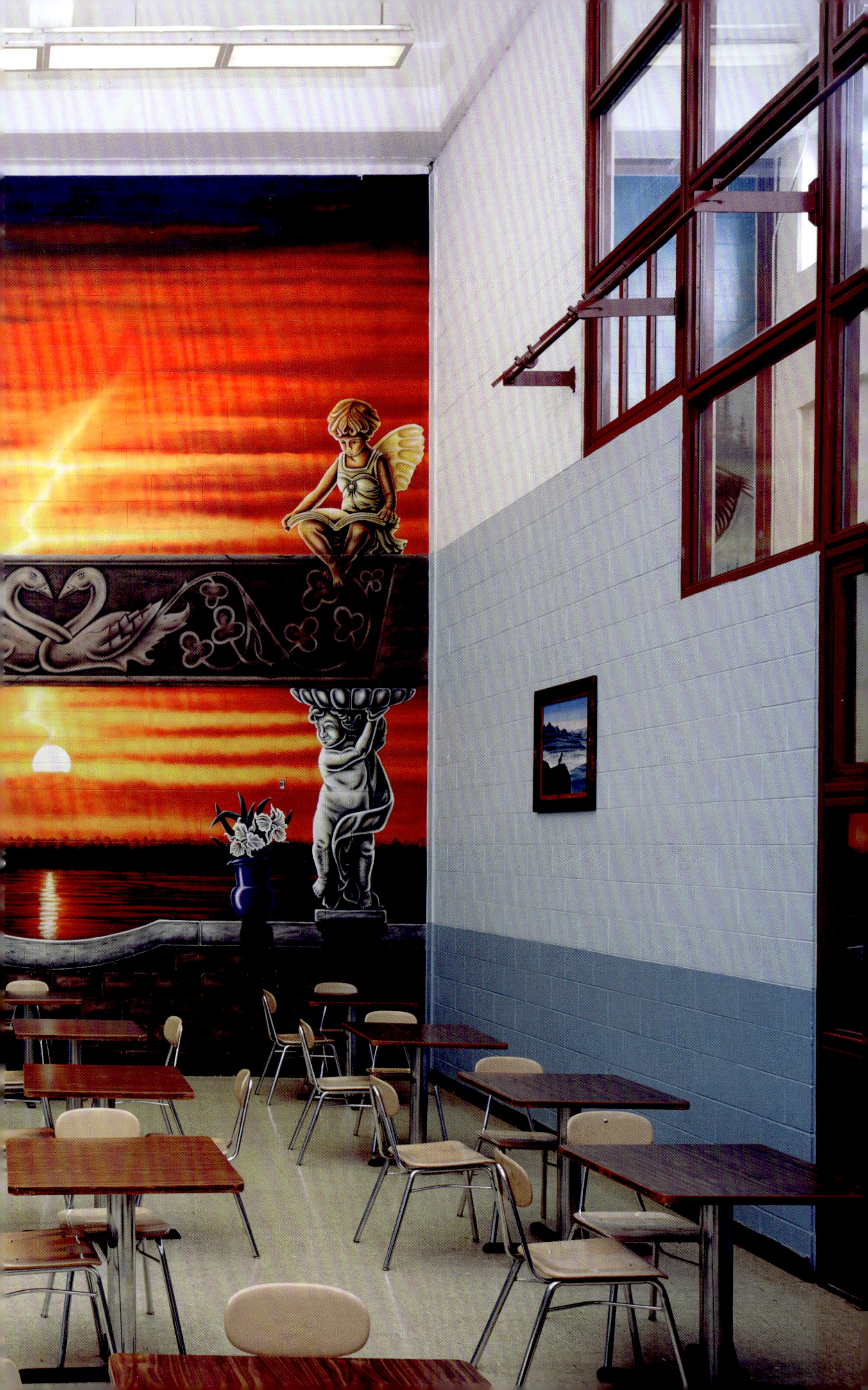

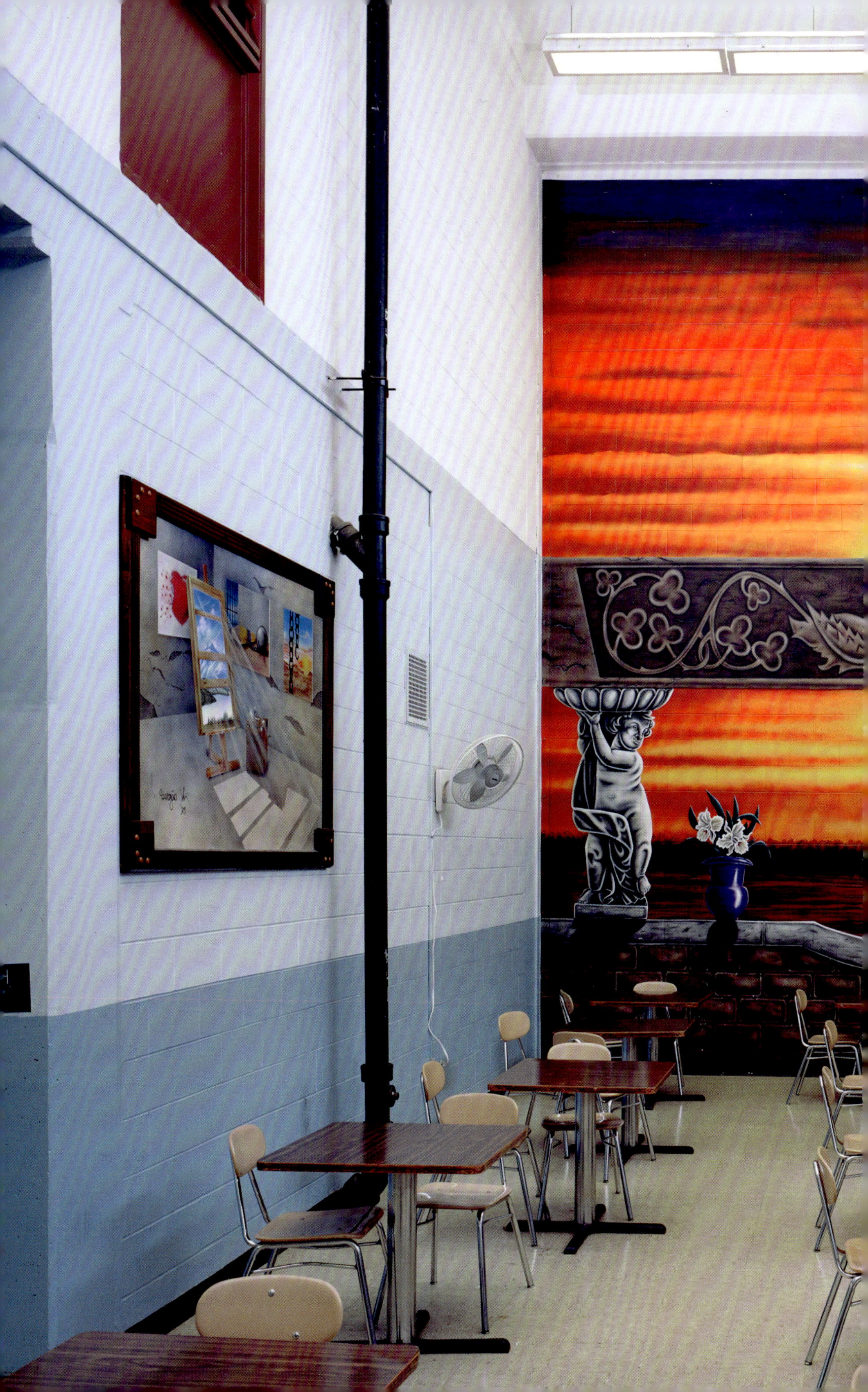

There have been very few times in
my life that I have been scared and
this was one of them. My heart was
racing. I haven't seen my family for
over 15 years.

What will they think of me when
they saw my picture? I don't even
know how to smile! It's just not in me.
I hope I don't send the wrong message.

Jaime Estrada, Pelican Bay State Prison,
Crescent City, California

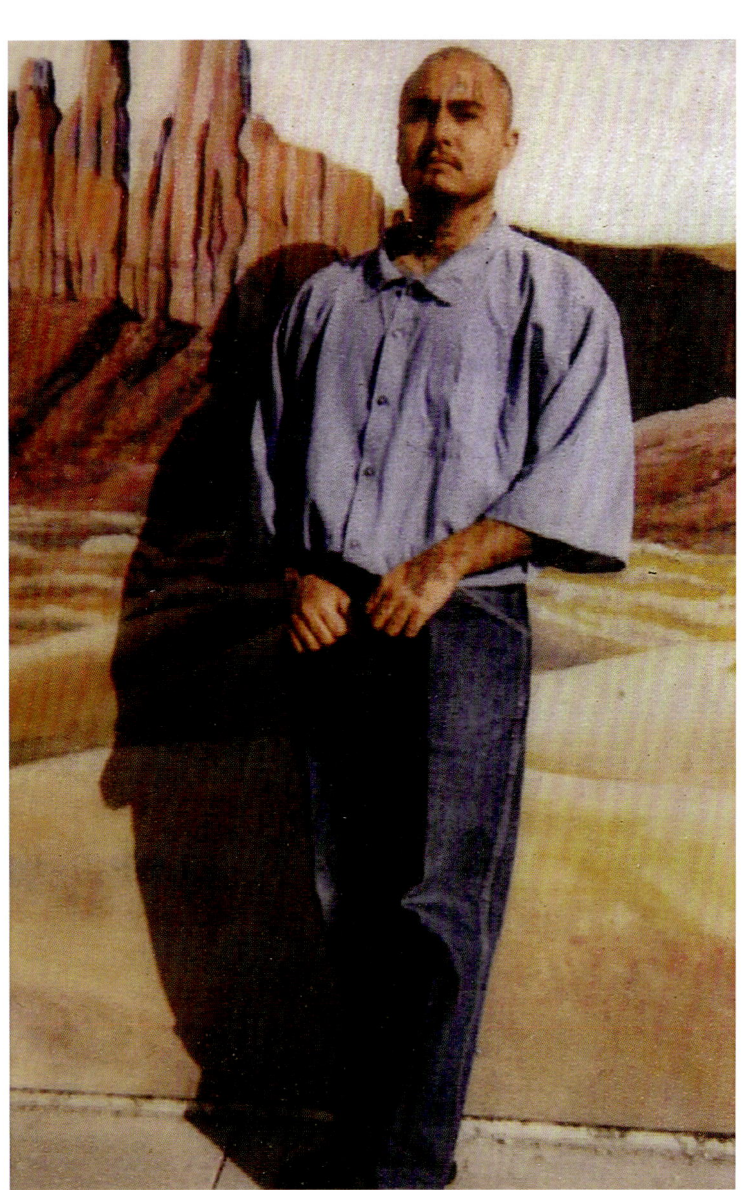

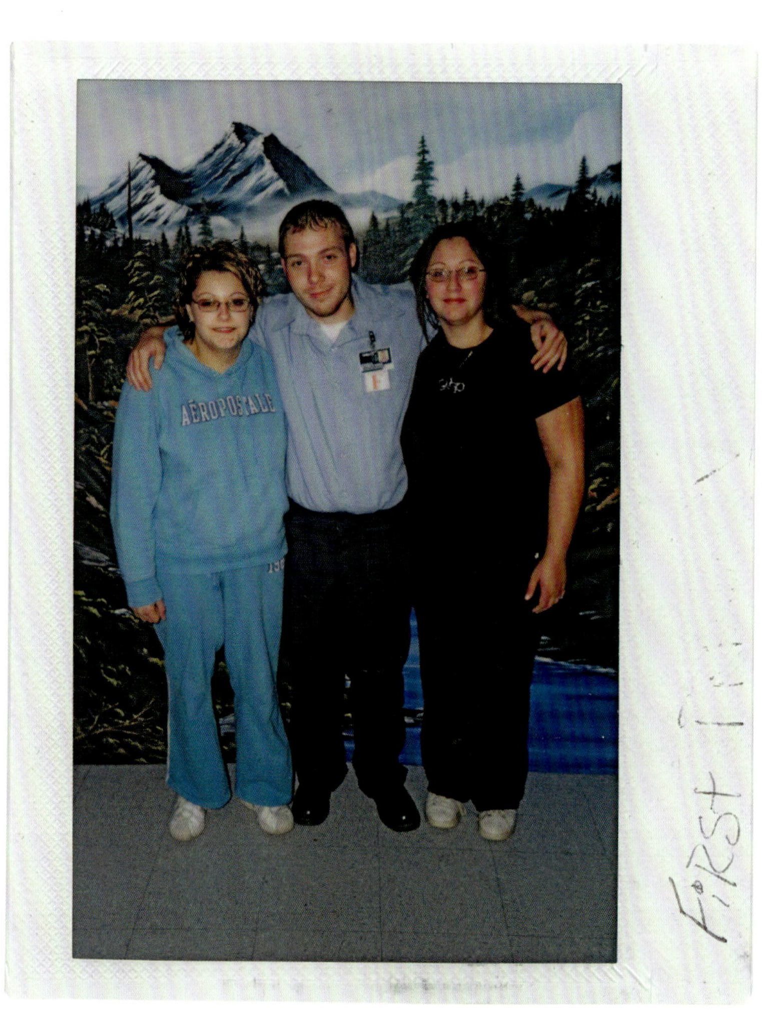

Matthew Wayne Ferman, Warren
Correctional Institution, Lebanon, Ohio

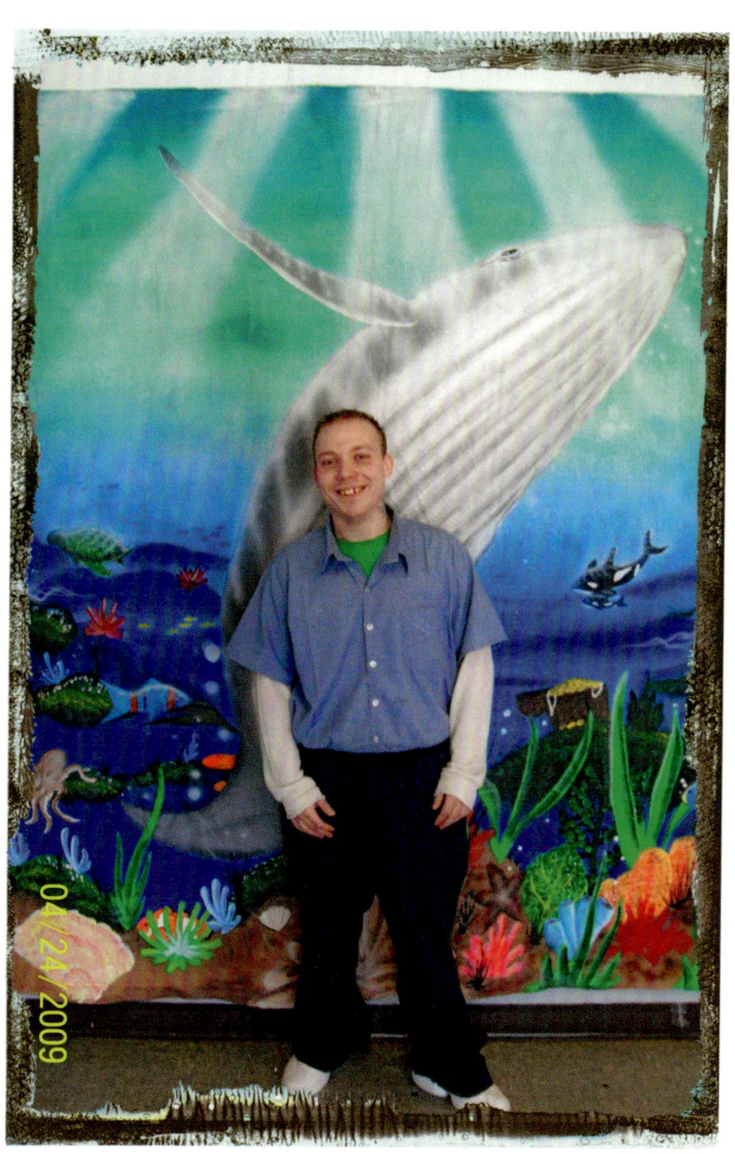
04/24/2009

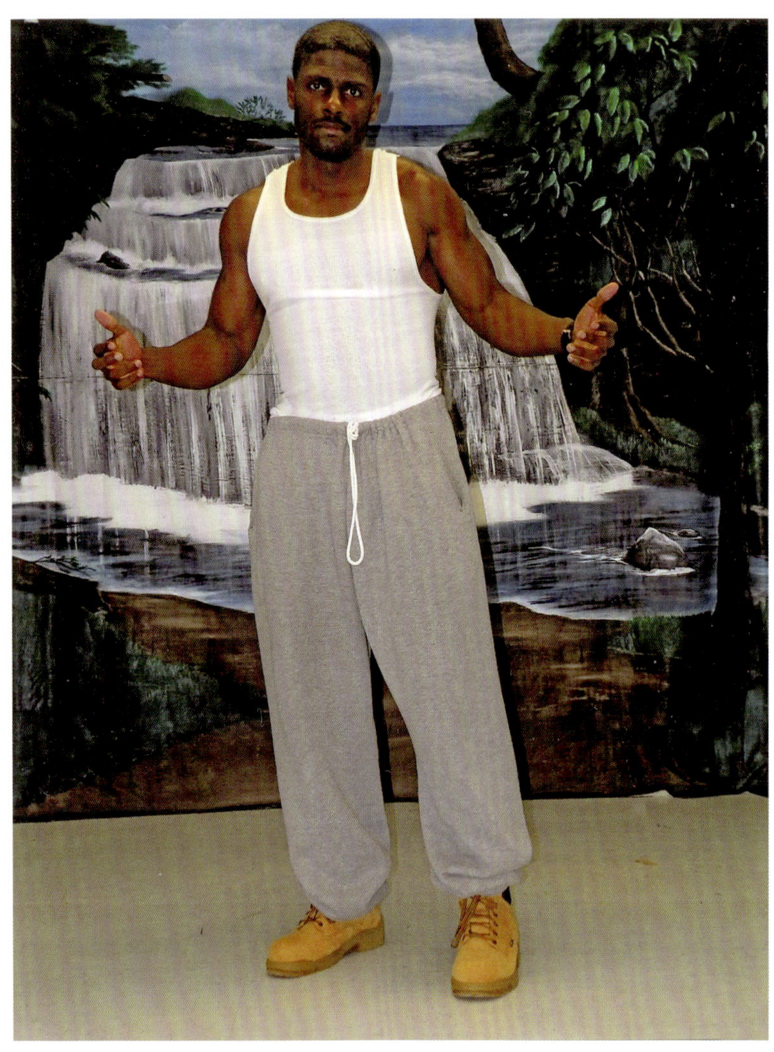

Riley Walls, United States Penitentiary
McCreary, Pine Knot, New York

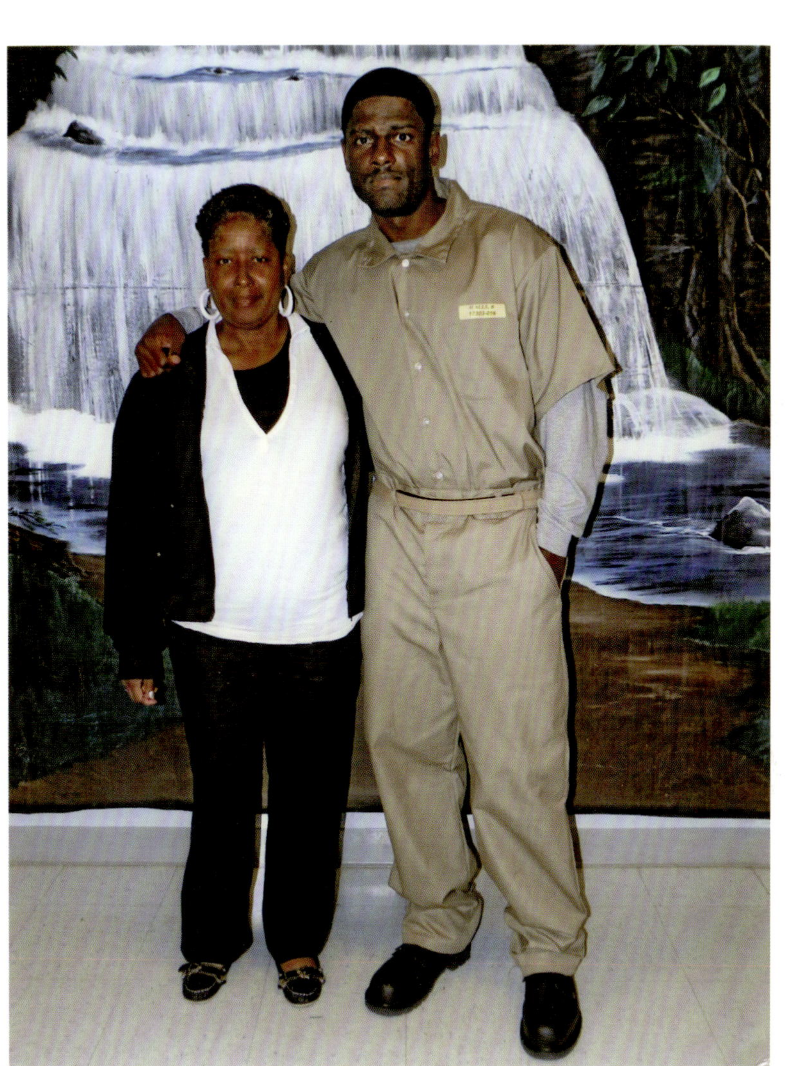

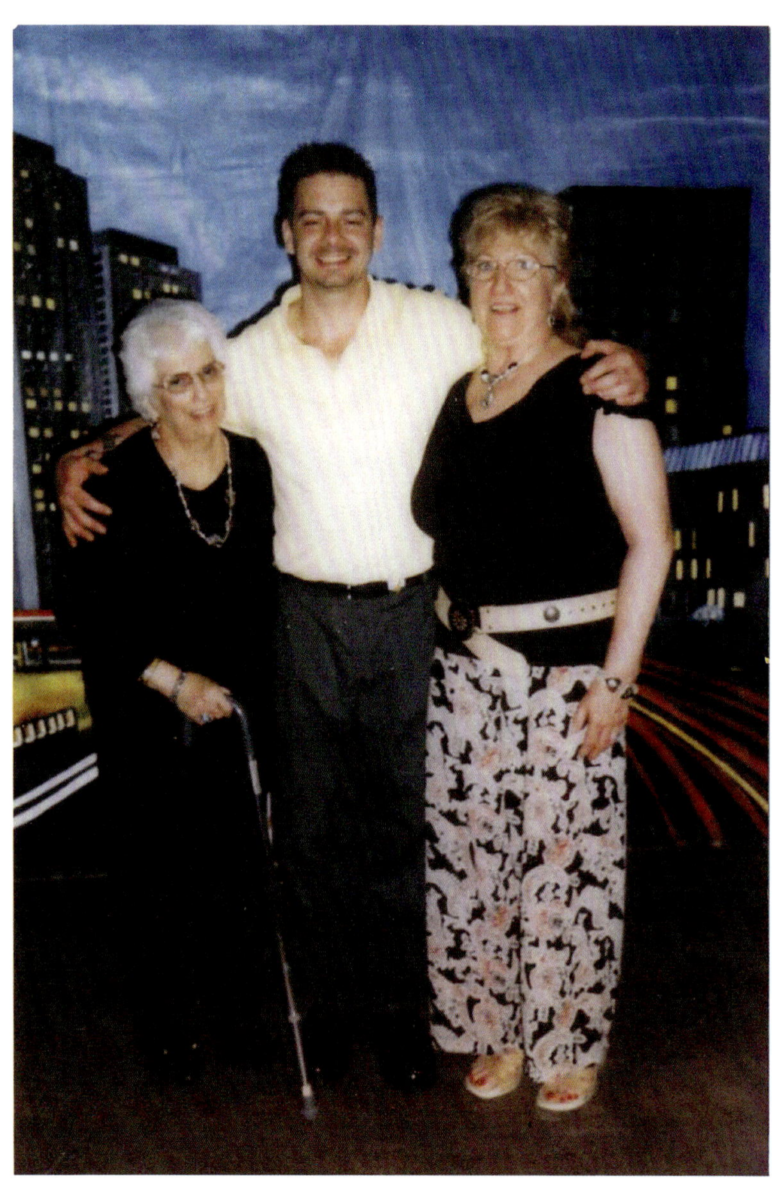

Christian Trunchali, Woodbourne
Correctional Facility, Woodbourne,
New York

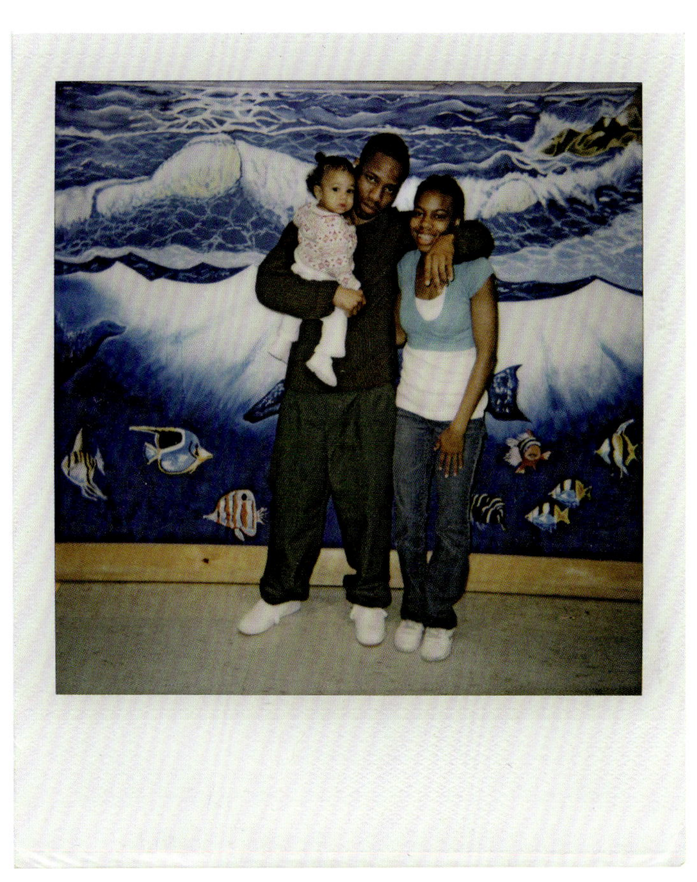

Kyon Jones, Eastern New York
Correctional Facility, Napanoch, NY

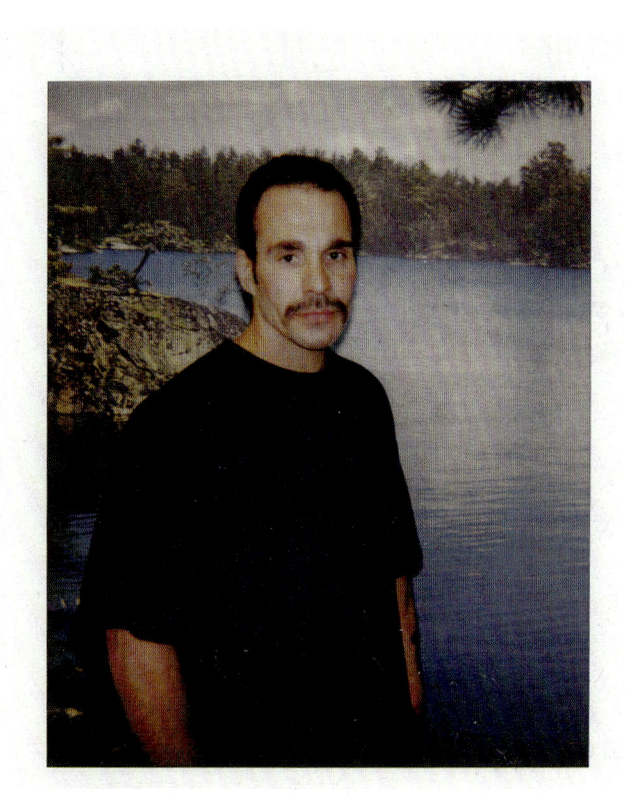

Anonymous, Alger Maximum Correctional
Facility, Munising, Michigan

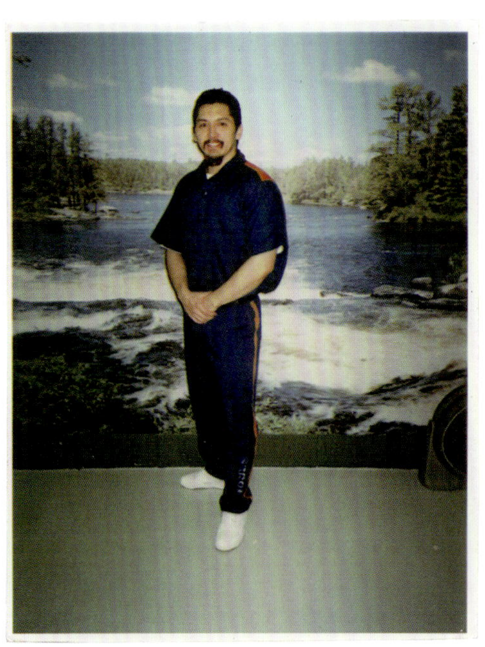

Anonymous, Alger Maximum Correctional
Facility, Munising, Michigan

Ottisville Correctional Facility, New York

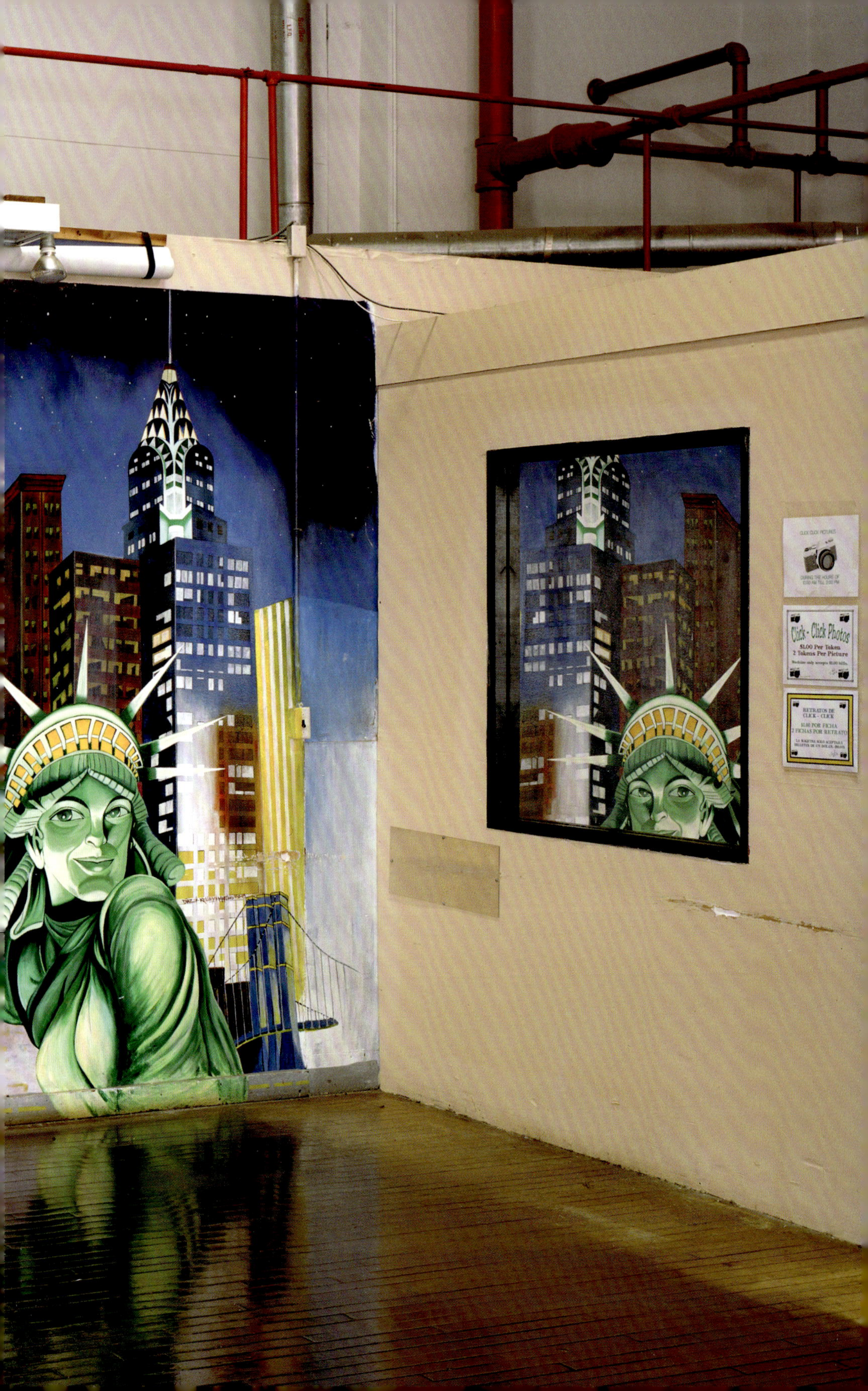
CLICK CLICK PICTURES
DURING THE HOURS OF
10:00 AM TILL 2:00 PM
Click · Click Photos
$1.00 Per Token
2 Tokens Per Picture
Machine only accepts $1.00 bills.
RETRATOS DE
CLICK - CLICK
$1.00 POR FICHA
2 FICHAS POR RETRATO
LA MAQUINA SOLO ACEPTARA
BILLETES DE UN DOLAR, $1.00

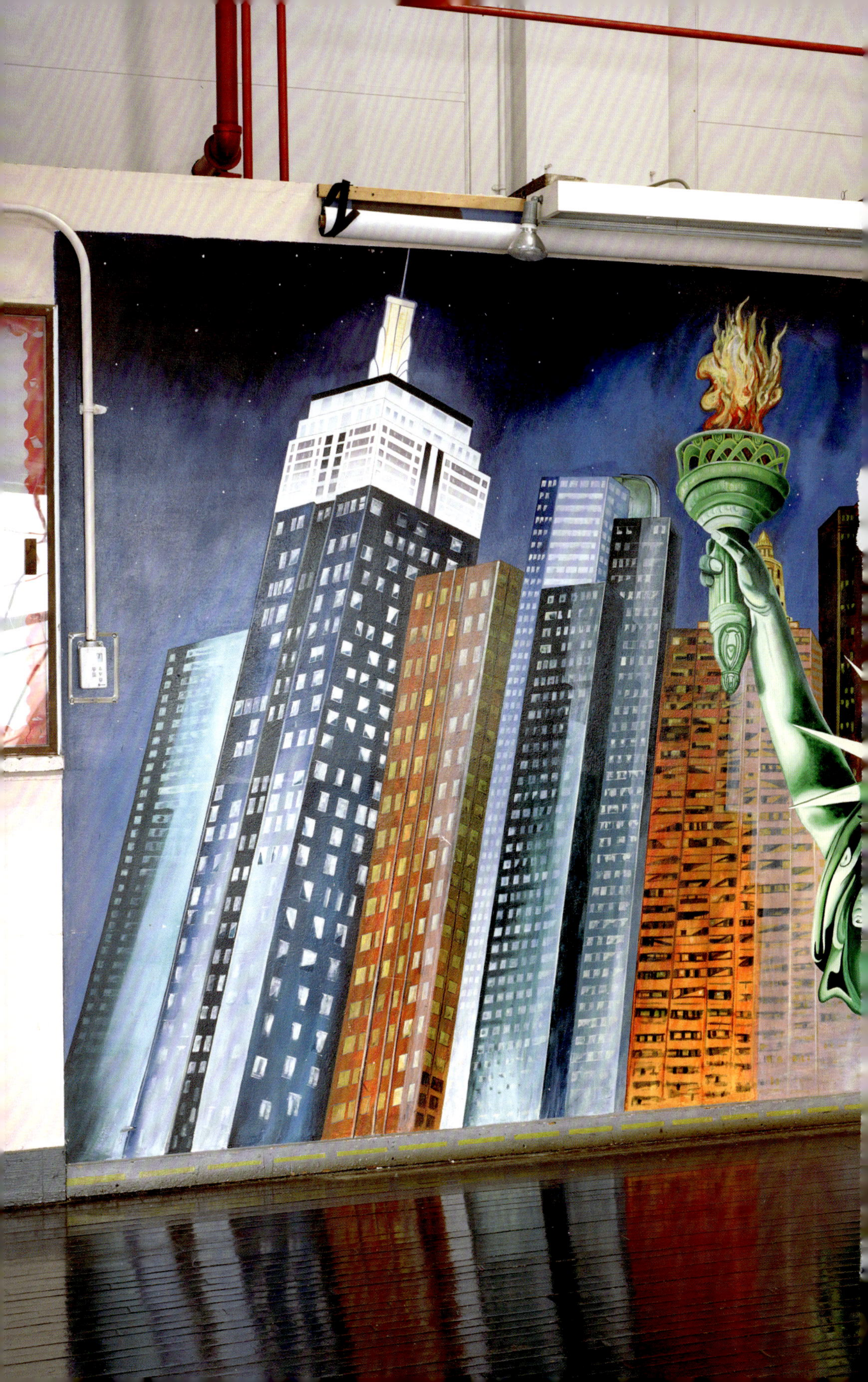

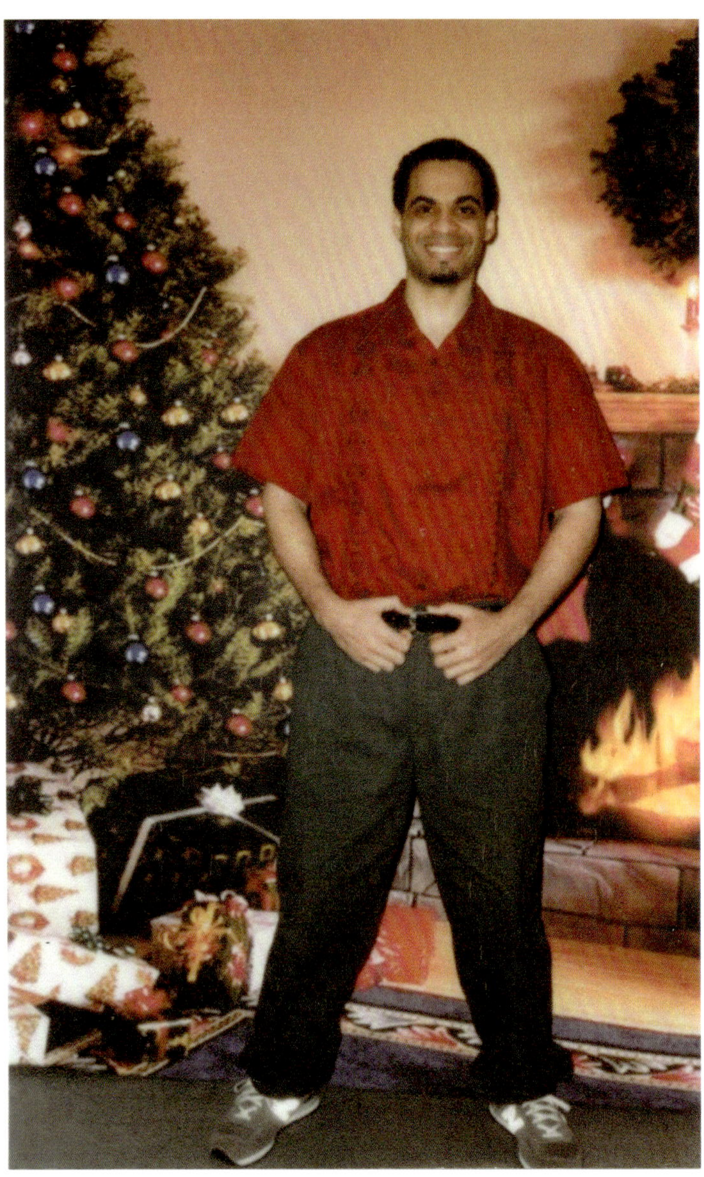

Cesar Mateo, Coxsackie Correctional
Facility, Coxsackie, New York

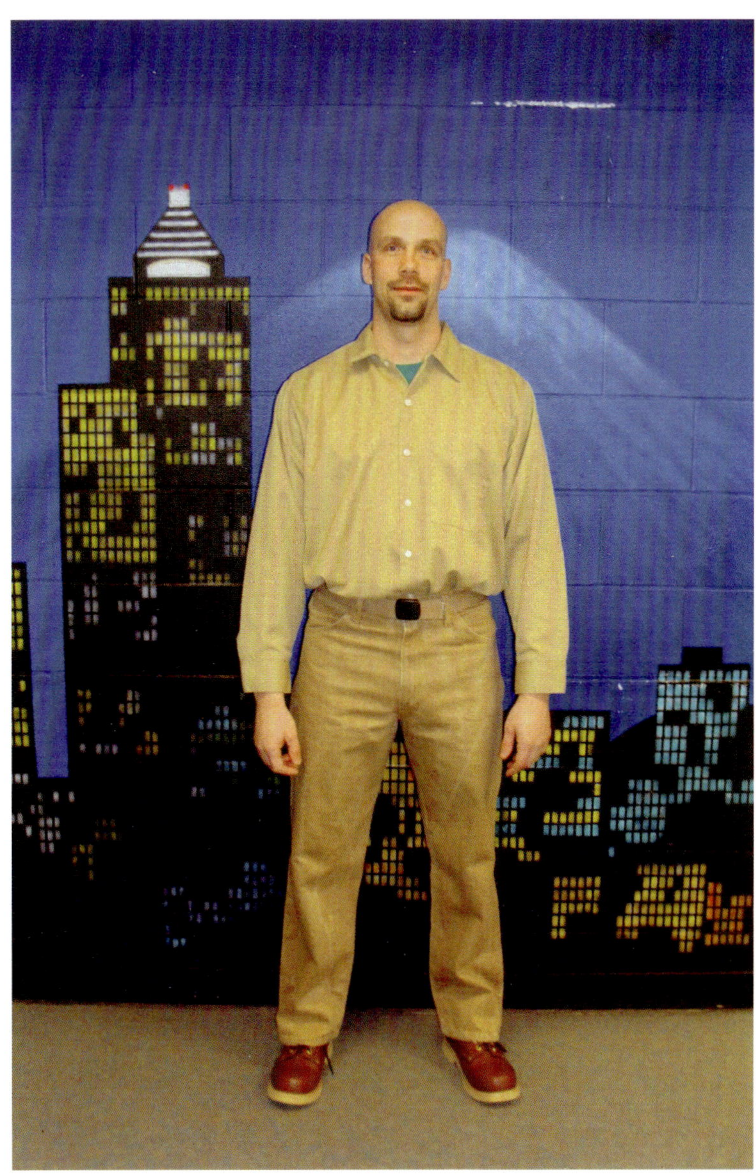

David Cobabe, Airway Heights Corrections
Center, Airway Heights, Washington

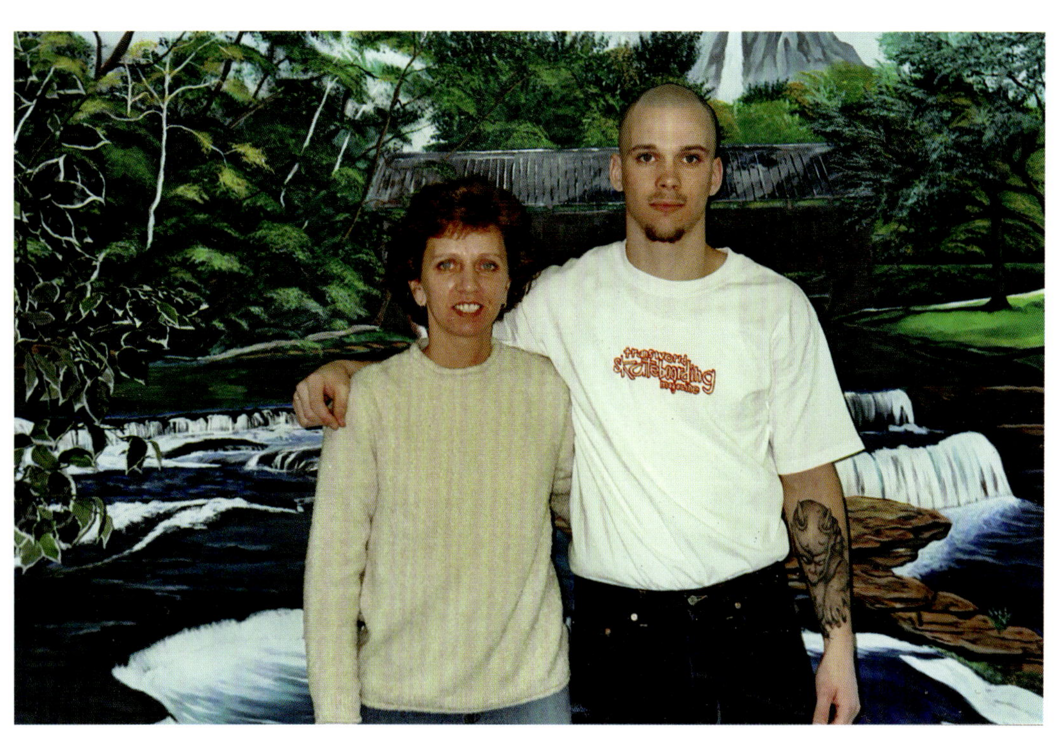

Joseph Vernetti, Maryland Correctional
Institution, Hagerstown, Maryland

April 29, 2009

Dear Lee Lana

I hope this letter finds you in the best of health and spirits.
I grew up in the south, mostly raised by my grandmamma.
My mama left us at age 12. My father was long gone. I moved to
Washington in 1994 to live with my father. He provided for me, but
he was a military man, so I never got the hugs or "I love you, son"
that I always longed for. He was always gone, so I started hanging
out in the streets, around the dealers and gang members. They
became my role models. I never joined a gang, but I loved the
respect they got. So I stole, robbed, sold drugs, became what
most people see as a thug. Mostly I was frontin, because I never
was an evil person. My heart was always in the right place. I had
one person I considered a friend. He died in '97. This is when
I stopped caring about life. This one night I was at this park with
a gun in my hand. I didn't want to live no more, but this white
girl came out of nowhere and saved my life. We became friends
and I fell in love with her. She was a good woman from a family
that didn't believe in dating outside the race so I wasn't liked,
but it didn't matter because I was happy. She became pregnant.
I tried to stay out of the streets and get a job. My daughter was
born on January 2. On the 4th the police raided my home and
took me away for a crime I committed ten months beforehand.
I received 150 months for first degree robbery with a gun. My girl
found another man. It took me a while, but now I'm a better man.
I could be dead, but I believe God did this to open my eyes and
realize he has a plan for me to do great things. I have two years
left. I try to stay reading something to better myself. I'm positive
about life, but I get scared because a lot out there has changed.
I've met a lot of good people in here that just made some bad
choices and it hurts my heart how the world looks at us like
we ain't shit. It's part of life, I guess.

God Bless,
B.

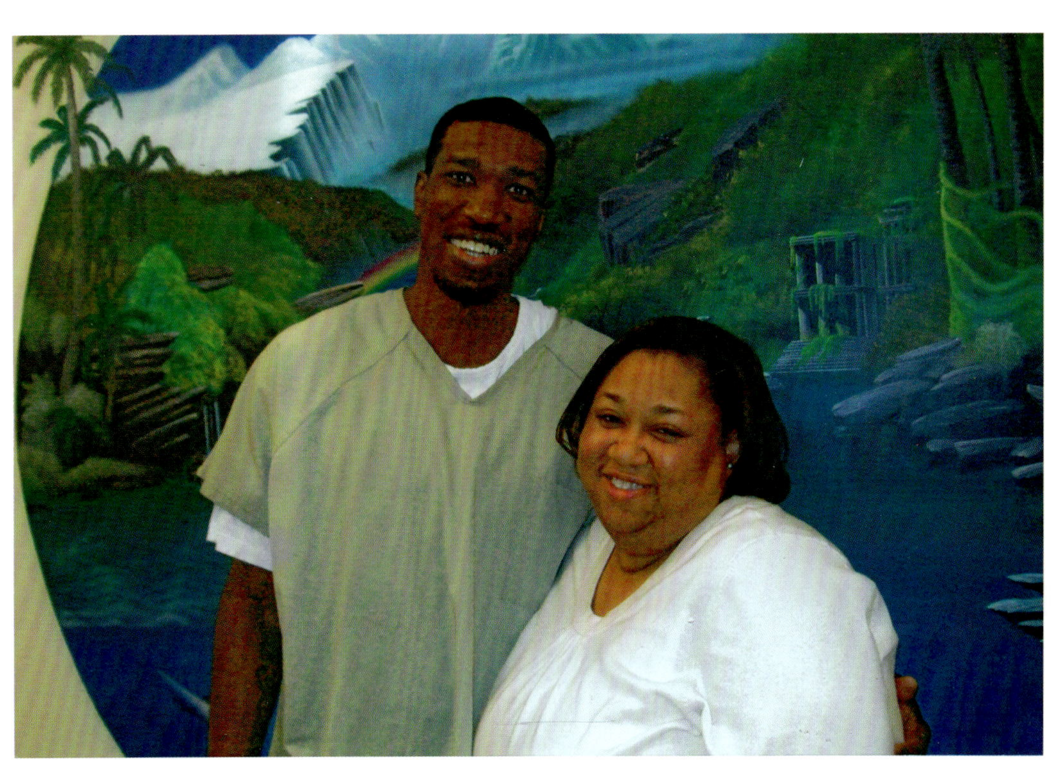

James "B" Louis, Prairie Correctional
Facility, Appleton, Minnesota

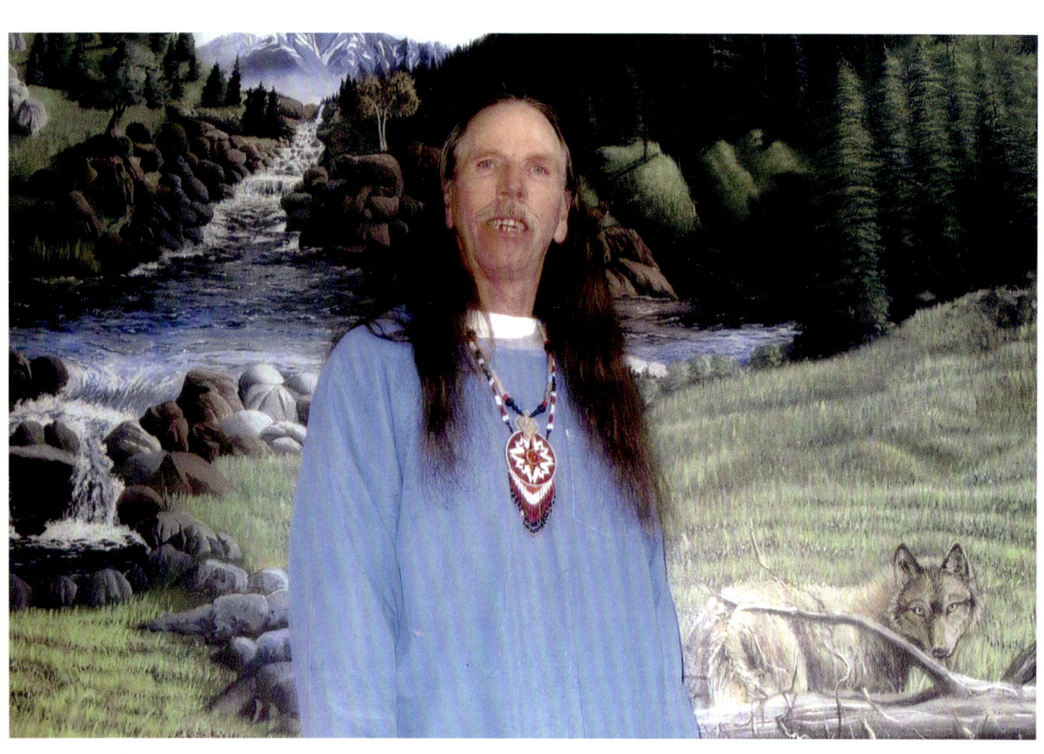

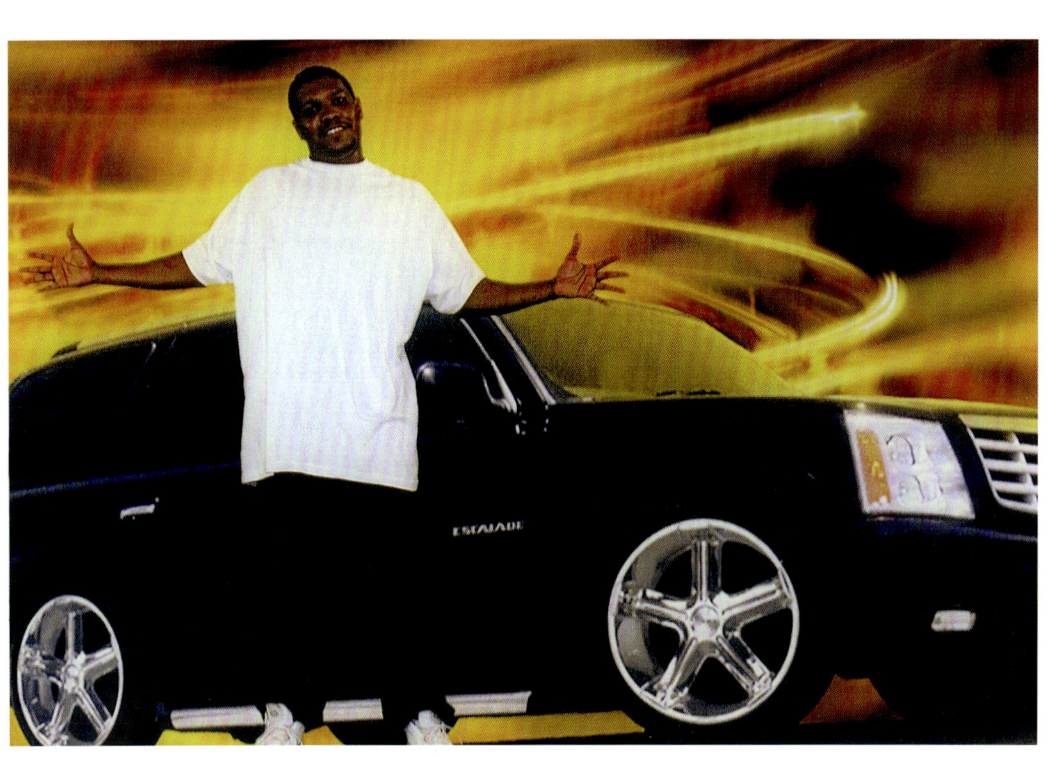

Baretta Wilford, Southern Ohio
Correctional Facility, Lucasville, Ohio

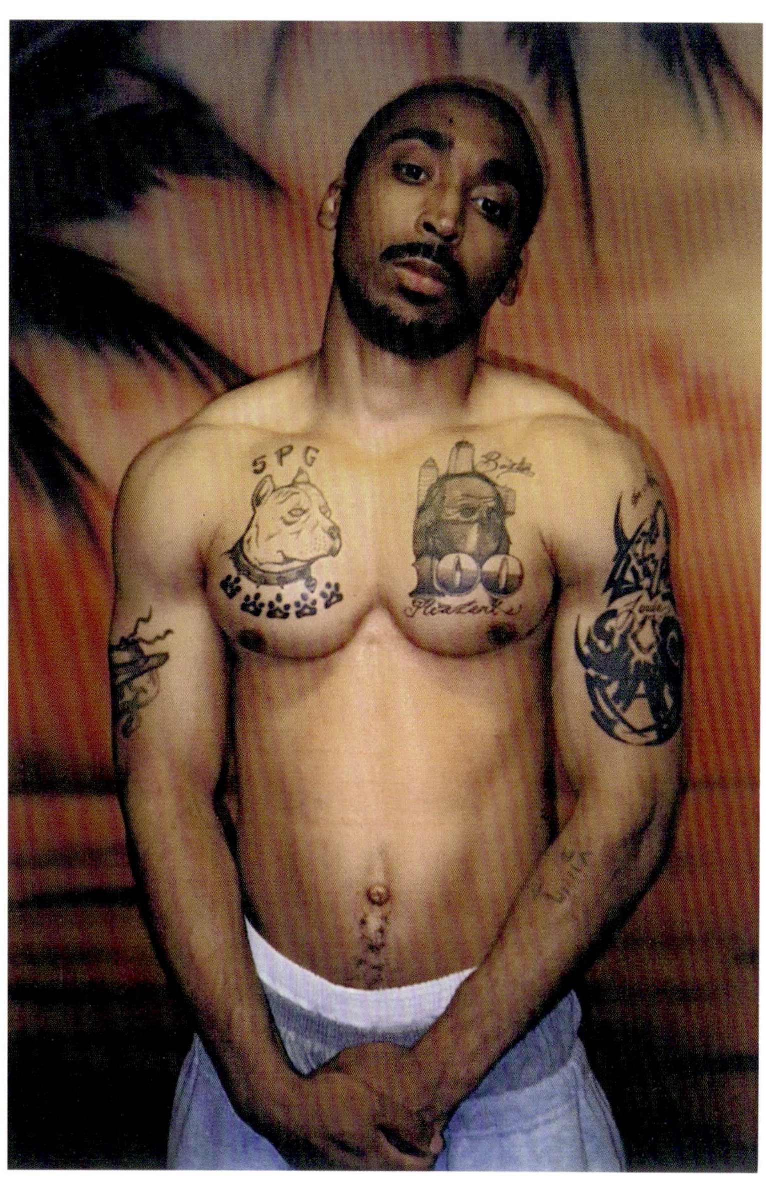

Keith Barboza, Federal Correctional
Institution II, Butner, North Carolina

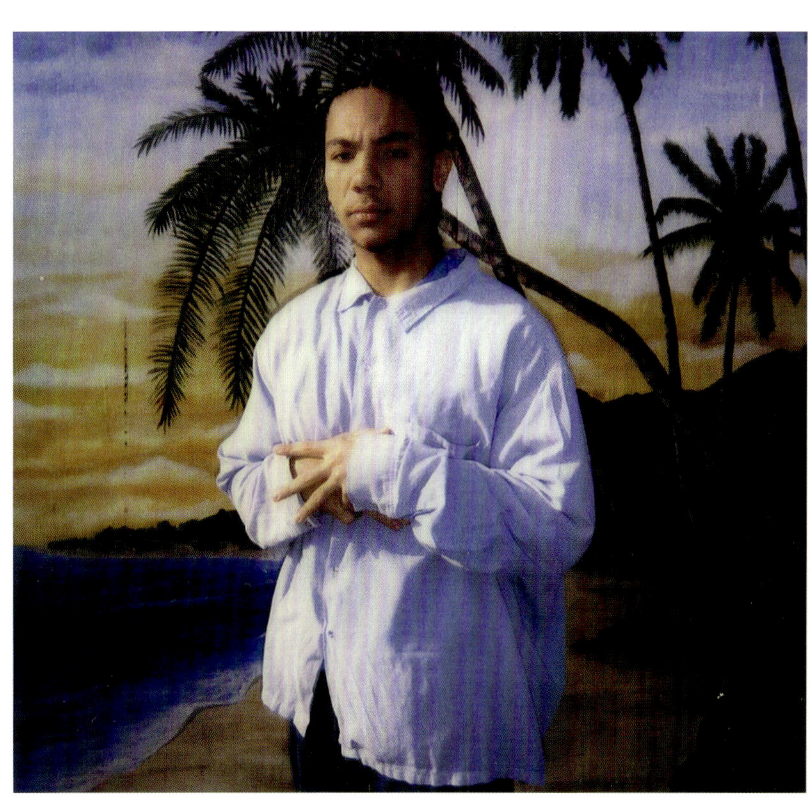

Shawn Jackson, Pelican Bay State
Prison, Crescent City, California

March 31, 2009

Hey Lana,

What's going on? How you doing? I got your letter about your art project. It's no problem. I got a picture I'll send now. It's old but it's all I got, and it might be too big for your project. But I got a visit coming in May and I'll take a picture. I hope it's not too long but I'll send it anyway.

I got the picture of you and your brother. I put it in my photo album. Just in case you become famous someday off your art. :)

Alright Lana, good luck with everything. And if you don't use my picture make sure you write anyway and let me know how everything went.

Be good,
Jerry

P.S.: I like the Sinatra stamp.

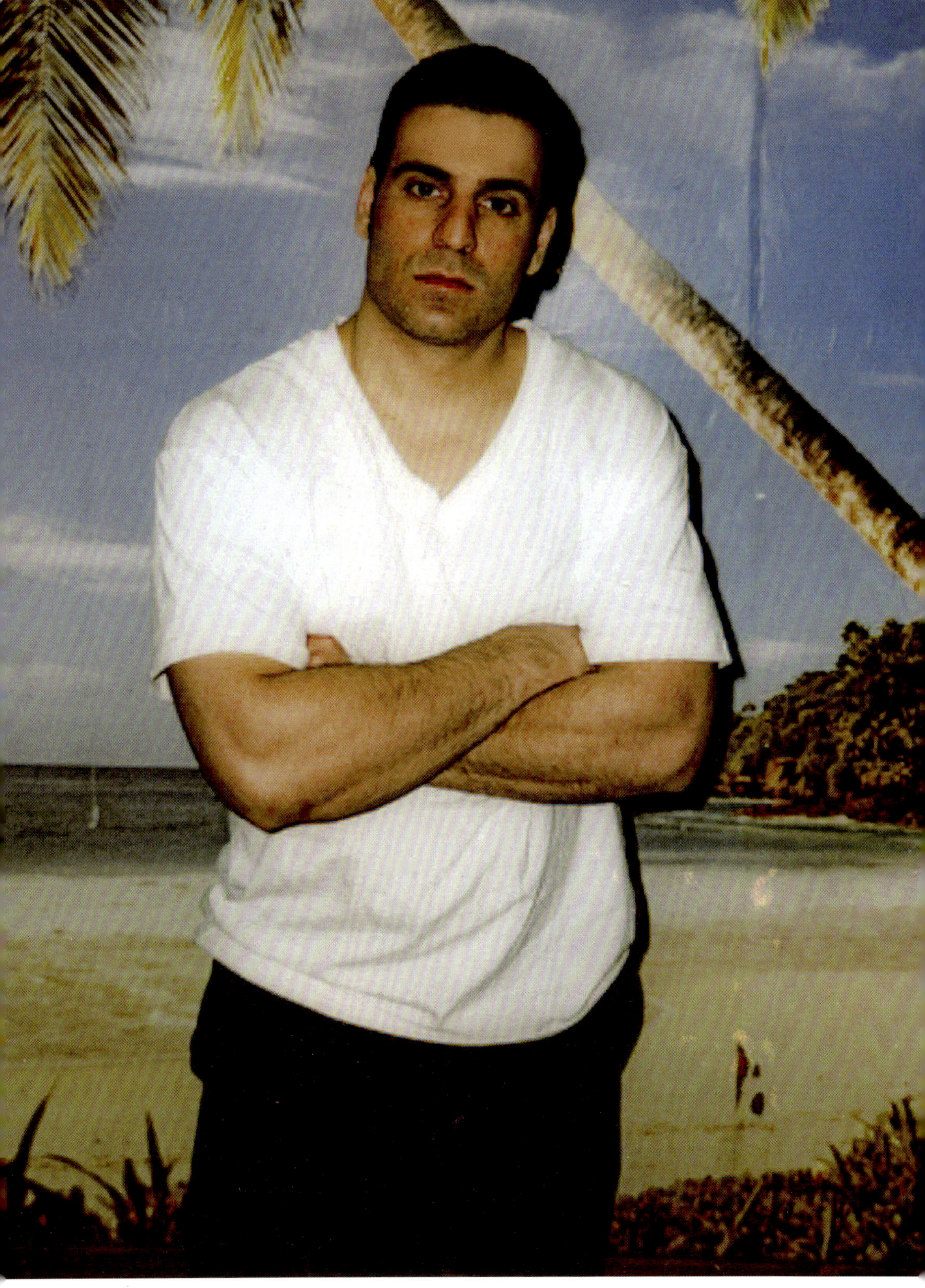

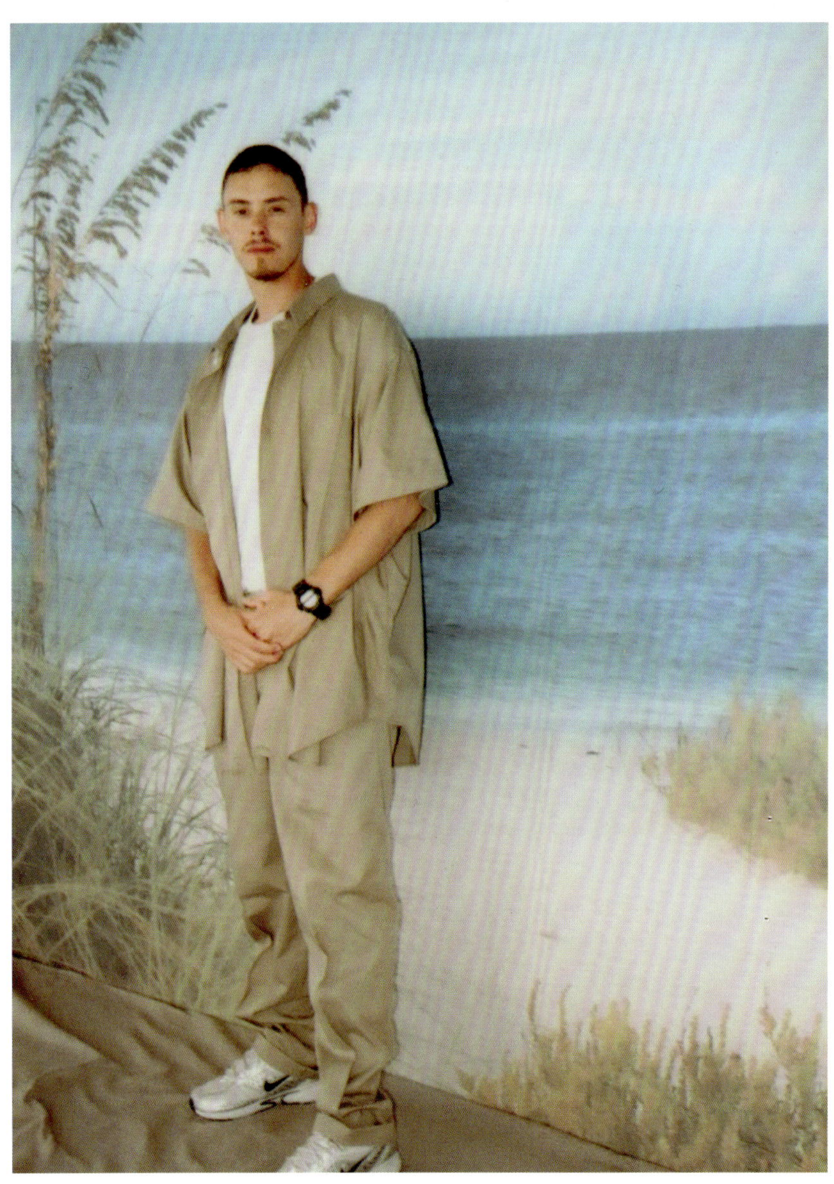

Charles Derrick Keller, United States
Penitentiary, Marion, Illinois

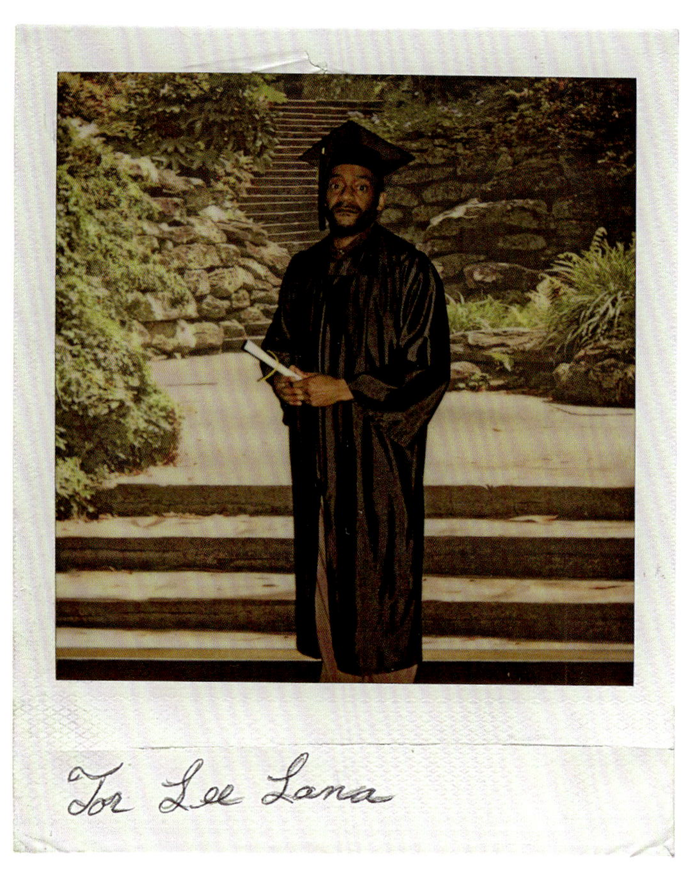

Anonymous, State Correctional
Institution, Coal Township, Pennsylvania

Woodbourne Correctional Facility, New York

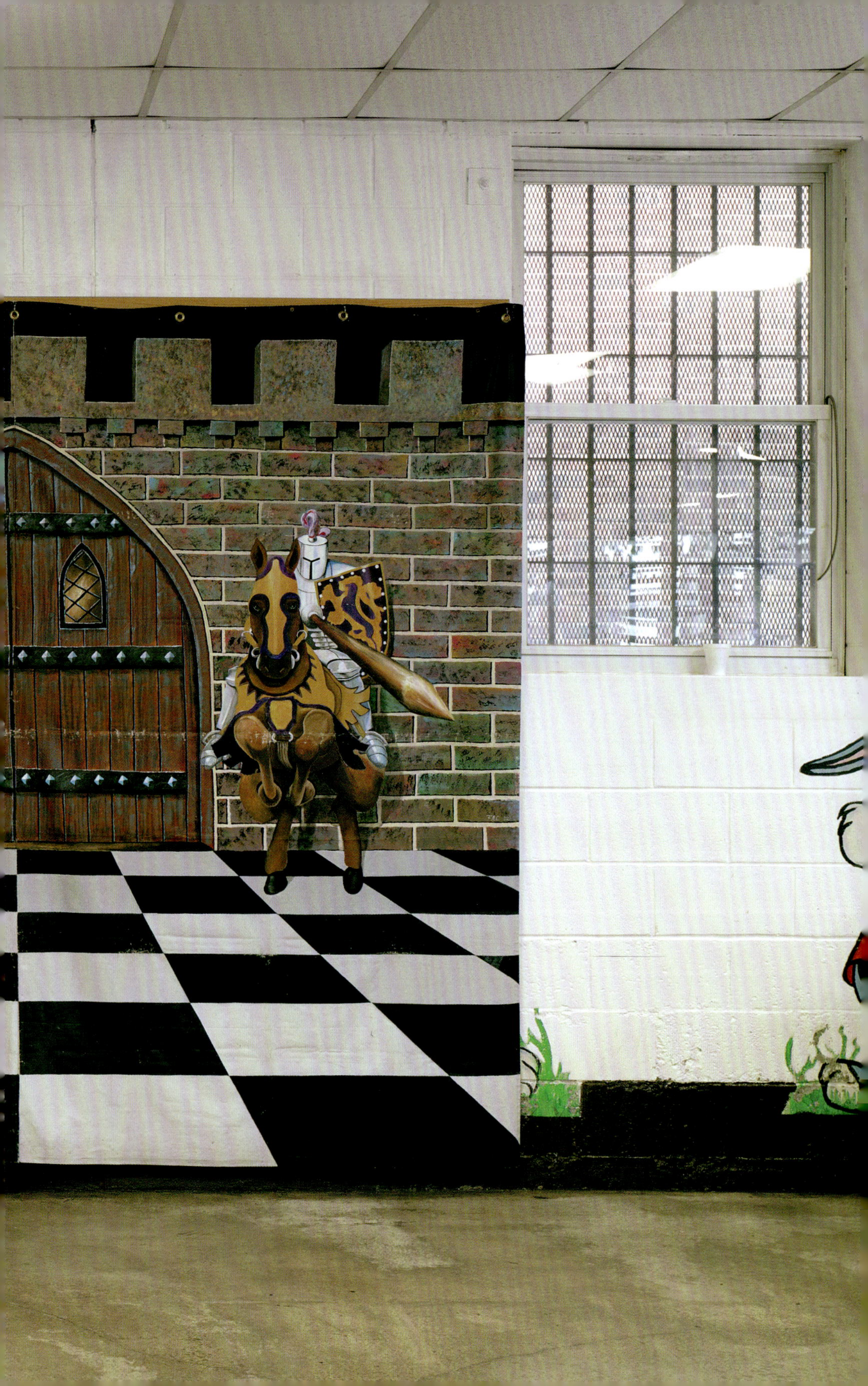

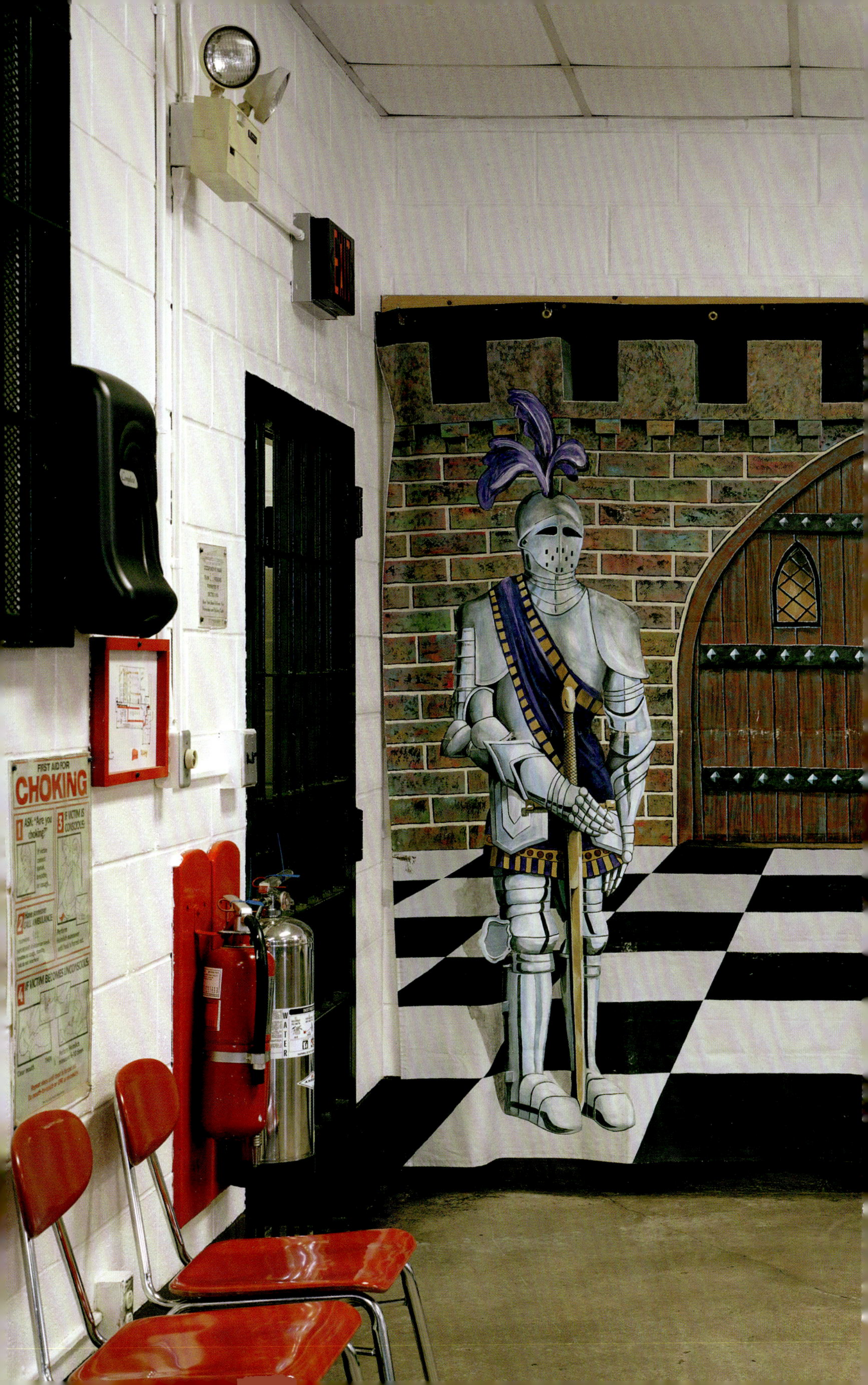

FIRST AID FOR
CHOKING
1 ASK: "Are you choking?"
3 IF VICTIM IS CONSCIOUS
2 CALL AMBULANCE
4 IF VICTIM BECOMES UNCONSCIOUS
WATER

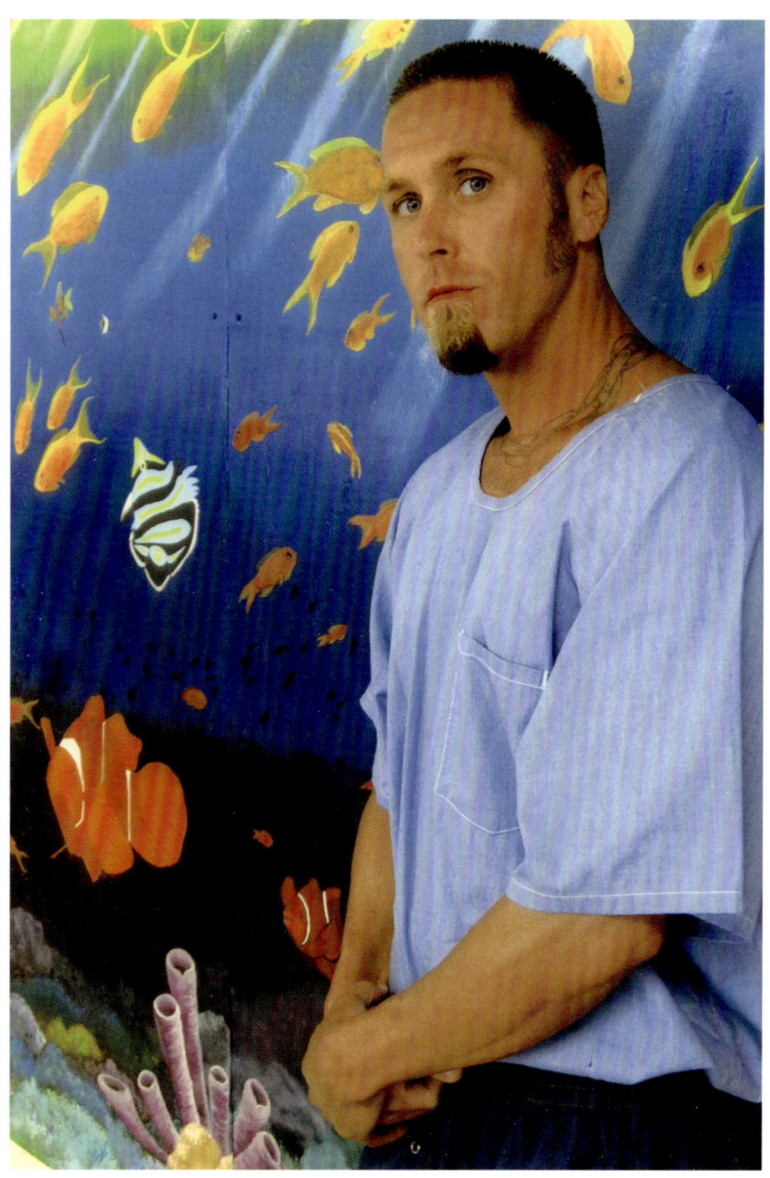

Marlon Connolly, Salinas Valley
State Prison, Soledad, California

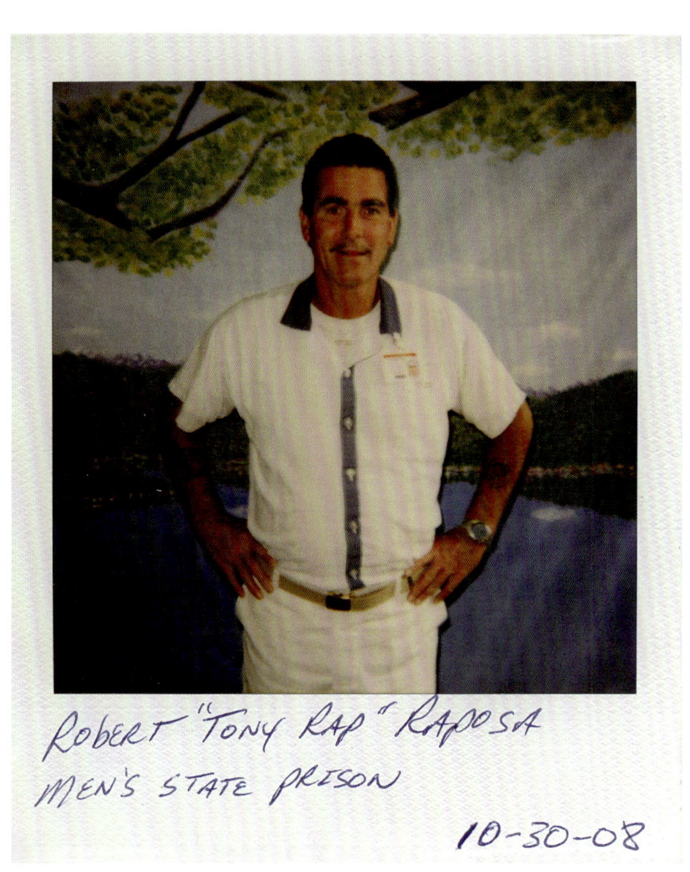

Robert "Tony Rap" Raposa
MEN'S STATE PRISON
10-30-08

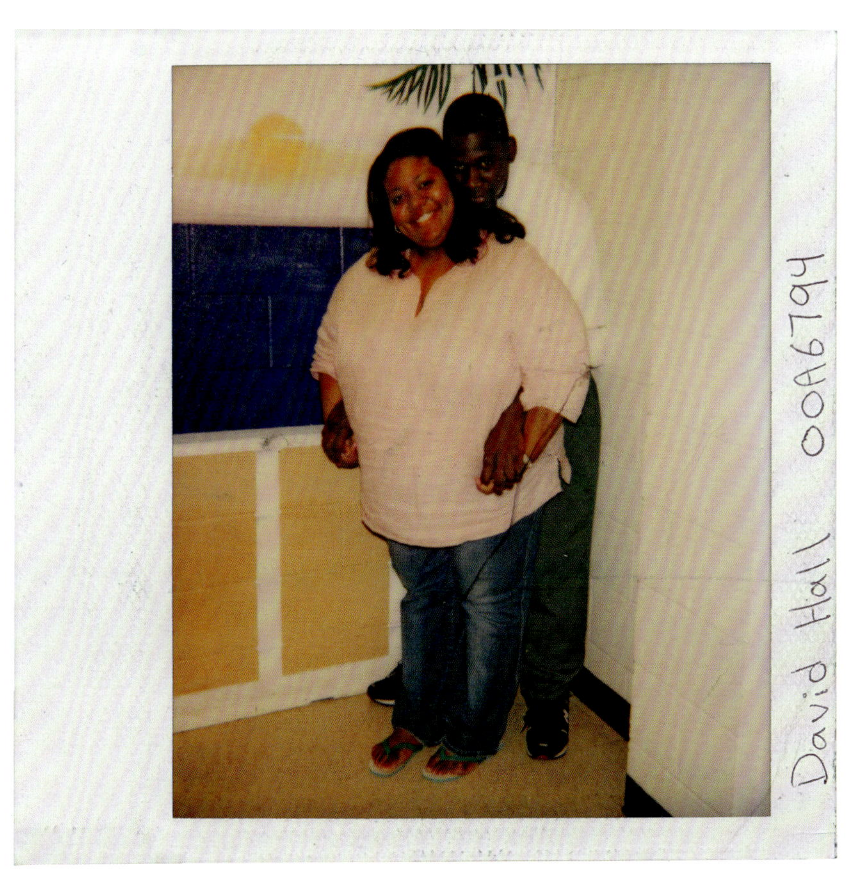

David Hall, Auburn Correctional Facility,
Auburn, New York

At the time of this photo I was thinking
about all my family in Chicago that
I haven't seen in almost a decade.
This photo was taken for them. I'm
originally from Chicago (born and
raised) and all my family resides there
and they can't afford travel expenses
to visit me here at the Louisiana State
Penitentiary. Over the years of my
incarceration (ten and counting) we
send each other pictures so as of now,
pictures like this are the only way my
family and kids can see me.

Leonard Stokes, Louisiana State
Penitentiary, Angola, Louisiana

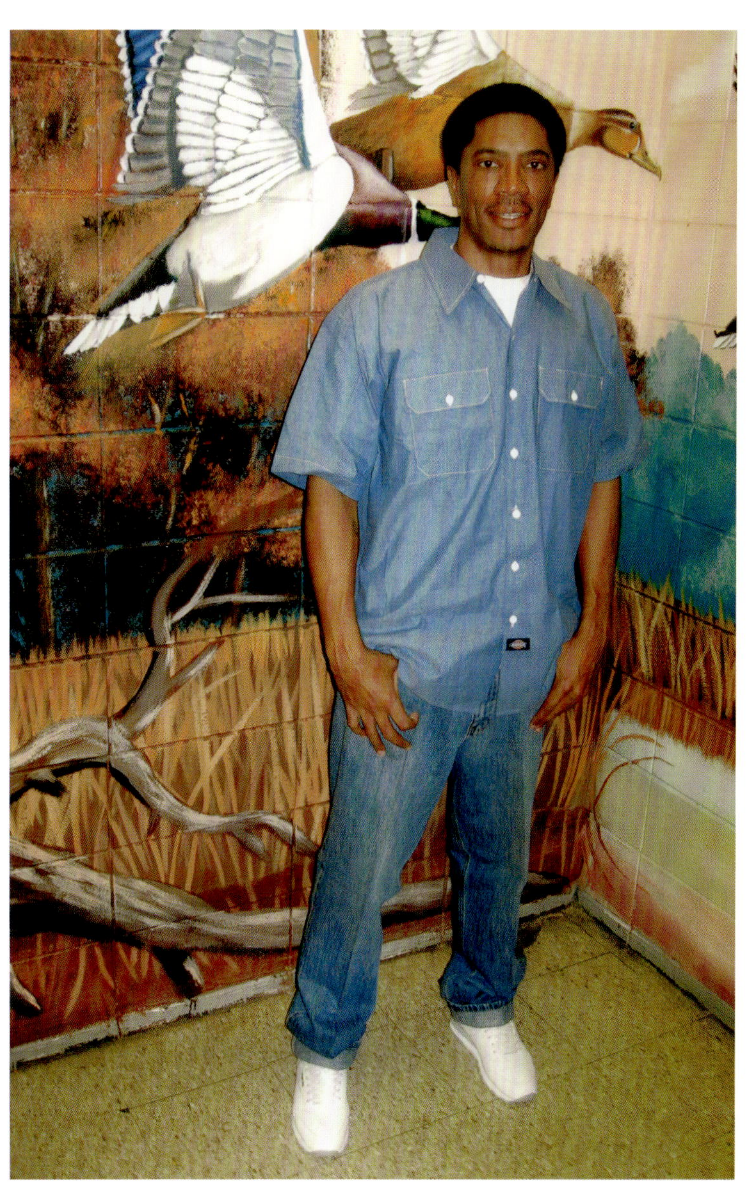

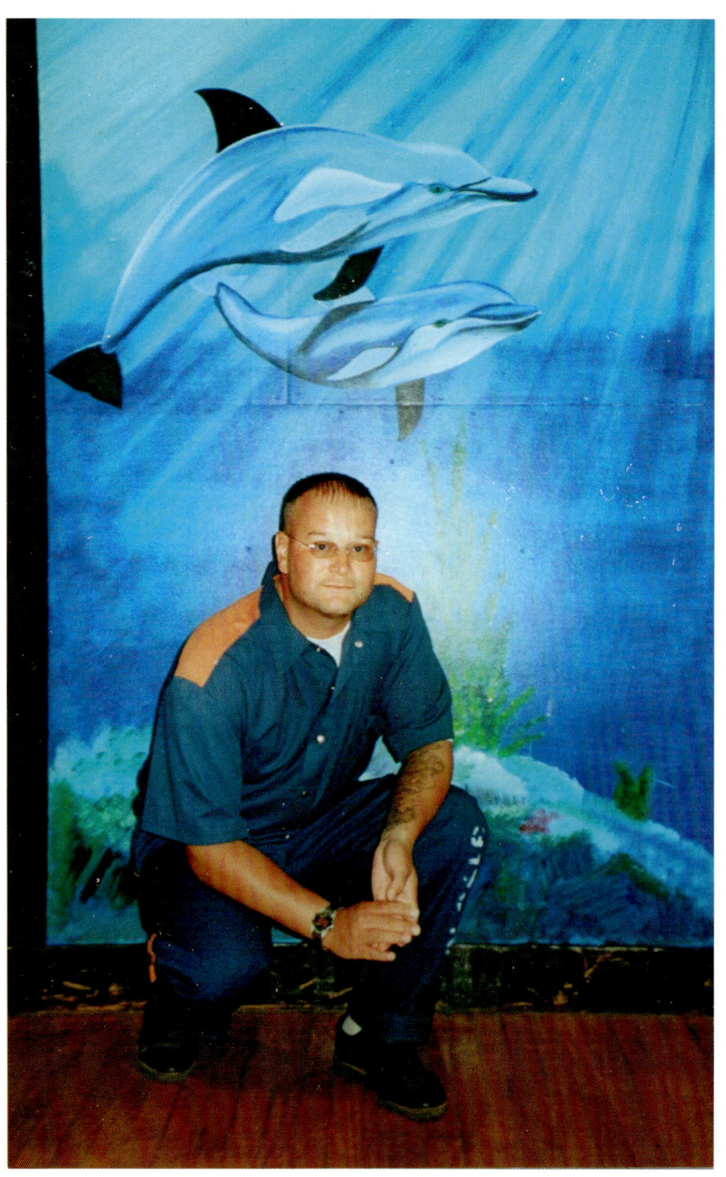

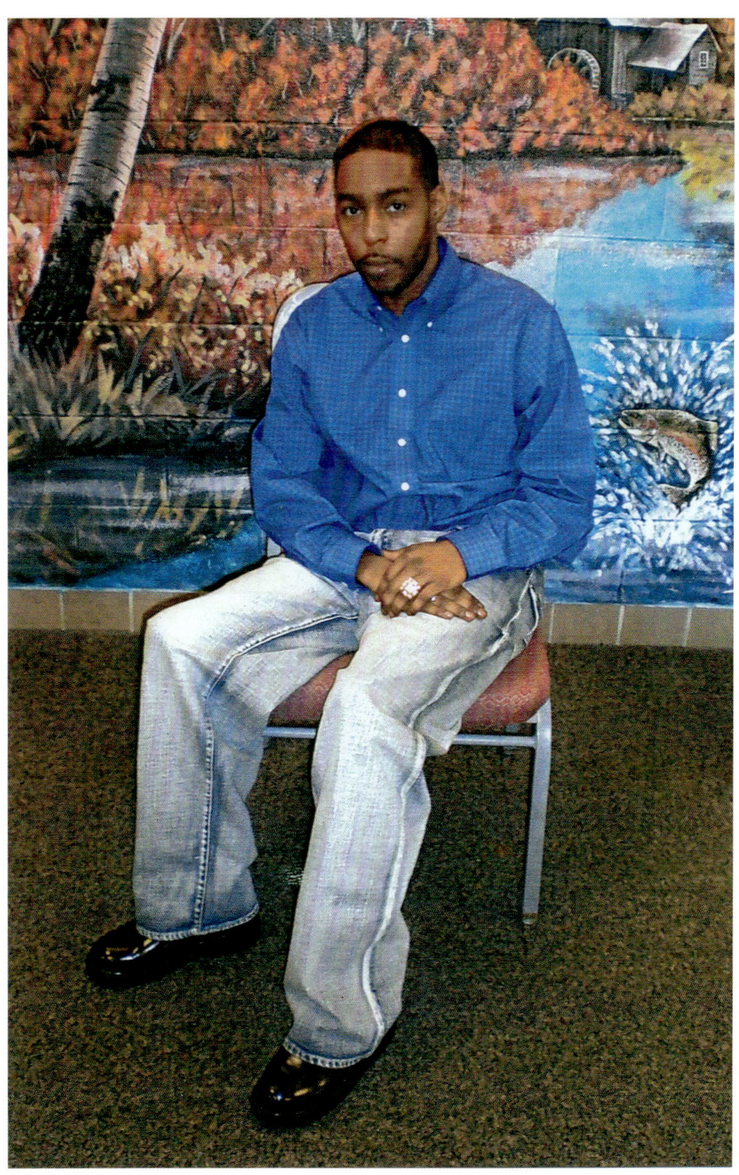

Jeffrey Richards, Thumb Correctional
Facility, Lapeer, Michigan

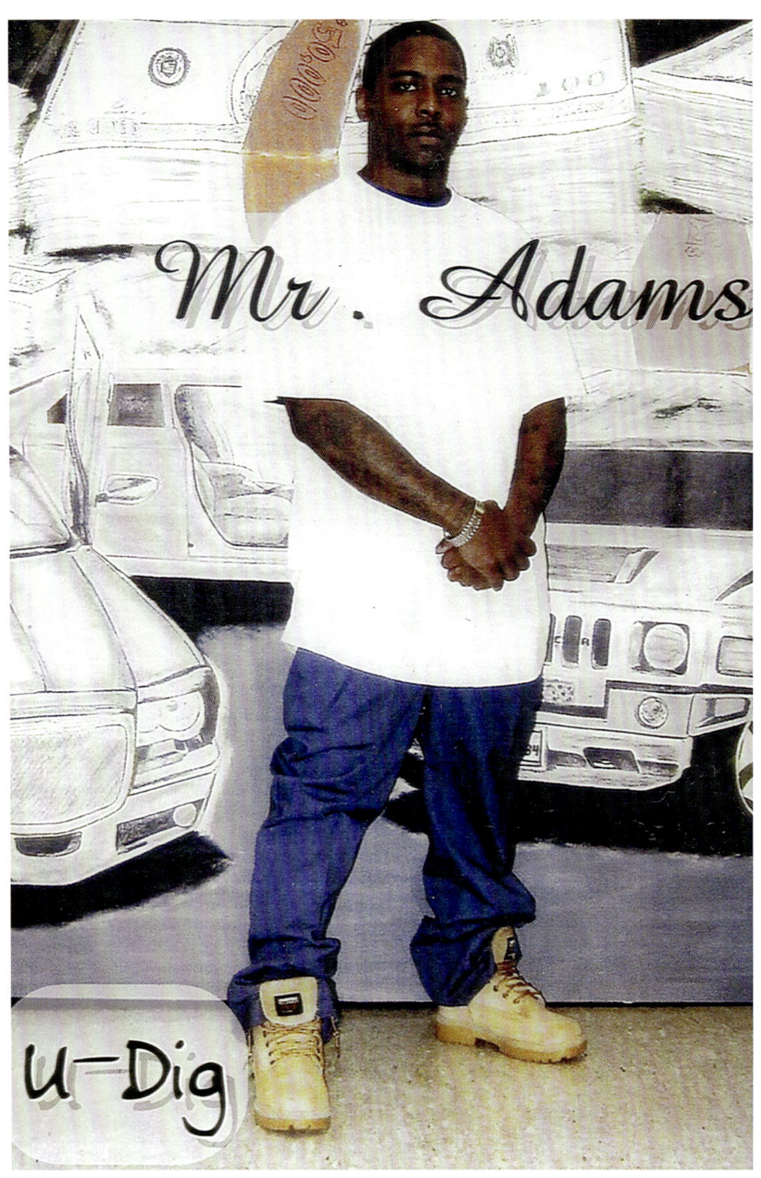

Mr. Adams
U-Dig

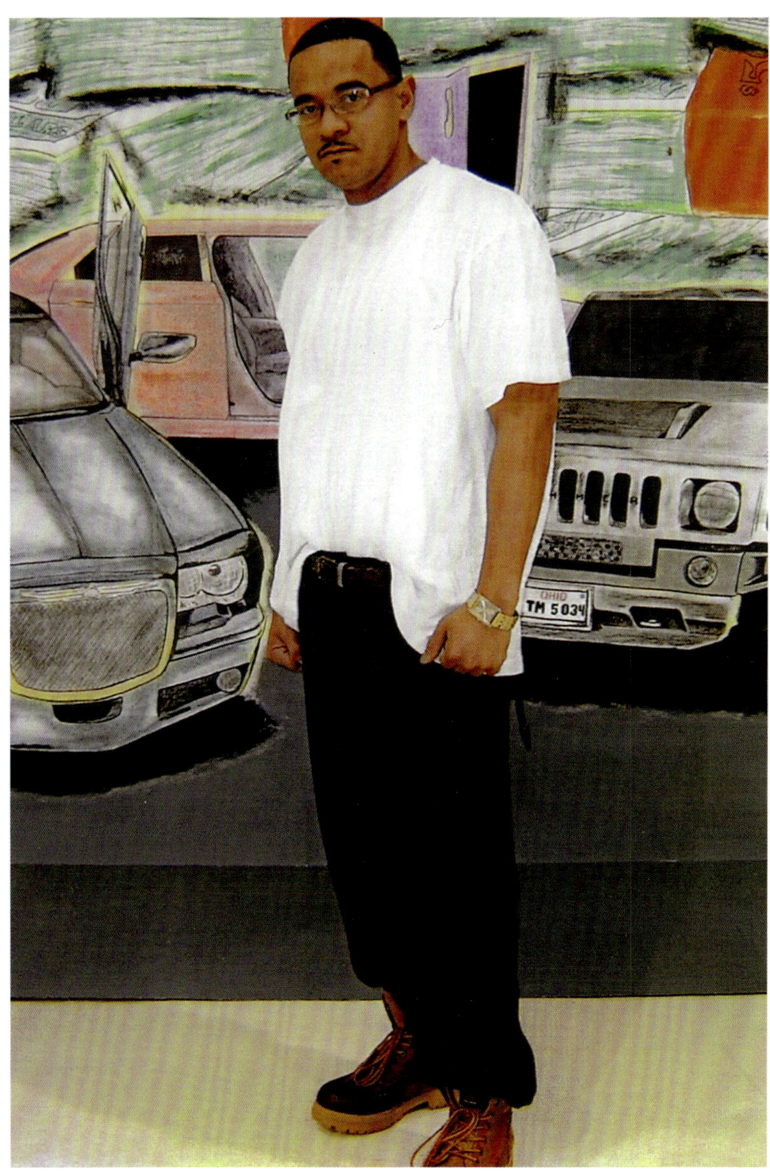

Salvador Molino Rivera, Trumbull
Correctional Facility, Leavittsburg, Ohio

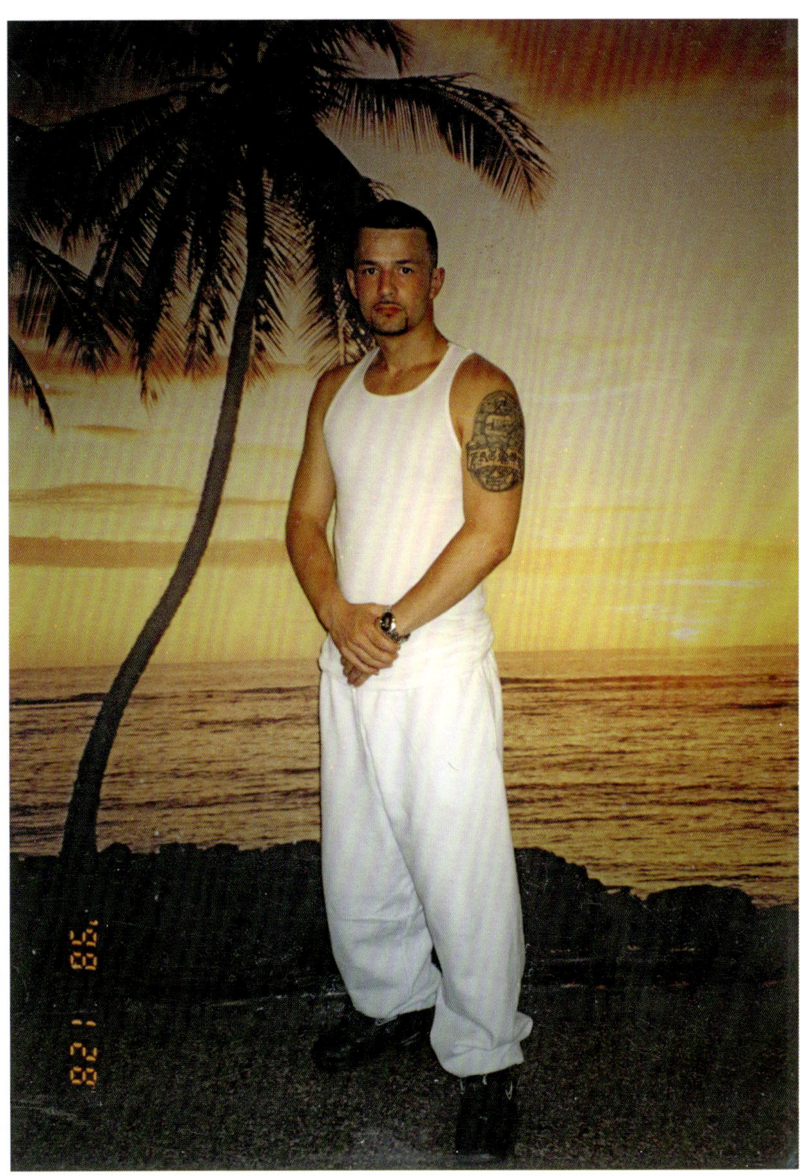

Anonymous, Ionia Maximum
Correctional Facility, Ionia, Michigan

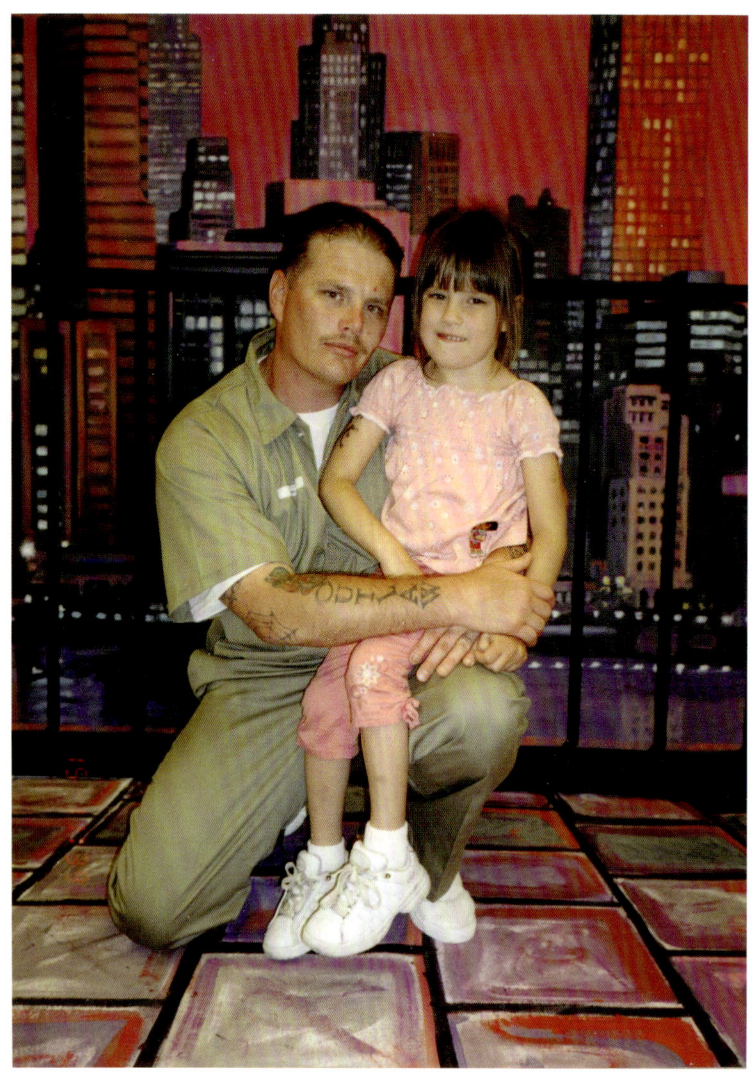

When I get home, I will give the magazine
you sent me to my son in the picture and
keep the book. I know this is going to
sound weird and I am not proud to be in
prison, but I am proud, in a way, to be in
your book. I mean. a book! Don't know if
you understand where I am coming from.

Jason Jordon, United States Penitentiary,
Marion, Illinois

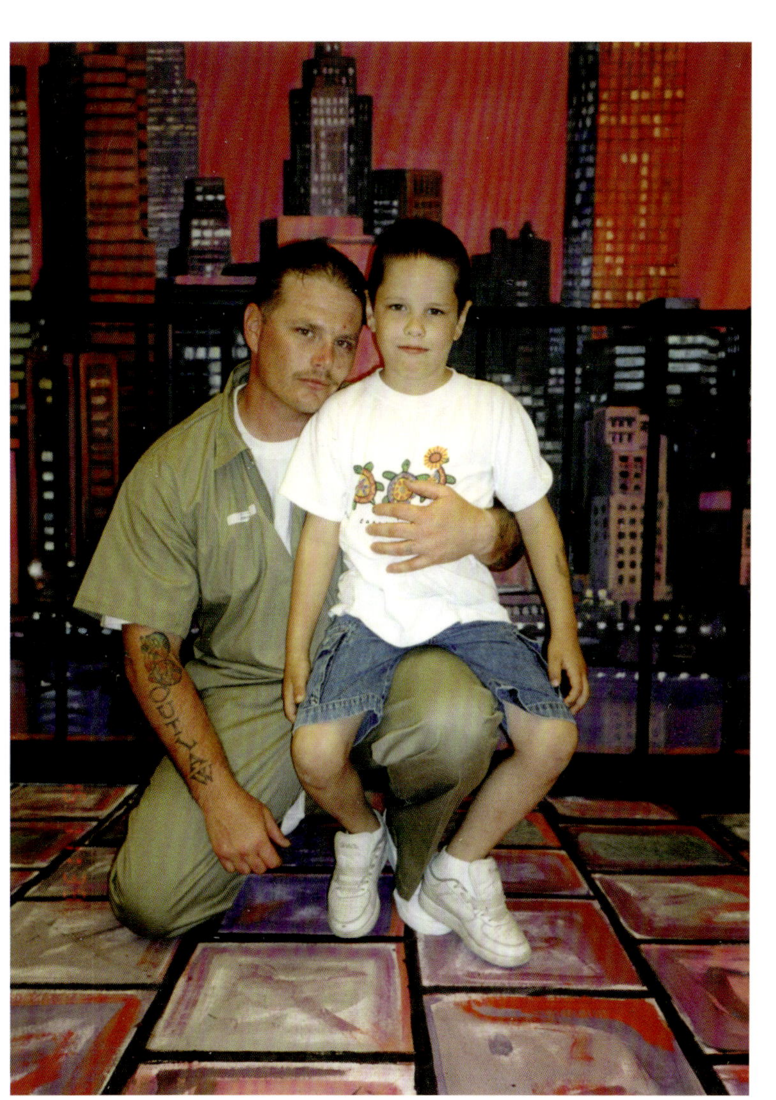

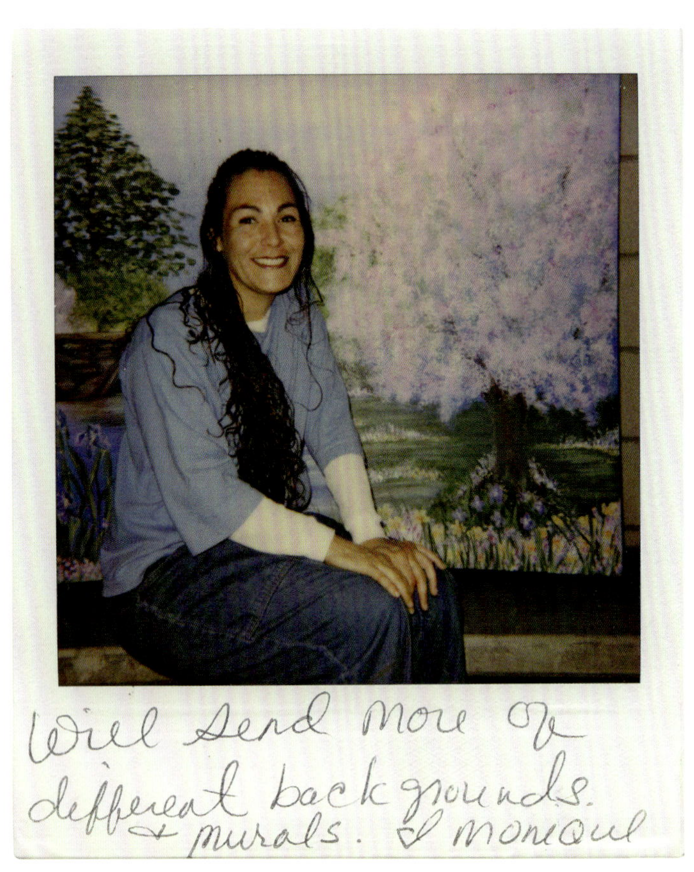

Monique Ramirez, Valley State Prison
for Women, Chowchilla, California

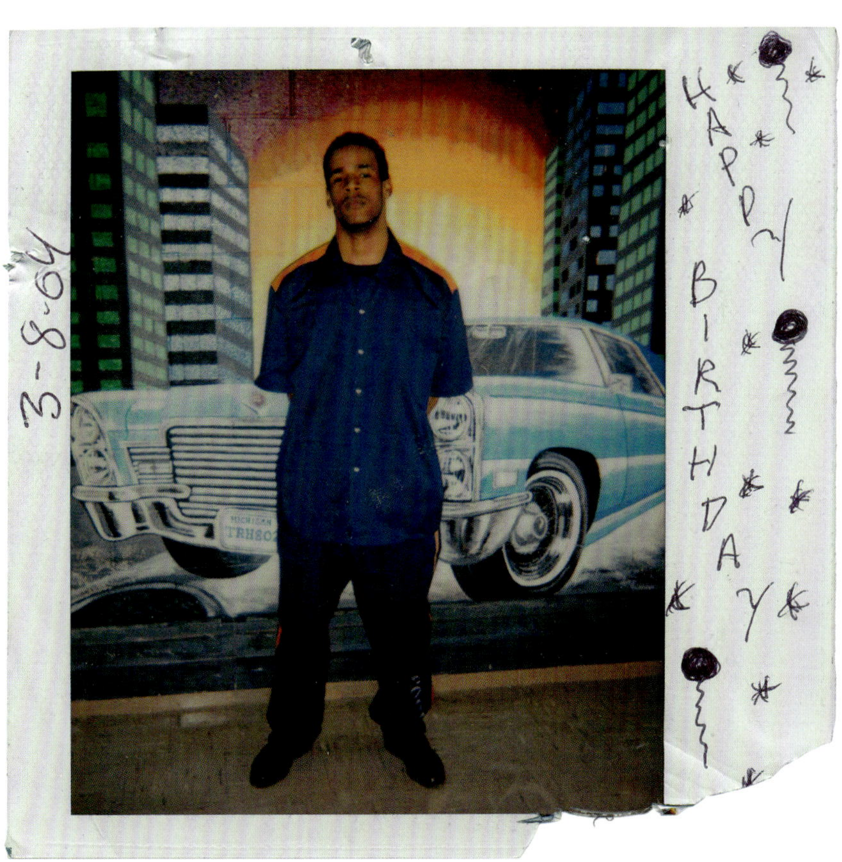

Anonymous, Parr Highway
Correctional Facility, Adrian, Michigan

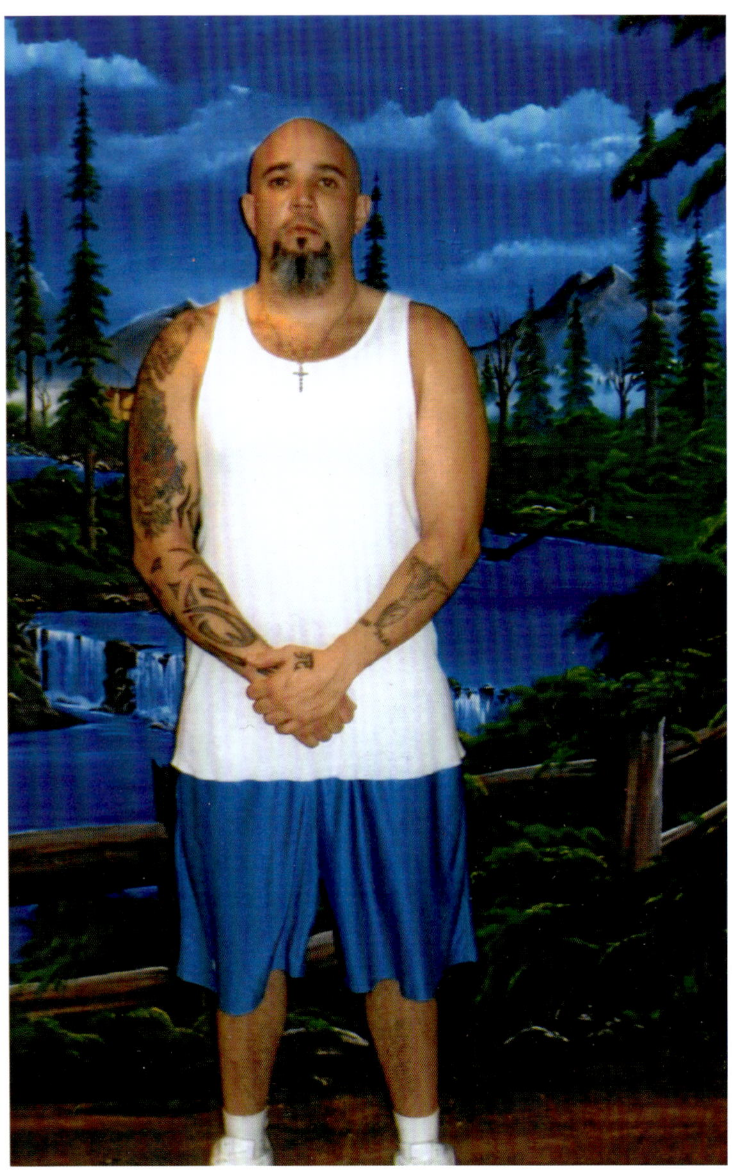

Johnny Russell, Allen Correctional
Institution, Lima, Ohio

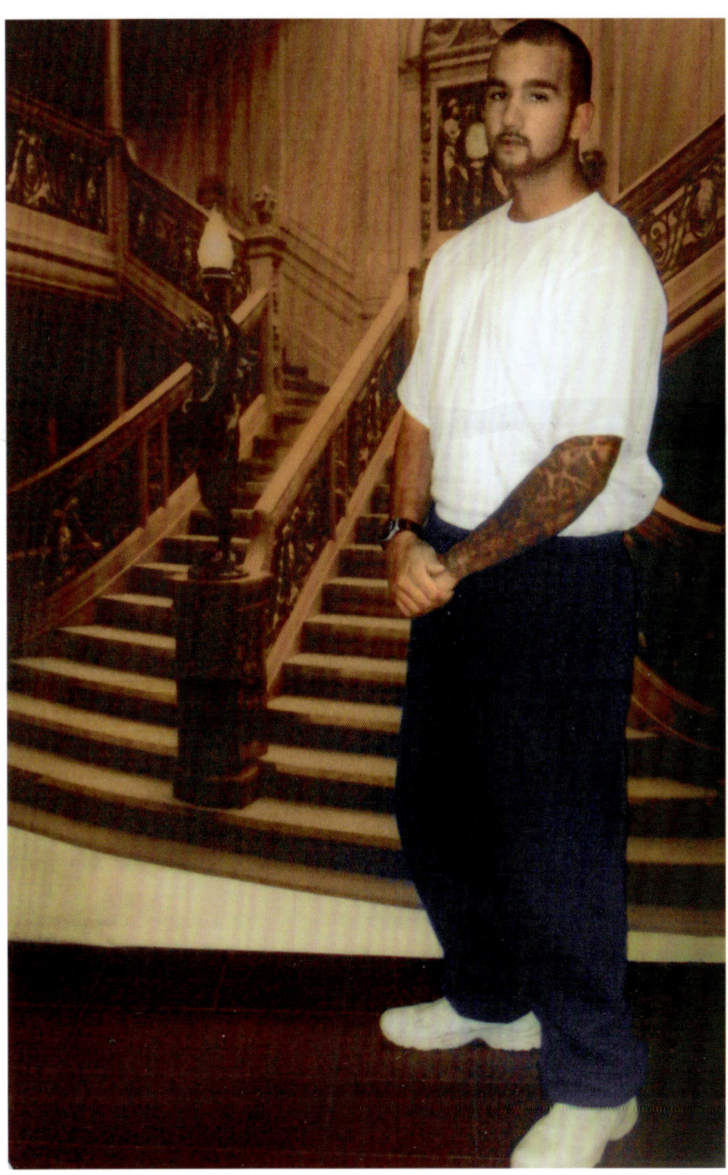

Josh Wilder, G. Robert Cotton
Correctional Facility, Jackson, Michigan

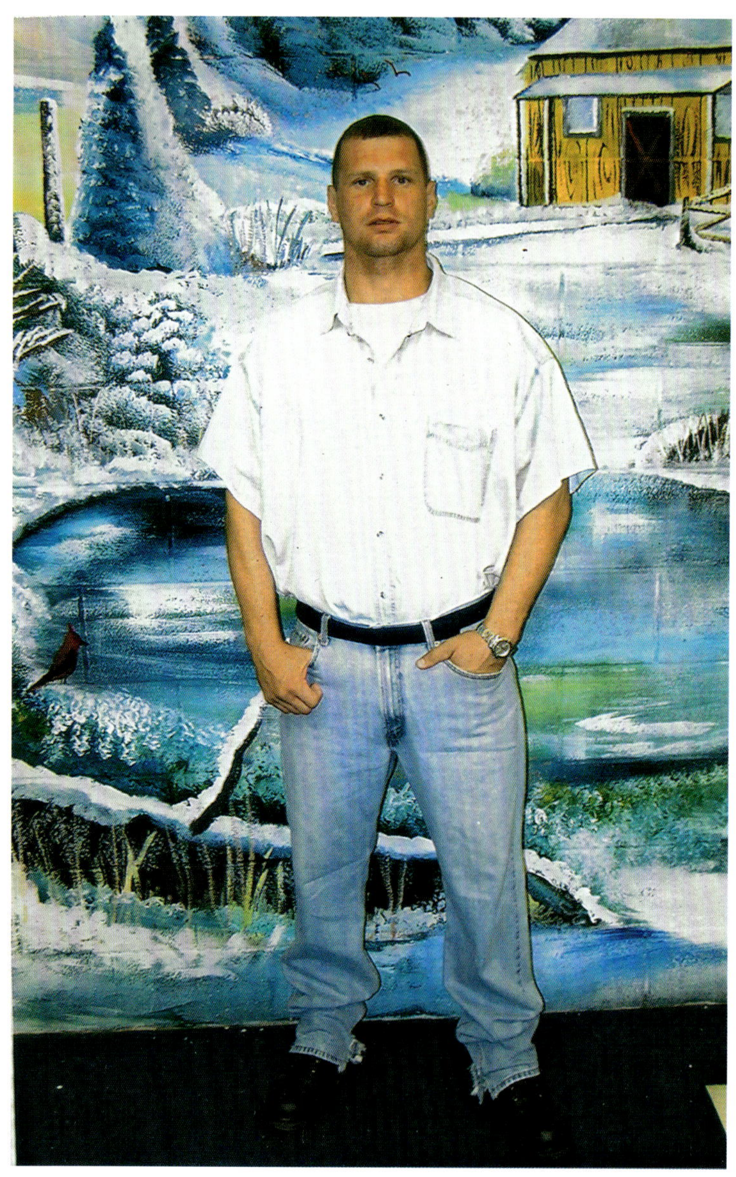

John Camden, Botetourt Correctional
Facility, Troutville, Virginia

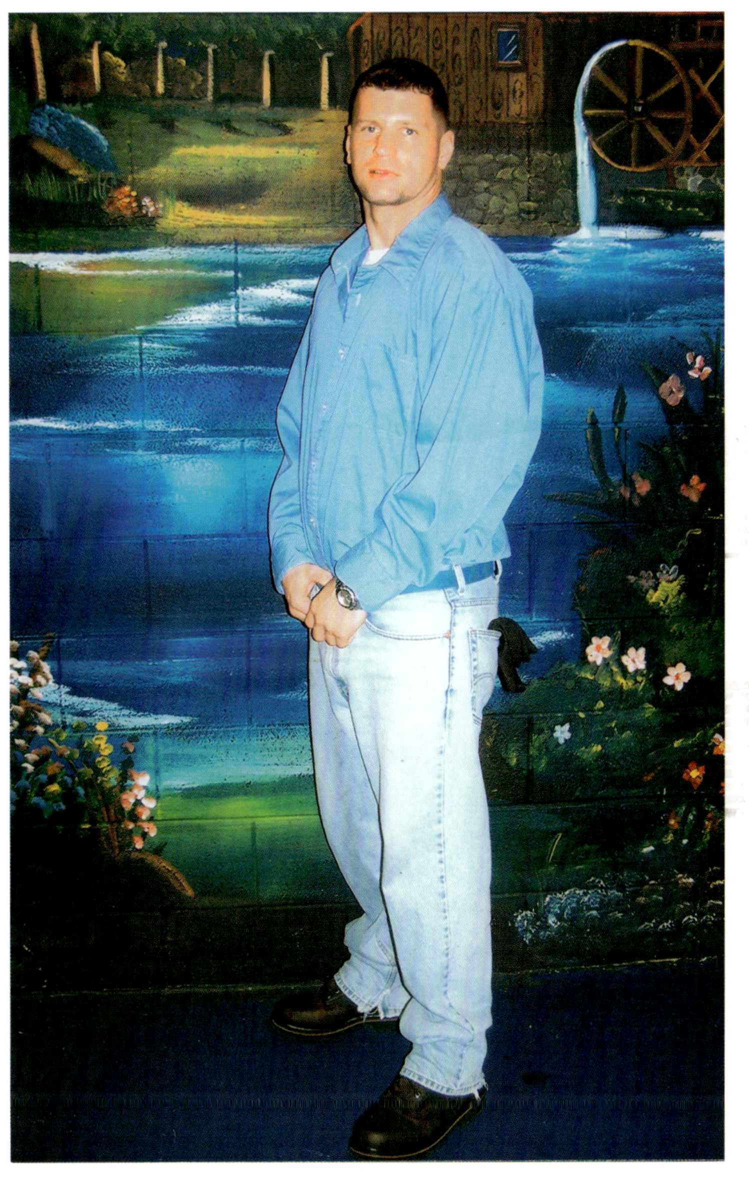

The pictures we take without the
backdrops are the pictures we get
to dress up in. They make us wear the
prison gear when we take the pictures
with the backdrops out in Visiting. The
ones without, we can wear our street
gear: shoes, jeans, tank tops, hats, and
glasses, go all out. All we can do in here
is make the best of what we got to work
with, and that's what most of us do
till we get the chance to be free again.
I've been locked up since I was 17 years
old for something I didn't even do. My
so-called best friend killed a guy and
I got charged with the murder too, being
that I was there and didn't stop it or go
to the police.

Clemeth Castille, California State Prison
Sacramento, Repressa, California

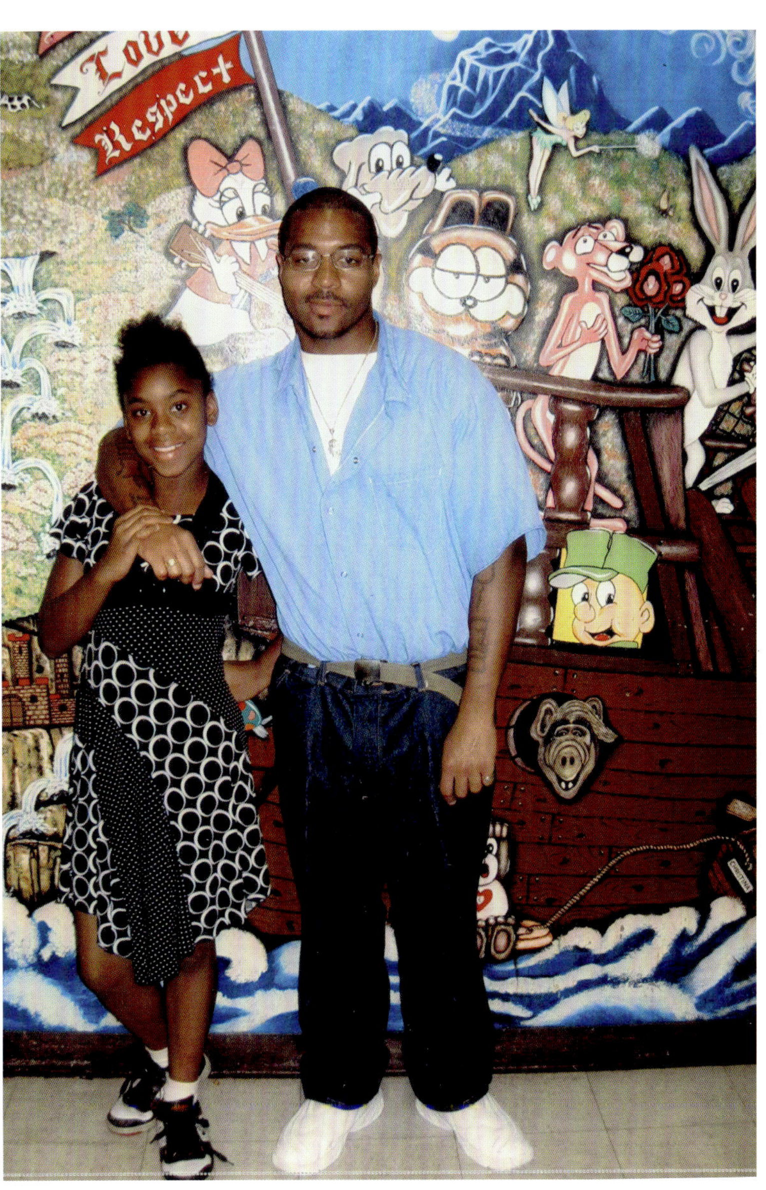

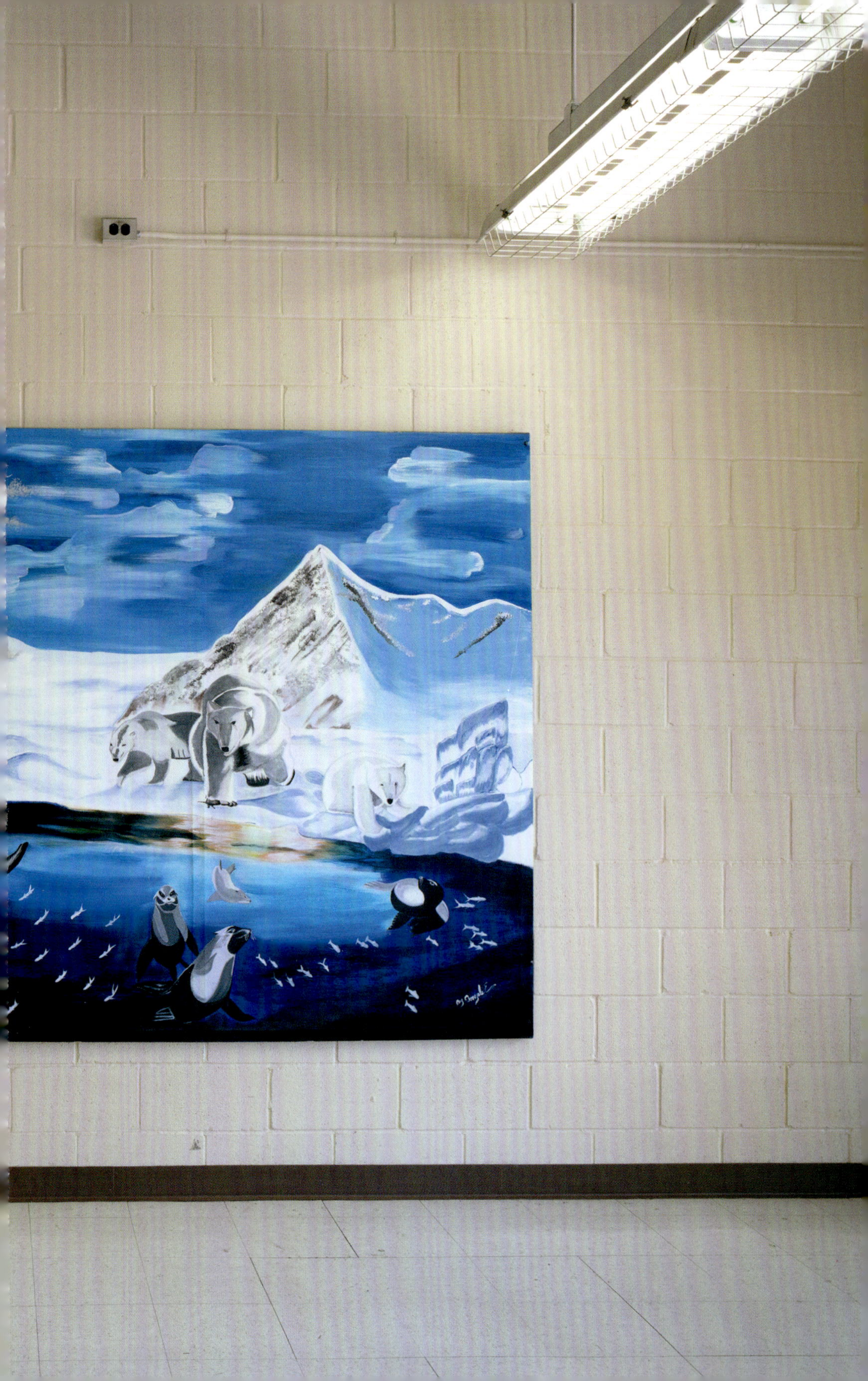

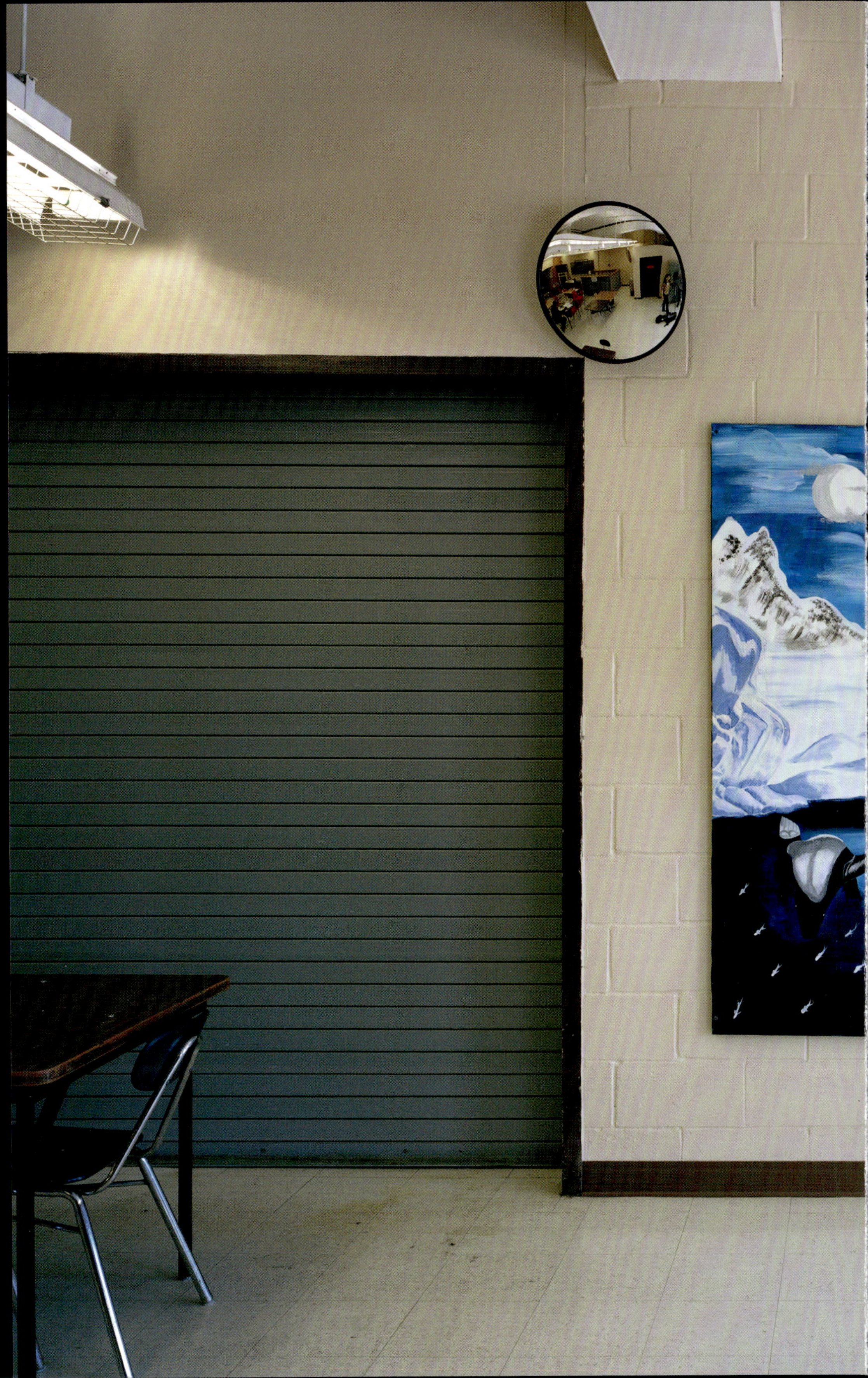

Wyoming Correctional Facility, New York

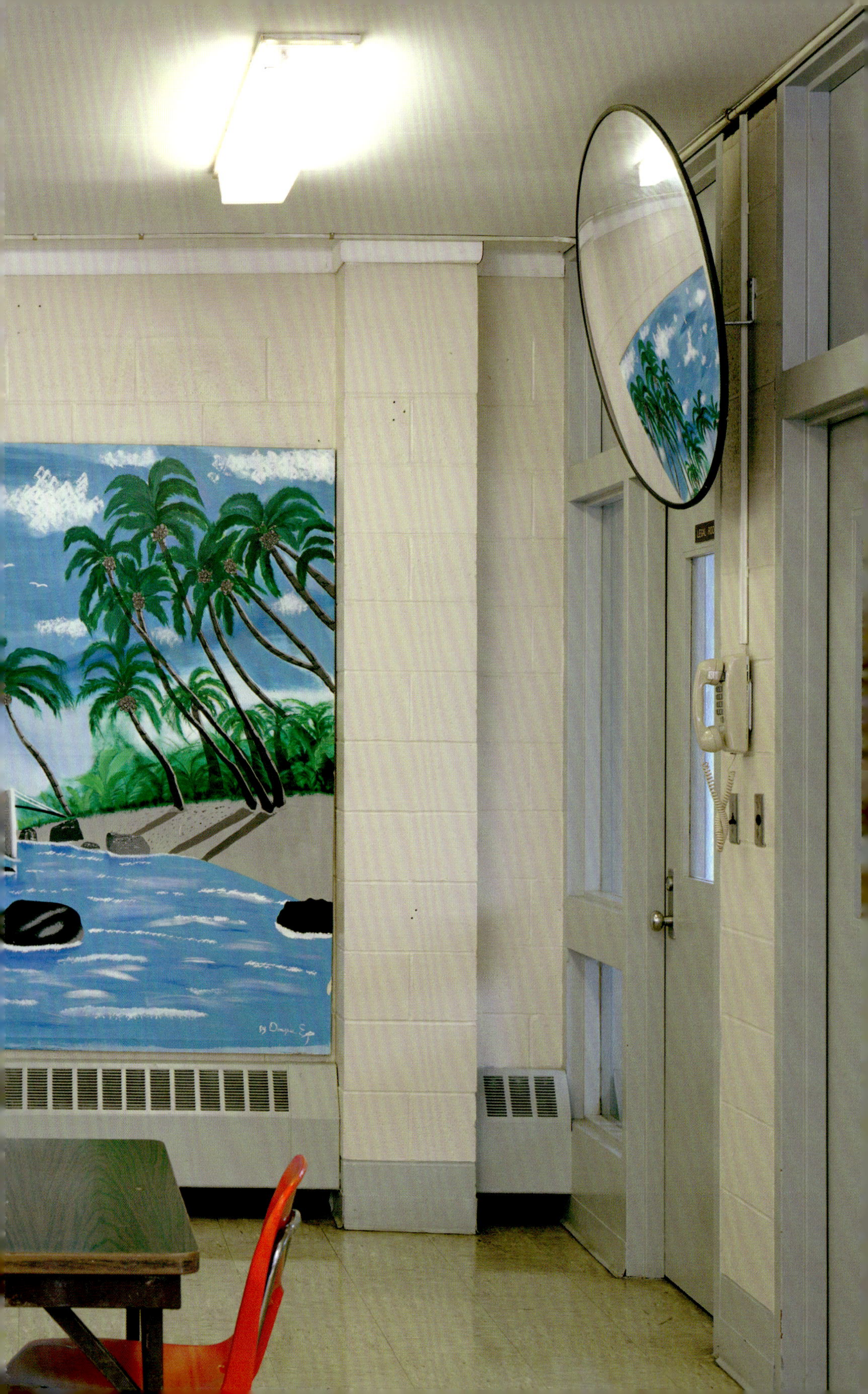

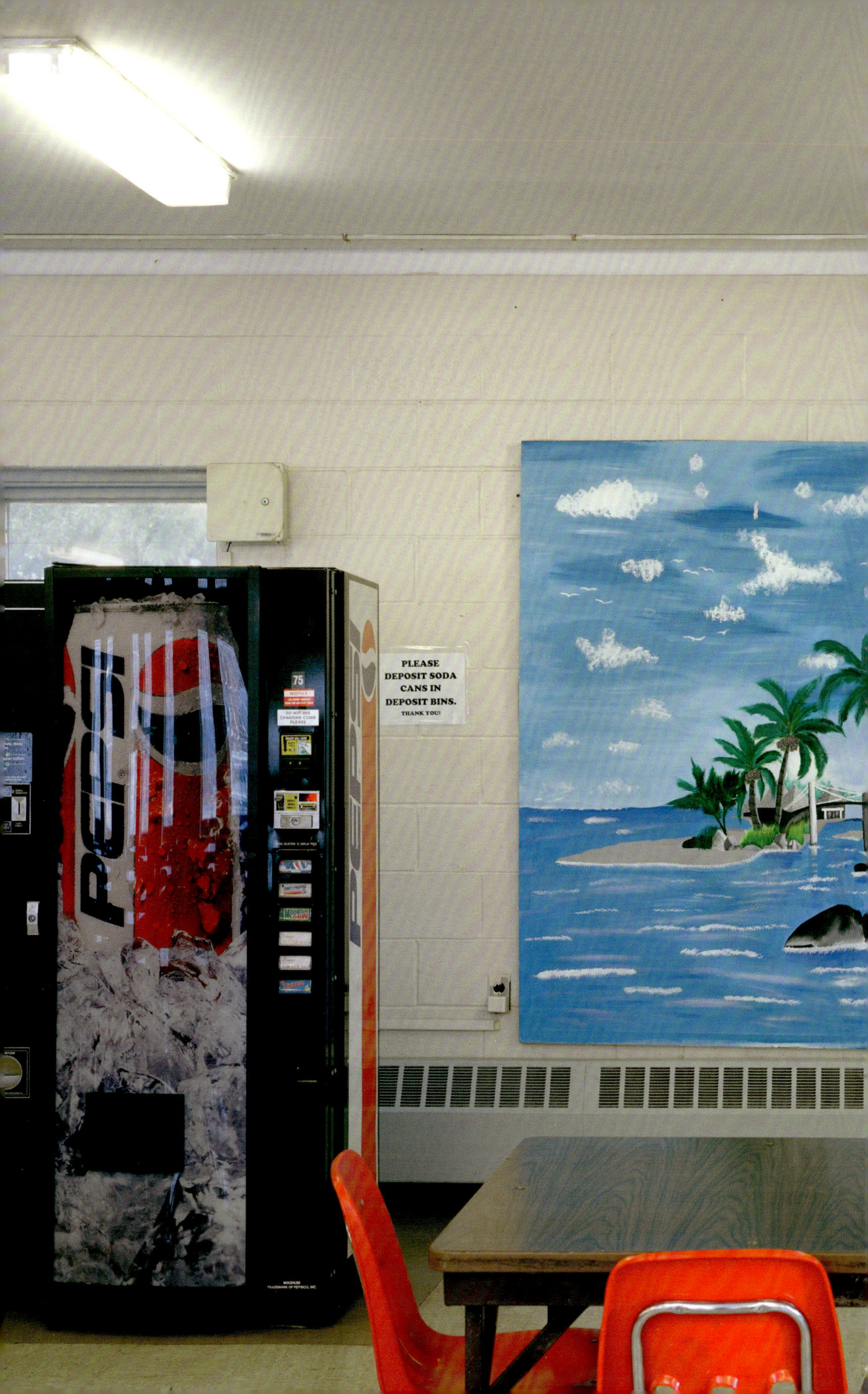
PEPSI
75
PLEASE
DEPOSIT SODA
CANS IN
DEPOSIT BINS.
THANK YOU!

Even though I'm in this place, it feels
good to know that people on the outside
still care enough to come and see me.
Taking pictures in front of the backdrop
gives off a better feeling despite my
surroundings. I remember when I was
posing for the picture, I was thinking
to myself, "I can't wait to be home
with my family and how this will all
be over soon."

Rahman Soto, Auburn Correctional
Facility, Auburn, New York

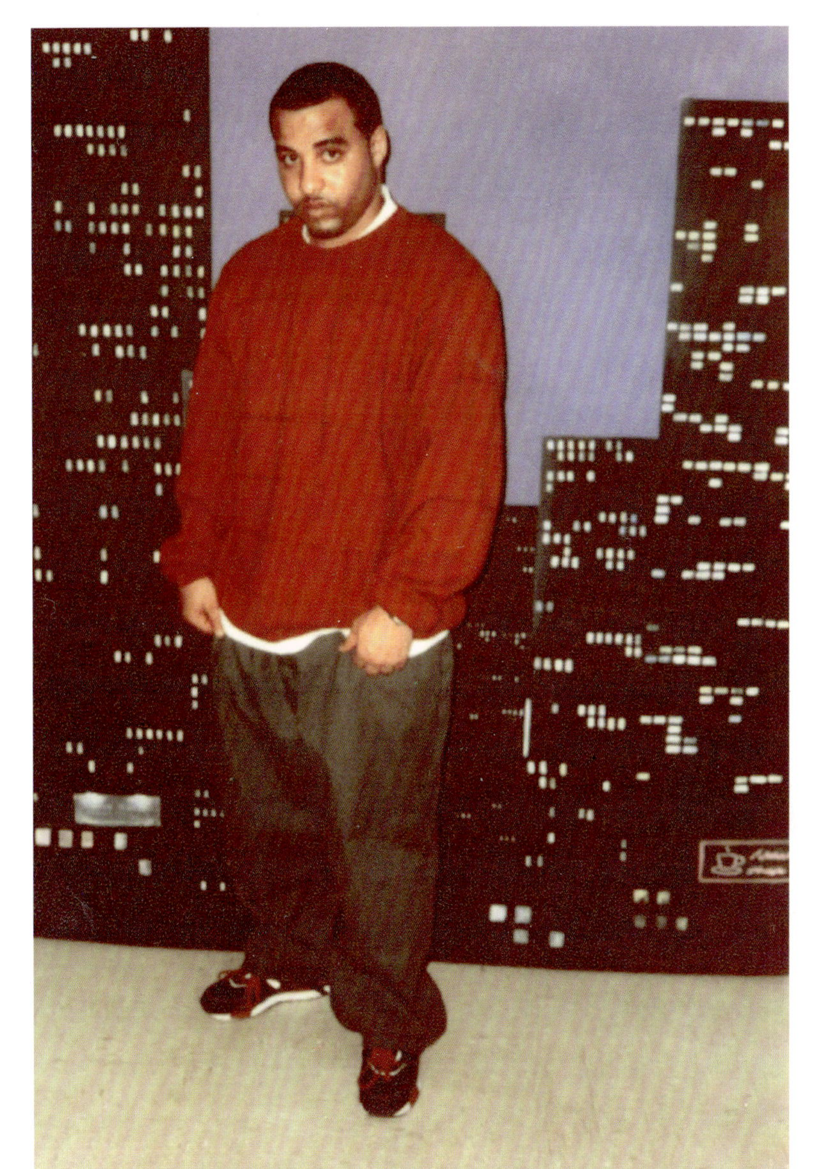

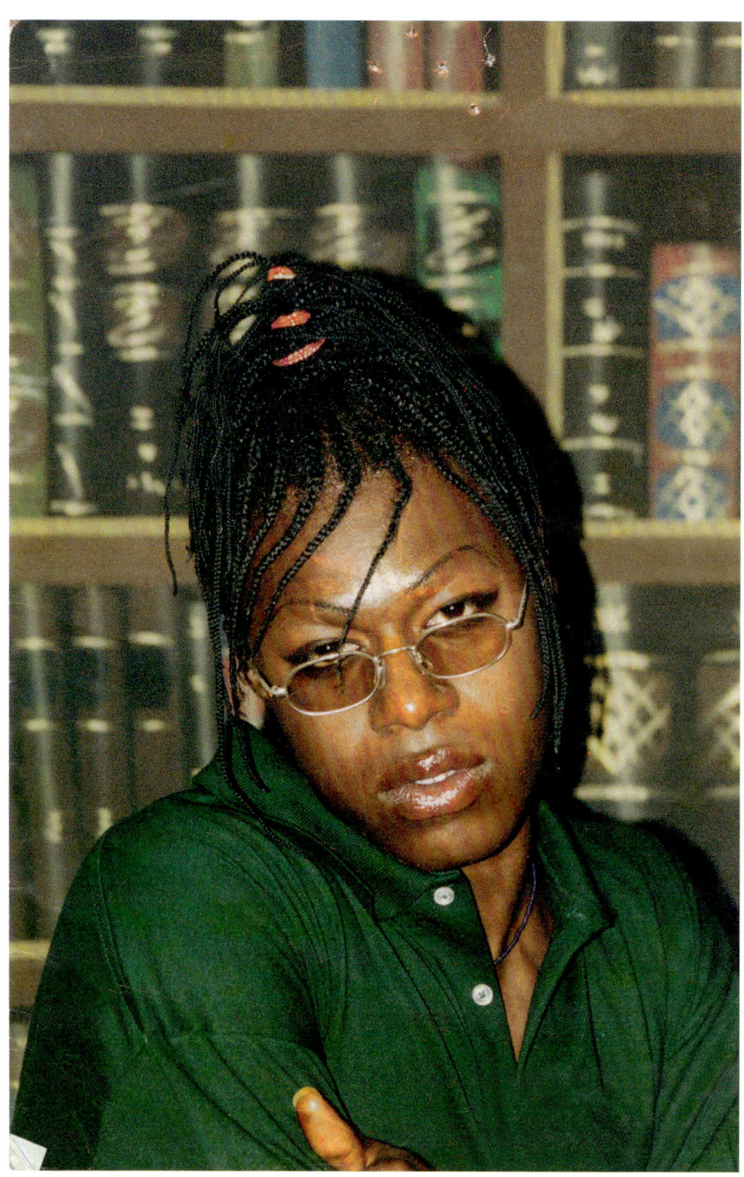

Shagasyia Diamond, Ionia Maximum
Correctional Facility, Ionia, Michigan

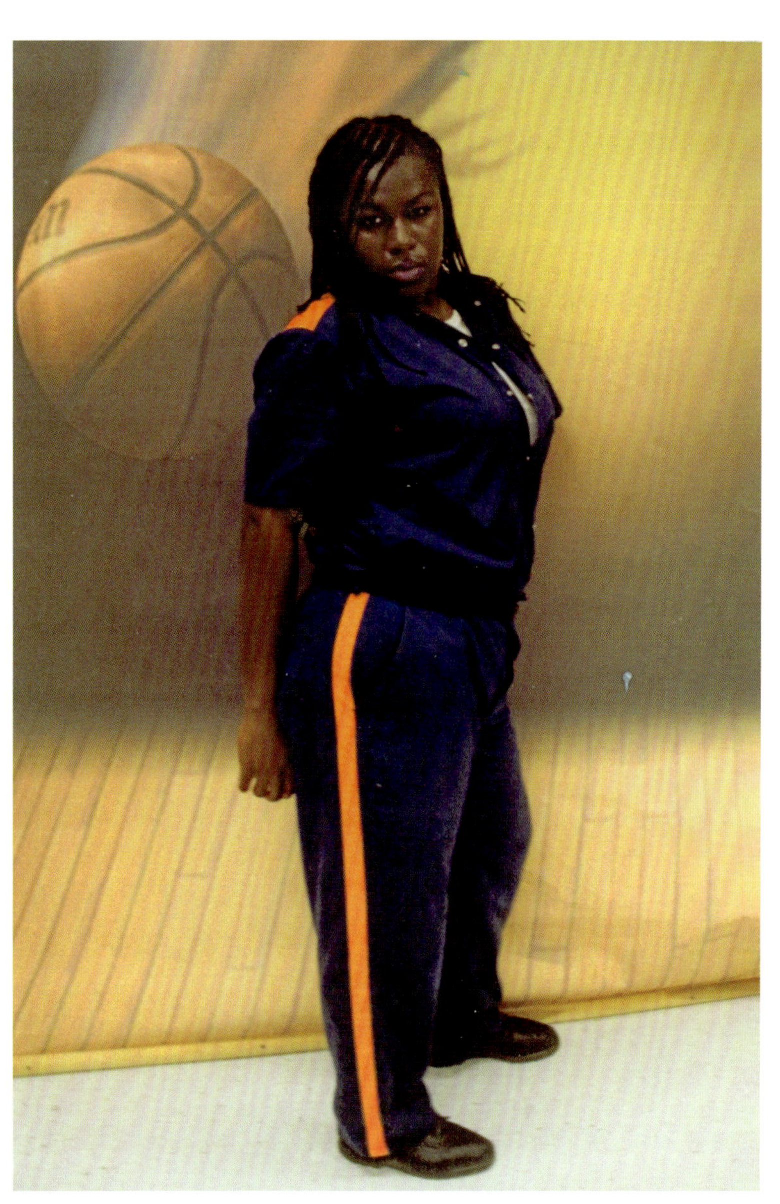

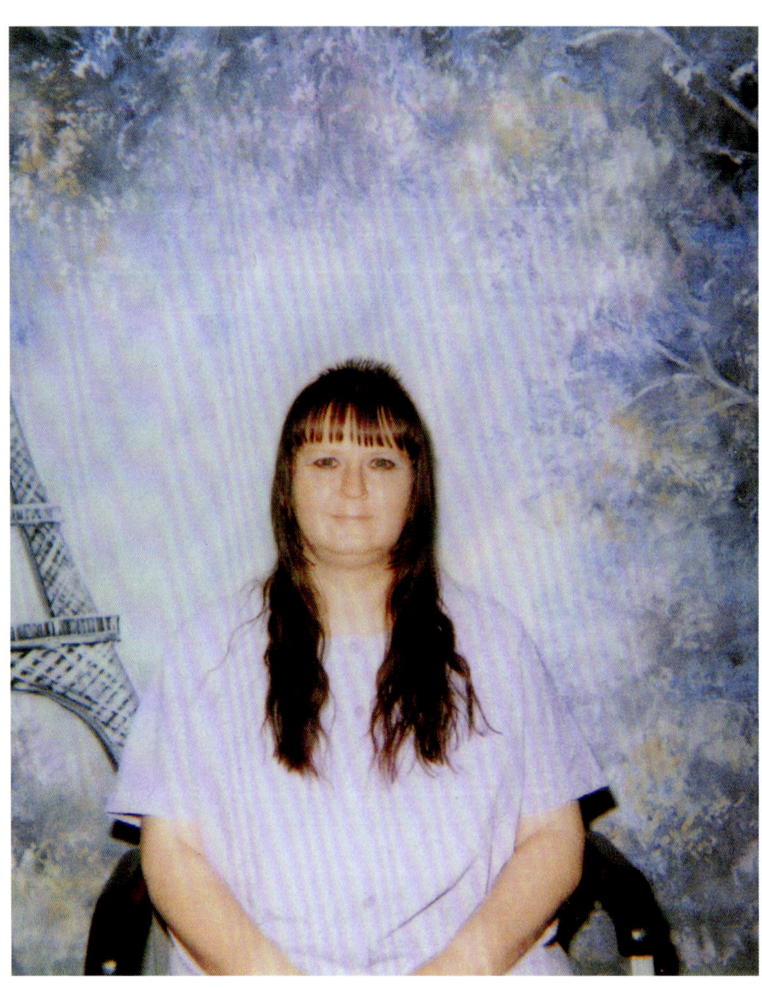

Barbara Jean Franzel, Women's Huron
Valley Correctional Facility, Ypsilanti,
Michigan

Dear Lee Lana   4-13-09

Hello I hope this photo's can give you what you want. A though alot of these photo's are old and not all that great. I would like to have them back. You see I've spent a decade here and thats alot of my life these photo's remind me of how I grew and changed. So I guess you wrote the right person not only have I been a very long time I've tooken many photo's over the years. If you have any further questions please ask when you send the photos back. I am a blunt straight foward honest person. So I will tell you like it is.

P.S. Take Care
        God Bless

                                    Love,
                                    Barbara
                                    Jean

Dear Lee Lana   6-21-9

          What's up Ms. Lady? I hope
this letter finds you in high spirits. It
was real cool of you to even take time
out of your busy productive life and get
back me. I understand and respect that
you have someone in your life you love
I really would like for us to be friends
and hears why I lack smart, positive
about something friends in my life plus
I can tell by your project that you are
a sensitive, careing, down to earth person.
All I want is friendship and for us to
stay in contact I mean Im a good
listener so when you like you feel
you aint being heard you know where
Im at plain and simple. Anywaup how did
your poncho makeing go? this might sound
crazy but I just find out what a poncho
was. What type of things do you plant
in your garden? My grandmama had pears
and fig trees oh yeah and pecans. Alot
of people claim they can cook but can
you really. I remember this chick made
dinner for me the rice was hard and the
chicken when I took a bite it was
still bloody talk about gross. I can't
remember if I told you my dad lives
in pensacola, florida and my mother who
I haven't seen sence 1989 lives stoughton,
MA. I also lived in bridgeport, conn

For three years I went to cathloic school up there. I hated wearing those tight ass micheal jackson pants. By the way what your doing is a beautiful thing and just knowing its somebody out who can see us as more then prisoners makes you feel good so thanks. when your done with this photo albuem if possible I would like to see it. I can tell by this drawing you got some skills. Im not going to bore you any longer take care and God bless!

Sincerly yours

James

Lee Lana,

Hello, I'm writing to let you know, that I received your letter, and to return the picture you sent. This is being done out of respect, from me to you. I think your art project is a great idea. However, I can not help you right now. I am in S.H.U (24hrs lock down). I also don't feel to comfortable with exposing the fact that I have been in prison. This is not something I am proud of. Who knows how far this little project of yours may go? You might end up on Oprah's book club, also sitting on her couch, on national T.V.! Look what happen to FRY, I know your book is going to be based on art. Please, relize "oops" that I would love to help you. The only thing that's going to come between that is that little discomfort. I have an only sister, so you touch me. I would like to know more, about how it affected you seeing your brother in jail alot. I think you mentioned someting in that regard. I still am undecided about the photo, when I get out of here I might send one to you. Please, understand my feelings about this. When I get out of S.H.U., I am going to see if people will be willing to do this. That I can promiss you. Is there anything I need to look for in a person, that would be good for your project? I just don't want you to feel neglect, or discourage, because people are not sending you the photo's you need. Lee Lana, it was nice to receive your letter. (even if you was soliciting me ☺). Has all we have to look forward to is mail. This is all for now.

STEVEN ROJAS

4/19/09.

4-14-09

Dear Lee Lana

Hello howa are You doing? I hope that life is seeing fit to wrap You & Your
Loved Ones in Peace, Happiness & Love! Well as for Myself I am in a constant
battle to maintain My Happiness & Inner Peace.

First off I would like to Thank You for being able to look past a situation
& show a peice of True Humanity. As I am sure you are aware most people do not
reconize what society calls it's worste. To know that there are still people
out there who's Spiritual Vision allows them to see a Man or Woman in bondage
as Human is Truly A Beautiful thing.

Lee Lana I was very intrigued by Your letter to say the least, I was not
sure if I was going to respond. As I read it over & over again the more I felt
that You deserve the Respect due to A Woman,. I would like to tell You a lil
about myself. Everyone calls Me Dayton. I am 36 years old, serving a double life
sentence. I have been in prison since a boy of 16. No I am not trying to ask or
seek pity. I made a mistake that can never be taken back. I won't try to make
an excuess. I was slipped PCP & went on a black out, comitting a rape kidnap,
robbery, assault & some other crimes against humanity. For which My Soul has been
in constant remorse. through this time I have became A Man of Morals, Character
& Understanding. Although I am far from perfect I continue to strive daily. I
hav alot of intrest from stocks, bizness, clowning, & learning. I have a zest
for life. Which is why I am excited about the project you are doing.

I must say that I would like to hear more about your project & You. I am
not looking for any type of romantic relationship. A Friendship would be very
much welcomed of course. You see I have a intrest in art. I be buying all type
of artwork in here & try to sell them. You having a back ground in Art I would
like to see if maybe we could assist oneanother. I have had alot of pieces made
but noone to share them with. Now I know that Trust must be earned. I am willing
to earn yours. I don't have alot but I am not out to misuse anyone. All I can
do is be who I am & ask you to let me show you.

I am enclosing a couple of pics for you to include in your works. I would
appreciate if you sent me a copy of them. Also a copy of the book when it is done.
I would also like to dig into the possibilites of a Friendship if it is possible.
Oneday who knows you may decide to visit, time wq will tell.

-Well Lee Lana I will close for now & I hope that I hear from you again soon.
Until then I wish upon You all the Gifts Life has to offer. I close as I openned,
with Respect!!   I Hope Your with A Smile!!

Eugene Cook H-15648   Take Care
Po Box 1050 D-7-108   You are Like a Light In a Dark Place!!
Soledad CA 93960   Sincerely
                                        Eugene Cook

4-13-09

Heyyy) Lee Lana,
Once again it was somewhat a treat to see your
mail land in my lap! As I attempt to gain
your attention, let me say to you that I whole heartedly
understand that your schedule is indeed full time!!
I also encourage you to continue to be all you can
be! Because it's oh so true that a mind is a terrible
thing to waste. As a matter of fact, that's exactly why
I'm taking the neccesary steps to step my game up too!
Besides that I guess it's safe to say that I'm like a
old coat in the closet — I'M HANGIN' IN THERE!!! ☺
Meanwhile back at da' ranch, I feel it's an honor that
you selected my photo (at least) to be a part of your
project. Get 'em girl! I've enclosed the original so you
can scan it, and then shoot it back to me. Reason
being that's the only one I have left with me being
able to perm my hair. ☺ ☺ They stop selling perms. ☹
Feel free to use my name too. Be it someone may
find the time to send me a "shout-out".
Well Ms. Lady, it's been a ball but that's all!
I'm looking forward to hearing from you at least
one more time. So until then — "Here's 2 Lookin' At You
Kid"!! ☺

P.S. While you're scanning pictures,
will you scan me a couple too?

Sincerely,
Greg

Hi Lee,
How are you doing on the holidays this year? How are things going for you and in finding a job?

I just found out on Dec 7th that my husband passed away on the 3rd. I got my transfer to Southern Calif on the 8th.

I have lot of support with my friends and family. I dont get visits but I am working on it.

You're in my thoughts and prayers.

Always,
Kimberly

Hi Lee   (6-11-09)   1

   Recieved your letter today dated 5/23/09. Thank you
for taking time to write me. Love to have a copy of
the book. It must be paperback though...
   People do often forget we inmates are people, not
crazed serial killers. We have families children, hopes
and dreams. Most of us just made mistakes and bad
choices.
   I really appreciate you seeing me as a human.
Me myself, i'm a kind, caring person. Who misses
my family. My three sons are growing to men
without me. My youngest will graduate High School
in 2012... Proud of the men their becoming
with-out me.
   I'm going to inclose a couple poems, you
might want to use them in some way...
   And a little of my art work hope you get a laugh.

   you know Lee, out of all the things i've lost,
I miss my mind the most. ☺ "smile"

what i've seen in here convinces me that society is
wrong when it throws away the key. Penitentiaries in this
country are little more than warehouses; the human
beings inside these walls often lose whatever remaining
fragile humanity that they had left when they entered...

But when you hear stories like stories of hope and transformation and amazing turnarounds.
Society considers the men who populate prisons as pariahs, some are, but not all. They just keep building prisons and filling them.
In this prison there answer to control is the big mace canisters. They've killed three inmates since 04 here with mace. Crazyness all around me...

"I'll just do what my Rice Crispies tell me too.

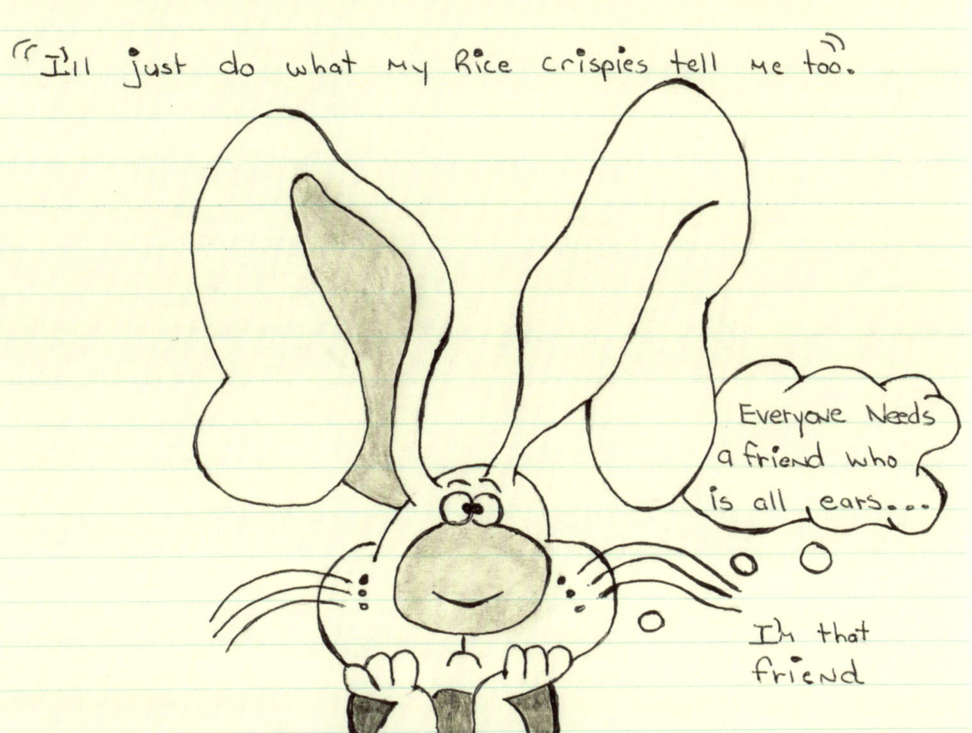

LEE LANA
655 S. FLOWER St. #166
LA, CA 90017

    What a wonderful suprize to hear back from you so soon!
Im happy to know you recived my letter. Its great to know your
doing well and your project is comeing along as planned. I will
signthe forms and send them back with my letter. If you think i
need to change anything pleaSe let me know, unless you want to
go ahead. You will not hurt my feelings. This is your project not
mine. If i can do anything to help pleas,pleas let me know!
    Idont think i toled you, i wrote a letter to the woman
who owend the citgo station i robbed. That was a really big step
for me. After writing it i felt so much better about myself. I went
toSchool with the womans kids. Whil laying on my bed one day GOD
would not let me stop thinking about them boys. I didnt know what
i was going to say, but GOD gave me the wordes. To think of the
fear i put that woman in, then think about the time i got stabed
brought tears to my eyes. Iknow if it wasnt for the(15) xanx i took
that day i would have never did what i did that day. Iwas so high
that day i went to jail and dont remember a thing. Ihad to ask
the c/o that sierved me brakfest that first morning why i was in
jail. YAH, that insanity!!! Never agin do i ever want to be like
that. Ithank the Lord ever day i never killed anyone or myself.
Thats a Blessing by its self!
    So you like to garden to? I love to be outside with my hands in
the dirt! You even planted some of my favorits. My mom got me eating
greens, beats and pritty much any vegtibal at a early age. She
loves makeing a big pot of greens with pork and i love eating them.
Im a very outdoorsy person! I like to fish, camp, hunt, hicking,
traveling, horse back riding, and grilling out. Im half Native
American maybe that has something to do with why i love the out-
doors so much? I dont know if you know or nott the chamomile the
Native Americans use it to make tea. All you do is boil it and
then drink it. You can even add a little suger and it tast grate!
We have it alot by the bss ball fieldes and ill make some sometimes. The sge the Natives use to smudge with. Smudging is the pr
cess of cleaning them self from any evil spirits. What are some
of the places you would like to travel? I would like to visit
Alaska, GERMANY, AND jAPN.The culters and the food really atract
me. Incase you dont know i love to eat ande cook thoughs are two
of my most favorit things to do.
    I would like to ask you apersonal qustion . How old are you
and what is your natanality? You seem like such a great person
but i dont know anything about you . Maybe you could send a pic
or two? That would really help mee know who im writing to.
Im sending you a couple pics with this letter of me the
to boys, my mom and grandma. There is one in ther also of Melissas
step dad wich is granpa from her side of the family. They are all
yours so dont worry about send any of them back.
    You said you have to write a thesis. My advice is to write about
something that means something to you, follow your heart and i know
you will do great!! I will contiou to keep you in my pryers !!
You want to teach after school. Would that be in art? I would like
a chance to get back to school. They dont offer any collge in here
any more. Its tuff because there hasnt ben anyone ive found that
will finacialyhelp me.

I would like to go for child sycoligy, phisical fitness and
busines. One day i would like to owen my owen busines. I have alot
of different ideas as to what i want to do but need to build up a
nuff money first.

The food is much like middle school cafeteria food. The best
thing they sierve is chicken and mac& chees once a month. The bred
is always hard and dry. The milke comes in little bags. Vagtables
are always mosh because they over cook them. They sierve alot of
potatos, noodls and rice. Basicaly what ever is the most cheep is
what they will give us. THats why its nice when i do get a visit i
get to eat foods i normaly dont get. NOt the best food for you but
it tasets good!!

I have five years in and four to do. TIme goes by fast aslong
as you keep yourself buisse. I do alot of reading, writing and
working out. At night i will usally watch a little T.V dapending
whats on. I'm not a big T.V fan. I watch foot ball the ~~Discovery~~
discovierie chanel and some CMT.

Thank you for sending the stamp. The only problem is i'm not
alowed to get stamps from the outside world. They have to come fro
the store. Also i'm not alowed books unless they come from name
venders. The book you want to give me you will have to send it
to my mother. I will give you that add's.

Well Ms. LEE, i thank you agin and hope to hear back from
you soon, hopfully you'll shar a little about yoursef. Tell your
sis hi!! I'll write agin when you write back. Until next time good
luck with school and your project!! YOU'LL BE IN MY PRAYERS!!!!

                    SINCERLY,

                    JOSHUA DAYTON WILDER

                    1727 W. blue water highway
                    IONIA, MI 48846

MY MOM;;
        1145 HARMONIA RD LT 63
        BATTLE CREEK, MI 49037

(269) 963-0319

11/2/2011

Hello Lana,

Along with this scribe I offer you my camaraderie and I pray that you're doing fine as well.

I'm really not a fancy writer, I guess because I don't practice at it. When I do write, I try my hardest, it has become a forced hobby of mine since I have no other vehicle to reach anyone I am corresponding with. My days go by incomplete whenever i donot receive any mail. I mean everyday is repeated like any other day will creep by slowly, and all through the day silence will connect with gloom like day is to nite. Most days are very hard to enjoy, atleast 10 minutes is to much to ask for.

I like listening to music that will soothe the soul, take away the tention, and relax my mind. I mostly listen to R&B, unlike tapes, CD players, and ipods, we have radios here. I try to tune out all the noise and keep my focus.

Right now, I'm really trying to use my time wisely and complete all the programs this institution has to offer. I just received my GED. I completed a few psychology programs too and I signed up for this personal trainer course to become a certified personal trainer. After studying I really learn more about the body. Doing these extra curriculum activities will not only keep me out of trouble but will also help me along the way when I am required to see the parole board.

Again I hope you don't mind me writing you as often as I do? You seem to be a very focused educated woman who love writing? Is your brother free? What is your origin? Will your book have an updated portrait of you on it?

Well until next time,
Riley

4/21/09

Hello, Lee Lana

I recieved your letter and photo
of your brother and you! I'll be
more than happy to help with
your art project, sorry for the
slow response, I didn't have any
money for envelopes."

Photos of me were never
returned from friends so I dont
have any more of me! I've never
been on a visit before anyway,
but usually when you take photos
anywhere in the prison there's
a back ground with different pictures.
So I sent photos of friends of
mine, th I just found an old
photo of me, before the breast "
w/ a library picture back ground!
Hopefully these pictures will
aid you in your project!
Although cameras aren't allowed
in the visiting room the facility
does have its own camera that
they would take of us togther.

There may be two opportunities to take it at two different facilities with different murals, cause I'm about to parole very soon (I'm only awaiting my parole papers, then I'll be transferred to another facility at a lower level! that's just an idea")

I'm unsure if you wanted your p photo of you & your brothes back, please let me know, please return these photos enclosed, you're welcome to use them I know everyone on there wouldn't mind most of them are at home now! &

take care and continue your great work of art!

I'm looking forward to recieving a finished product (Book)

Bless you
Ms Shagasyia Diamond

Chris Stark   # 281586

Boyer Road/Carson City Correctional Facilities
P.O. Box 5000
Carson City, MI 48811-5000

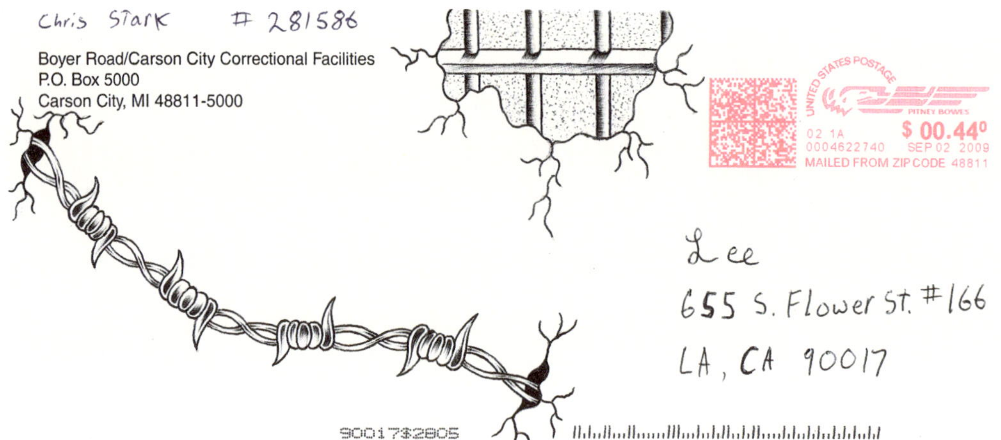

UNITED STATES POSTAGE
PITNEY BOWES
02 1A
0004622740   SEP 02 2009
$ 00.44⁰
MAILED FROM ZIP CODE 48811

Lee
655 S. Flower St. #166
LA, CA 90017

90017$2805

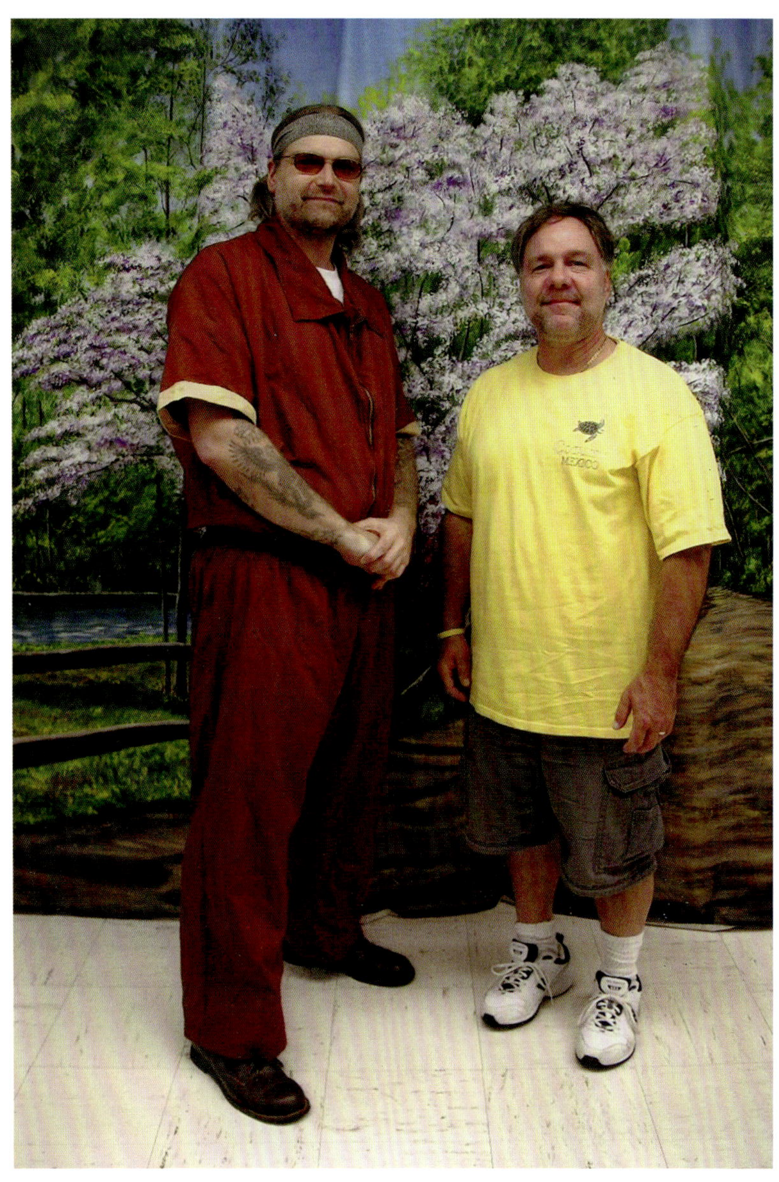

Darrell Van Mastrigt (left), State Correctional Institution, Graterford, PA, 2011

An interview with Darrell Van Mastrigt

This interview was conducted via the US Postal Service between July 2010 and September 2011. Darrell and I have met once in person in the Graterford visiting room the day I photographed his painting (front cover) in August 2011.

DVM: Yes, prison has changed me a lot. Although I was in college at the time of my arrest, I was really a naïve stupid teenager caught up in a drug and alcohol lifestyle with no clue as to what life could or should be. I didn't appreciate things and really didn't care about a future. Prison made me grow up fast. It made me find strengths and parts of myself I didn't know existed. You can't be weak (physically or mentally) if you want to survive and not be victimized in prison. You either adapt to a new way of life or suffer the consequences. Over time you learn to temper strength with positive growth. Prison taught me what kind of man I want to be.

DVM: No

DVM: Mostly trial and error. I volunteered to work for the Philadelphia Mural Arts Program after watching an outside artist give a demonstration on under paintings to prisoners in the program. The best advice I was given was, "Don't be afraid of the paint. Just paint. There are no mistakes because if you don't like it, you can always paint over it." I bought some books but painting was my best teacher.

DVM: Eric Ogdeh, who gave the demonstration, started working with us regularly and has become our inside coordinator for the Mural Arts Program. He still critiques my work and provides references and encouragement.

DVM: Yes, they are pretty basic drawing and painting classes. The most valuable art class I have taken was offered through Villanova University. They sponsored a teacher from the Barnes Foundation to teach a two-semester course on art appreciation. These classes really inspired me and taught me a lot about composition and how to evaluate art based on the plastic elements of color, light, line, and space. The classes improved my work and influenced my subject choices.

AE: Has painting changed you?
DVM: Yes, It allows me to see things differently. I notice things everywhere that I never noticed before – an interesting gathering of objects, a unique perspective, the effect of attention. Painting itself is a powerful emotional experience. Every painting requires a part of myself, how I feel, what I see, and what I want to show others. It makes me much more aware of the beauty that surrounds us always.

AE: What inspires you to paint?
DVM: Painting is very much a stress reliever. To create something of beauty also alleviates frustration and depression. Feeling love, joy, sadness, and other emotions inspires me. Painting is a way to express such feelings when there is nobody to immediately interact with.

AE: How often do you paint with the Mural Arts Program?
DVM: 3–4 days a week for about 6 hours.

AE: Are you compensated for your work with them?
DVM: Yes, 51 cents an hour. Not much but it is one of the top paying jobs in the prison plus, every little bit helps.

AE: Does the Mural Arts Program supply paint for your personal work?
DVM: About twice a year we are given brushes, stretched canvas or panels, and paints (usually to prepare pieces for a show). Mural Arts isn't just a job, it is also designed as a class to teach painting techniques to beginners and encourage advancement of personal skills.

AE: What art supplies are you permitted to own in prison?
DVM: As a painter, I am allowed to own 12 brushes, 12oz jars of acrylic paint, 2 bottles of gesso, and up to 6 canvas panels no larger than 24"×36". However, with special permission, I can use stretchers or larger panels and more supplies for projects with MAP. It would be impossible to do the paintings I do without working for MAP in some cases. Personal supplies are very limited.

AE: Does the library at Graterford have an art section?
DVM: There are some art books in the library. They are not the best but some of the museum and collection books are good. There aren't many instructional books. I usually buy my own books when I have the money. I get a lot of magazines for reference materials.

AE: Are you able to dream? What is your dream for the future if you get out?
DVM: Interesting question. After more than 23 years in prison, you tend not to dream of anything outside these walls. Music and painting give me balance and help me maintain sanity in this negative and dehumanizing environment. Everyone needs to feel a purpose, to see beauty, and know they are still connected to something good. As you experience art and music as your dreams, it gives a glimmer of hope for the future. To really dream, I think you need to love. Love what you do, love who you are, and love someone enough to share your dreams with. I didn't dream for a long time in prison. I do now. My dream is to marry the woman I love (my soul mate), raise our family, and grow old together. I may never get out but I will never stop dreaming of love.

AE: How much is escape part of your life in prison?
DVM: Physical escape is virtually impossible but no one can imprison our minds, creativity, emotions, or dreams, except ourselves. You have to accept the reality of life in prison to survive. You have to protect and defend yourself from guards and other prisoners alike. You have to eat the unsuitable food provided and accept the rules and procedures (no matter how stupid or bizarre), or it can get worse. Without the ability to escape through reading, writing, art, music, and some social interaction, prisoners could not hope and dream of freedom and beauty. Without hope, you give up on life. You have to find a way to escape the oppressive environment of prison and make the best of it or you wont survive. A critical part of survival is finding ways to escape through positive and meaningful activities in our prison life.

AE: I understand Pam lives in Florida and you are incarcerated in Pennsylvania. Can you share with me, how do you keep a relationship going in such challenging circumstances?
DVM: It's not easy. Any relationship with a prisoner is strained by rules and restrictions. With a life sentence hanging over your head, it's even harder. You want to tell those you love to go on with their lives because you can't truly be a part of it but you have to be willing to face the pain and hardship of separation because the relationship is more than just

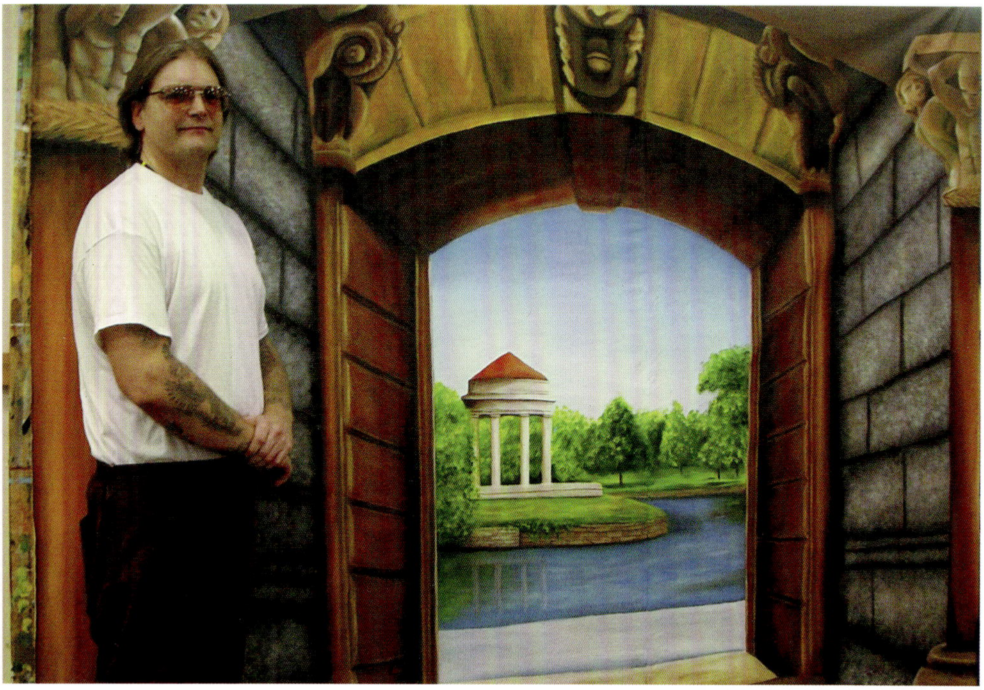

Darrell Van Mastrigt, State Correctional Institution, Graterford, PA, 2011

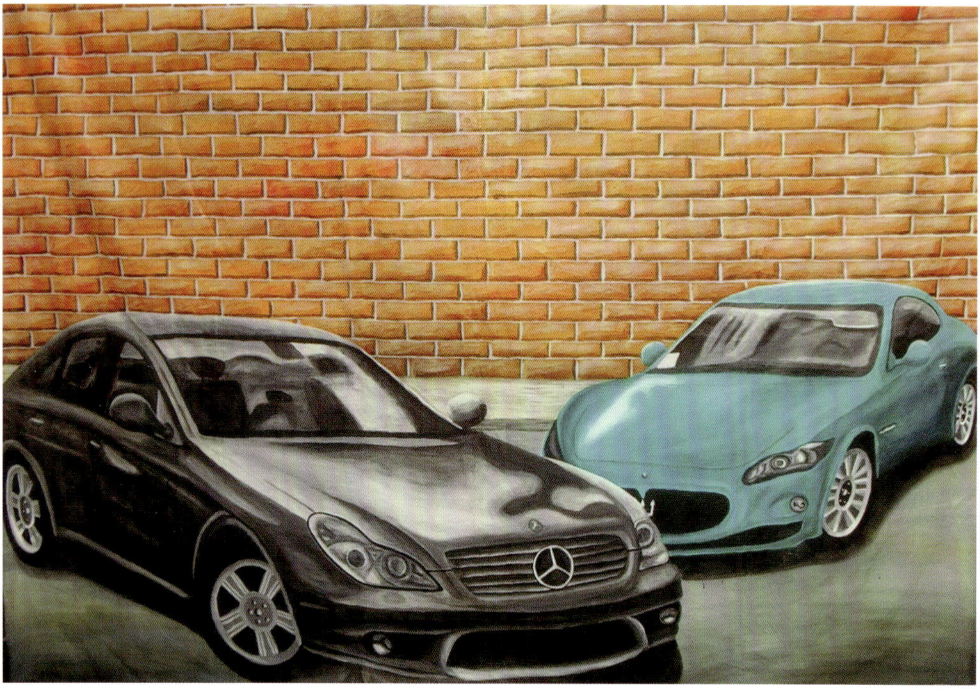

Backdrop painting by Darrell Van Mastrigt, 2011

physical presence. It's always being there emotionally and in support of the others goals and aspirations. It's never letting each other lose hope of a better future. It's giving all you have despite the distance and challenges, to be their friend, partner, and support network. In many ways, it is a sacrifice of immediate wants and desires to make your partner's life better. That's what makes my relationship about love and keeps it strong.

AE: Are visits sometimes held outside in a yard?
DVM: In the summer, there is a yard with picnic tables and a play area for kids. It's only open weather permitting and if staff is available. It is nice to go outside once in a while though.

AE: What do you usually do during a visit? Do you mostly catch up and talk? Or do you play games?
DVM: We talk a lot! Although there are times we are content to just be together and hold hands. It is amazing how much a reconnection after being apart means. We don't play games. There really aren't any games available even if we wanted to. There are some toys for the kids but not much else.

AE: Are marriages allowed in Graterford?
DVM: Yes. They are conducted in the visiting room on regular visits. I've seen two but not been part of them.

AE: I understand that wedding pictures are also taken in front of the backdrops. Have you and Pam considered marrying in Graterford?
DVM: I don't want to get married in prison. However, if all of our efforts fail to get me a new trial and vindication, I would consider it. A wedding day should be special and personal. This is a hard question because love overcomes all but I don't think it's fair (or romantic) to ask somebody to marry you in a prison visiting room.

AE: Do you take a photo in the visiting room every time someone visits you? Do you usually take two photos, one for you and one for your visitor?
DVM: With Pam, yes. With my nephew, yes because I want photo memories of him growing up. With everyone else, we usually take photos once or twice a year. I usually have my visitors take the photos with them and then send me copies of them when they get a chance. It's less expensive this way and everyone gets their own copies.

DVM: I like the visiting room backdrops but always wished they could
be more diverse and rotated more often. They definitely change the
ambience of the visiting room and make it less drab and sanitized. I have
received a lot of compliments since one of my backdrops was recently
placed in the visiting room. By this response, I believe most people
want them.

DVM: Before I started painting, I really only paid attention to what
my visitors or I looked like in the photos. As a painter, I see the
value of backdrops and can appreciate a touch of color and beauty
to enhance the visiting experience. Personally, I love photos because
they are memories I will never forget. I wish we could be in the idealized
landscapes but, until that is possible, I like reliving the memory with
beauty and promise always possible in the background.

DVM: Yes. In other areas and in my cell because I'd like to let others
see how a prisoner lives, both good and bad. The visiting room is
an overcrowded area I rarely see. Unlike in other areas of the prison,
we must wear our jumpsuits in the visiting room.

DVM: The four basic poses: 1) Standing partly sideways with your
hands crossed in front or behind you. 2) Arms crossed in front of
you. 3) Squatting down with one knee higher than the other. 4) Four
is really two variations. Hands spread wide as though inviting somebody
to hug you if you are alone in the picture. (I don't have any of these
because they were taken to be sent out) or if others are in the picture,
a hand around their shoulders. When you ask someone to take a picture
in prison, these seem like the four types of poses you get. It's funny,
but true.

DVM: Prisoners take the photos. An NAACP prisoner chapter owns
the camera and printing equipment. They sell tickets for photos.

The cameramen are members of the organization and paid by the organization for taking photos. The prisoners are specially approved by the prison administration for this position. I believe there are 3–5 at any one time that rotate working days and hours.

AE: Are cameras allowed in the prison (aside from the one used in the visiting room)?
DVM: No.

AE: Are photos allowed to be taken anywhere in the visiting room, or just in front of the backdrop?
DVM: No. At Graterford they must be taken in front of the backdrop or a little set of steps for children. At Christmas, if there' is a tree, photos can be taken in front of the tree in the portrait area.

AE: How many years have you spent in prison? In this time, how many photos do you estimate you have taken in front of visiting room murals?
DVM: I've been in prison almost 24 years. Probably about 200 minimum. My last prison didn't really have murals but the one before that did. At Graterford, I've probably had 500–700 photos taken but a lot of them were not in front of a mural – many were from special events and musical shows. It was easier to get photos in my last prison. Here, all photos are taken by NAACP members. In my last prison, the prison provided the camera in the visiting room. These same cameras where available through the activities department for special photo sessions in the chapel, auditorium, or band room. Prisoners who worked for the activities took the photos. However, only certain spaces could be photographed, i.e., no pictures in front of doors or windows, and group photos became banned sometime in the early 2000s. As a general rule, photos are only allowed in the visiting room. Exceptions are made for special events (banquets, award ceremonies, graduations) at Graterford. Over the years, photos have become more of a sensitive security issue and their availability restricted further and further.

AE: How do they decide who paints the backdrops? Is there a competition?
DVM: Usually reputation. When enough people request an artist to paint a backdrop, they are asked to paint. Basically it comes down to talent and if the artist is willing to do the work.

DVM: For the most part, it's at my discretion but I get their approval before starting. I have to keep in mind not to make a backdrop too regional specific. (like Pittsburgh or Philadelphia) because prisoners here are from all over the state and the backdrops need to be usable by everyone. I also have to avoid gang color schemes – dominant red, blue, or black objects. The cars I recently painted could not be red, blue, or black so I made one grey and the other green. I usually prefer landscapes and non-specific city scenes so it's not a problem for me. I ask the NAACP what they want and then try to find a reference for it or create it from scratch. I'm given a lot of freedom of expression because they know my painting style is for beauty and realism, not shock value or confrontation.

DVM: Except for the colors, it's common sense. No graphic violence, nudity, or political statements. The visiting room is not the place for that. Restrictions don't affect my painting style because my paintings are an appreciation of beauty (sometimes in unique ways). They help me be thankful for life.

DVM: Yes. It's not a job but I do get some free photos as compensation for my work.

DVM: No, the parts I do at work for Mural Arts, I just have my normal supervisor there. In my cell, I like to work at night. Often, the guards, who make their rounds will stop to see what I'm working on. I get a lot of compliments from guards for my paintings. Some stop by just to see what the new project is. We used to be able to sell our artwork to prison staff until it was forbidden by a new policy about two years ago. A lot of staff members own my artwork and have seen it displayed in the prison or at art shows on the outside.

DVM: The last one was done about a year ago but nobody seemed to like it and it didn't generate much revenue. A new one is completed about every year. They are a lot of work. I don't think there has ever been more than two new backdrops in a year.

DVM: Yes. I was given two new canvases and four old ones to paint over. The one I sent you a picture of is on an old canvas painted over. The next two will be on new canvas.

DVM: Just one at a time but they are rotated. They want me to paint three more to be put in the rotation.

DVM: Prisons have always controlled the images exported outside. I think the backdrops were kind of an idea from the outside that developed in prisons over time. Like standing in front of a scene, wild animal, or those muscle cutouts you stick your head through. As prisoners are transferred around the state or across the country, ideas tend to transfer with them about what other prisoners are doing. Some companies offered to change the backgrounds of photographs for prisoners. I think a lot of prisoners just thought, "Why don't we do the backgrounds ourselves?" The prisons probably allowed them at first because there was no legitimate reason not to. As with everything else in prison, prison administrators found a way to control an activity that prisoners wanted to do first. Permitting photos in front of backdrops allowed the prison to control what images are permitted to leave the prisons in a supervised and uniform way. Some activities just sort of make themselves into policy after being done for a long enough time. You wont ever find an official prison policy that says photos must be taken in front of a backdrop but then, you also probably wont find anything in official prison policy saying they allow photos at all!

DVM: I don't think the prisons try to make a profit off the photos. Photos are more expensive at Graterford because they are organized as a fundraiser for the NAACP organization. The cost for copies of photos at my last prison were half the price they are here and most of that probably went back into buying new cameras and film.

DVM: There are other murals in the field house, basketball court, hallways, auditorium, and the outside visiting yard. There are also three murals in the hospital area. The new warden just asked us to plan one for the office's dining hall and the main corridor.

AE: What are the most important possessions you own in prison?
DVM: Photos, letters, and things I've created or accomplished are the most important to me. They are memories and connections to the people I love and respect. There's about a box worth of stuff I would fight for and die for. The rest of the stuff in my cell is nice and convenient but expendable – my TV, radio, typewriter, clothing, and everything else can be replaced. Even my trumpet and paints can be replaced. When they shake me down, I don't care what the guards take. I can get it back, usually the same day or by the end of the week with something of equal or greater value. Until they touch my photos, letters, or binders, I don't pay much attention to them or care. I'm not a materialistic person and am used to having things confiscated at a guard's whim. My memories of relationships and items of emotional attachment are all I care about.

AE: Are artists in Graterford respected for their talents?
DVM: Yes and no. Other prisoners respect and admire prison artists if they are good or can bring something positive or beautiful into the world. Mural artists are greatly respected at Graterford – even by many on the outside. There are outside segments of society that greatly respect prison artists' talent. Though the formally trained and highbrow art world seldom appreciate prison talent, though many people don't want to recognize and respect the humanness, creativity, goodness, and beauty a prisoner may create. Out of retribution and vengeance, we are supposed to be shunned, ignored, and forgotten, not praised. This is a tough question and basically is determined by whether an observer is seeking an experience of beauty or only seeking beauty where they believe it can be found.

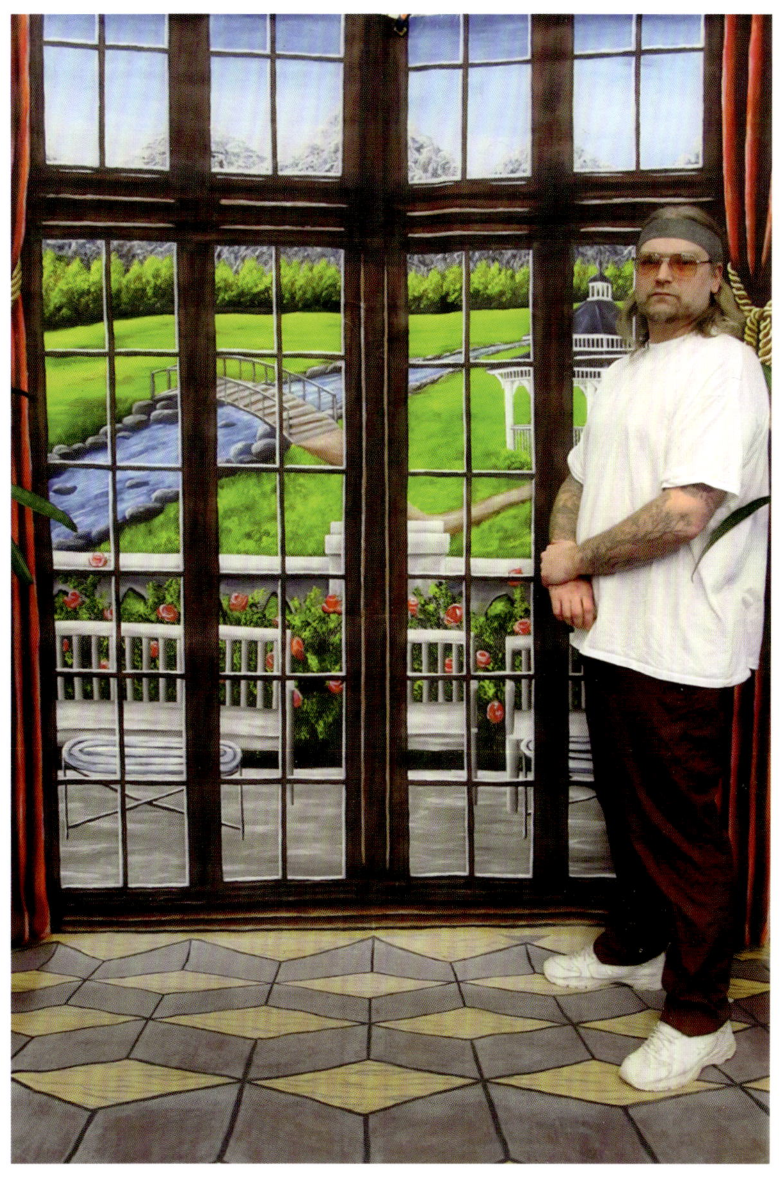

Darrell Van Mastrigt, State Correctional Institution, Graterford, PA, 2012

Acknowledgments

My deepest appreciation goes to all of the contributors for their trust
and generosity in sharing their personal photographs and insights.
This world would be invisible without you.

Due to issues of privacy and confidentiality, prisons have withheld
the names of the artists who painted the backdrops in this book.
Thank you to all of the unknown backdrop artists and visiting room
photographers who helped make these images.

This book is dedicated to my brother Bruce. Thank you for your
openness and honesty as you have reflected on your years in prison
with me.

I would like to acknowledge the following people and organizations for
their hard work and support:

Lisa Anne Auerbach, Robyn Buseman, Jack Bowers, Doug Ashford,
Pete Brook, Christian Cummings, Jim Drain, Elizabeth Dwoskin, Fred,
Helene, Marla, and Remi Emdur, Roxanna Eslemia, Harrell Fletcher, Adam
Garson, Christopher Gianunzio, Robby Herbst, Jane Kassavin, Anthony
Lepore, Sharon Lockhart, Rebecca Loftchie, Darrell Van Mastrigt, Chris
and Michelle McNulty, Christine Osinski, Pam Piterski, Jeff Schwartz, Niels
Van Tomme, Charlie White, Andrea Zittel, the Lambent Foundation, the
Philadelphia Mural Arts Program, Printed Matter, the William James
Association, and all of my friends and colleagues who have given me
feedback over the course of this seven year project.

In addition, I am grateful to Gadsden Correctional Facility's Public
Information Officer Richard Crutcher, the New York Department of
Corrections Public Information Officer Linda Foglia, the Pennsylvania
Department of Corrections Press Secretary Susan McNaughton, as well
as all of the Superintendents and Public Information Officers in the
following institutions for granting me access, offering their perspectives,
and working with me to photograph the portrait studios:

Gadsden Correctional Facility, Auborn Correctional Facility, Ottisville
Correctional Facility, Wyoming Correctional Facility, Shawangunk
Correctional Facility, Woodbourne Correctional Facility, State Correctional
Institution Dallas, State Correctional Institution Graterford, State
Correctional Institution Houtzdale, State Correctional Institution Muncy.

I especially thank Michael Parker for accompanying me in the above
ten prisons and for helping me think through nearly all the details
in this book. I am grateful for your unflagging love and support.

Finally, thank you Sarah Newitt and Fraser Muggeridge for the design,
Martin Lee for print production, and above all, thank you Richard Embray
and Elinor Jansz of Four Corners Books for publishing this project and
for encouraging me to go inside prisons. Richard, as I worked closely
with you, your sensitivity, experience, and critical engagement has
profoundly shaped this book every step of the way.